Educating Hearts and Minds

EDUCATING HEARTS AND MINDS

Reflections on Japanese Preschool and Elementary Education

Catherine C. Lewis

Director of Formative Research
Developmental Studies Center

CAMBRIDGE UNIVERSITY PRESS

PUBLISHED BY THE PRESS SYNDICATE OF THE UNIVERSITY OF CAMBRIDGE
The Pitt Building, Trumpington Street, Cambridge CB2 1RP, United Kingdom

CAMBRIDGE UNIVERSITY PRESS
The Edinburgh Building, Cambridge CB2 2RU, United Kingdom
40 West 20th Street, New York, NY 10011-4211, USA
10 Stamford Road, Oakleigh, Melbourne 3166, Australia

First published 1995
Reprinted 1996, 1997

Printed in the United States of America

Typeset in Palatino

A catalogue record for this book is available from the British Library

Library of Congess Cataloguing-in-Publication Data is available

ISBN 0-521-45197-3 hardback
ISBN 0-521-45832-3 paperback

To my mother
Marguerite Garber Lewis
(1911–1985)

CONTENTS

vii

ACKNOWLEDGMENTS

OVER THE PAST 14 YEARS, MORE THAN 50 JAPANESE PRE-school and elementary teachers have opened up their classrooms to me for periods ranging from a day to nearly 4 months. Teaching is, by its nature, personal and full of risk, and I feel enormously grateful to the many teachers who have welcomed me into their classrooms. The more than 90 Japanese teachers and principals I interviewed showed patience with my endless questions, willingness to talk about their difficulties and doubts as well as their successes, and willingness to disagree with me. I could not have asked for more.

I would also like to acknowledge the tremendous support, over the past 14 years, of Dr. Shigefumi Nagano, of Japan's National Institute of Educational Research. Frank, caring, and endlessly energetic, Dr. Nagano introduced most of my original school contacts, shared his own observations of classrooms and his extensive knowledge of the Japanese-language research literature, and challenged my thinking in many ways. He has given generously of his time to help me, and I hope this volume begins to do justice to his extraordinary mentoring. Drs. Keiko Kashiwagi and Hiroshi Azuma have also helped and encouraged me over many years with their interest, thoughtful questions, support during my stays in Tokyo, and the inspiring example of their own work.

During my six trips to Japan to observe in schools, I have inconvenienced many more people than I can name here. In Nagoya, Dr. Masami Kajita helped me in just about every way conceivable: arranging school contacts, introducing colleagues, locating research, settling my family. Dr. and Mrs. Yasuhiko Nakano, Dr. and Mrs. Katsumi Ninomiya, and Dr. Masako Kiriyama also went to extraordinary lengths to make possible my family's stay. In Tokyo, Masayo Itoh, host "mother" from my AFS high school days, provided a home away from home for me and my family. She earned her host grandmother credentials the hard way, caring for my whole family when my husband and I were ill and helping my children over their initially difficult adjustment to Japan. I also owe a special debt to Yumi Kato, Nobuko Usui, Toshiaki Yukimatsu, and the other teachers of Asahi Yochien and Naeshiro Elementary School, where my sons attended school. They were unfailingly kind, upbeat, energetic, and welcoming, both to my sons and to us. And no one knows more about the importance of belonging and friendship in children's education than Penny Rix, of Alamo School, and Laeta Siri, of Methodist Preschool, who spent much time and energy keeping my sons in touch with their classmates across 6,000 miles of ocean.

One of the best things about studying Japanese education is the good company along the way. My thinking has been shaped in many ways, over many years, by conversations with Tom Rohlen, Ineko Tsuchida, Lois Peak, Merry White, Nancy Sato, Jim Stigler, Harold Stevenson, Joe Tobin, Gerry LeTendre, Robert LeVine, and Sarane Boocock. I have tried to acknowledge these influences in the text, but no doubt I have fallen short in many places. I owe a special debt to Tom Rohlen and to the participants in his seminar on Japanese education, an important source of ideas and feedback for me. Full of lively, thoughtful exchange and good fellowship, the seminar is an inspiring model of "whole person education" at the graduate and professional level.

An interdisciplinary training fellowship from the Social Science Research Council (1978–79) allowed me to study anthropological approaches to education and to conduct my initial observations in Japanese preschools. My observations of elementary classrooms were funded by the Grete Simpson Fund of the University of California (1985 observations) and by the Spencer Foundation Small Grant Program and the Association of Asian Studies (1989–90 elementary school observations). I am greatly indebted to the Nippon Life Insurance Foundation for funding observations and videotaping of elementary schools in 1991–93 and for enabling me to meet regularly with a network of researchers of Japanese education. My 4-month stay in Japan during 1993 and subsequent research were made possible by the Abe Fellowship Program of the Social Science Research Council and the American Council of Learned Societies, with funds provided by the Japan Foundation's

Center for Global Partnership. I particularly wish to acknowledge the flexibility and generosity of the Abe Fellowship Program, without which it would not have been possible to reconcile the needs of my research in Japan, my ongoing longitudinal research in the United States, and my two young children.

Several conferences sponsored by the Joint Committee on Japanese Studies of the American Council of Learned Societies and the Social Science Research Council (with support from the Ford Foundation and the National Endowment for the Humanities) have also been instrumental in the development of my research and in connecting me with others interested in Japanese education. These include the Conference on Child Development and Education in Japan (also sponsored by the Center for Advanced Study in the Behavioral Sciences), the Conference on Social Control in Japanese Early Education (also supported by the Society for Japanese Studies), and the Conference on Teaching and Learning (also supported by the Society for Japanese Studies).

While I was writing the manuscript, I was very fortunate to be given an office by the Developmental Studies Center (DSC), a nonprofit research organization where I have been affiliated since 1987. Within this unusual organization, classroom teachers and basic researchers work together closely on a daily basis. They bring differing expertise to a shared mission: helping elementary schools foster children's development as good learners *and* good people. Although I had conducted and written up most of my observations before I ever met the staff of DSC, the sense I now make of Japanese education has very much to do with the work going on at DSC. The introduction and final chapters of this book owe much to the thinking and generosity of Eric Schaps, Marilyn Watson, Sylvia Kendzior, Dan Solomon, and Vic Battistich. An idea basic to this book – that children develop an attachment to schools that meet their needs – is central to Marilyn Watson's work and to the Child Development Project. I cannot acknowledge each of DSC's 50 or so staff members by name, but I do feel a debt to each for the many things they've taught me about classroom education and for creating an organization that has enabled me to learn. In many ways, it embodies what we all want for schooling: a place where individuals feel cared for, yet challenged, and where they feel safe to take intellectual risks, to disagree, and to recognize their own shortcomings as well as strengths.

I would like to thank Julia Hough, Keiko Kashiwagi, Merry White, Judy Babbitts, Howard Gardner, and two anonymous reviewers for feedback on drafts of the manuscript and Carol Mann (of Carol Mann Agency), for help bringing the project to fruition. Responsibility for shortcomings is, of course, my own.

Not every husband is willing, even temporarily, to exchange his medical practice for a position as a Japanese house-husband, a precipitously dropping dollar-yen exchange rate, and reliance on a 4-year-old child as interpreter. My husband, Andy Leavitt, was well equipped for this mission by his sense of humor and his boundless curiosity, both of which enriched my own experience. His mother, Peg Leavitt, stepped in many times when I traveled, and was inexhaustibly generous with her time and affection. Finally, to my sons, Daniel and Matthew, I give my thanks for their willingness to venture into schools where, initially, they understood little. They worked hard to adapt to their new settings and showed great patience and resourcefulness. They have often (and appropriately) asked, "Why do you work?" For them, and for children on both sides of the Pacific, may this book contribute to school years full of friendship, belonging, and challenge.

INTRODUCTION

We should hold Japan up as a mirror, not as a blueprint.
> Merry White, *The Japanese Educational Challenge*

To know one's own country, one must know another country.
> Seymour Martin Lipset

WE HEAR A GREAT DEAL ABOUT THE HIGH ACADEMIC achievement of Japan's students. Yet we know little about the roots of that achievement. Is it the longer school year? The national curriculum? Greater family support for education?

This book explores a fundamentally different explanation: that Japanese education succeeds because, early on, it meets *children's* needs – for friendship, for belonging, for opportunities to shape school life. Consider the following:

- Japanese kindergartens center on free play, not academic instruction. Japanese kindergarteners spend almost *four times* as much time in free play as their American counterparts.

- Japanese elementary schools emphasize kindness, collaboration and persistence – *not* test scores. Without ability-grouping or tracking, Japanese children cooperatively master a challenging academic curriculum.

- Japanese students assume much authority. Even first-graders quiet their classmates, help solve disputes, lead class meetings, and shape class rules and activities.

- Small groups are at the heart of elementary school life. The four or so members of a group together pursue a wide range of activities – from art to lunch to science. Only when small

1

groups become "like families" do teachers expect learning to occur.

When we are urged to "learn from Japan," the social side of Japanese education is rarely mentioned. In the chapters that follow, I try to bring alive the Japanese preschool and elementary classrooms that I have studied over the past 14 years. What I was told, again and again, was that when schools meet the needs of the whole child – for friendship, for belonging, for contribution – children will in turn develop an emotional bond to the school. They will come to see school as a place that has their best interests at heart, and they will be motivated to do their best – to work hard at learning, to care for others, and to reflect self-critically on their own learning and behavior.

Like their Japanese counterparts, many American teachers see friendship and belonging as central to children's growth. Caring, supportive relationships are at the heart of the successful American schools discussed in chapter 8. Yet the American system as a whole – our curriculum, testing, grouping, discipline – is not designed with these goals at its heart. Indeed, it often erects formidable barriers for teachers who would make close, caring relationships central to school life. What should be our goals for preschool and elementary education? Japan may provide a valuable vantage point to reflect on our own goals.[1]

THE METHOD

I first encountered Japanese education during the 1967–68 school year, when I attended Nihon Joshidai High School as an exchange student. That year was full of surprises. I expected intense competition among students but found, instead, tremendous camaraderie and sense of shared purpose. (Like many elementary, junior high, and high school classes, my high school class still gets together regularly to reminisce and renew friendships.) I expected authoritarian control by teachers but found that students ran many aspects of school life, from school trips and club activities to discipline and landscape maintenance.

My experience in Japan challenged many of the assumptions I, as a 16-year-old, held about human nature. Why did my Japanese classmates rush to give each other hockey sticks and kneepads rather than grabbing their own first? Why did they earnestly pursue class discussions and lessons even when no adult was present?

In trying to understand the puzzle of my own high school experiences, I have found the most compelling clues in Japanese preschools and elementary schools. I have come to believe that preschool and elementary schooling are both central to Japanese educational success and widely misunderstood in the United States. This book focuses on preschool and *early* elementary education in Japan.[2] It draws heavily on my own observations and interviews, totaling about 8 months, in a wide range of Japanese preschools and elementary schools. I conducted all observations and interviews in Japanese. In addition, I draw upon both Japanese and Western research.

My study of preschools began in 1979, when I spent at least 2 full days in each of 15 diverse Japanese preschools: private schools; public schools at the national, prefectural, and local level; schools known for their academic or arts programs; and schools in urban, suburban, and rural areas of Japan. I observed classes for 5-year-olds. This sample, described in the appendix, was a convenience sample introduced by friends and colleagues. Initially interested in how the "indulgence" of early family life gives way to discipline at preschool, I was greatly surprised by what I found: child-centered, unregimented preschools focused on free play. These findings were subsequently confirmed by several ethnographic and quantitative studies.[3]

But the mystery remained: How *do* "indulged" Japanese children become self-disciplined elementary students? Reasoning that the "real" discipline must begin in elementary school, in 1985 I began to study classroom management in Tokyo public elementary schools, initially spending at least 1 full day in each of 15 first-grade classrooms in 13 schools. This convenience sample included schools in wealthy and poor neighborhoods of Tokyo; the oldest elementary school as well as one of the newest; classes that ranged in size from 23 students (in central city areas of declining enrollment) to 45 (in

3

rapidly expanding industrial areas); and teachers ranging from 1 to 40 years of teaching experience.

During the two studies, I collected certain information systematically, including spot observations of where children were and what they were doing at 20-minute intervals throughout the preschool day; tape recordings and narrative notes of all academic lessons in first-grade classrooms; and records of all materials posted on first-grade walls and blackboards. In addition to these systematic observations, I made many additional, often longer, visits to these and other preschool and elementary classrooms in Tokyo, Kyoto, and Nagoya, both during the original visits to Japan and during four subsequent stays in Japan (in 1987, 1989, 1990, and 1993). The longest of these was in 1993, when I lived in Nagoya for 4 months, observing intensively in 2 elementary schools over that period and visiting about 10 other elementary schools for periods ranging from a day to a week. My sons attended the neighborhood schools in our mixed neighborhood of factories, apartments, and single-family residences, giving me the opportunity to see something of Japanese education from a parent's viewpoint. My older son was a third-grader at the local public elementary school, my younger son a member of the 4-year-old class at a private preschool of 350 students. Neither school had previously had an American student.

On my visits to Japanese schools, I interviewed classroom teachers after observing them teach. I asked them standard questions about their goals and teaching practices, and I also questioned them about incidents I had seen during my days of observation. For example, when children were disruptive or fought, I asked teachers why they chose the particular responses they did and what they thought about other possible responses. I tried to understand the thinking about children's development that lay behind teachers' choices – to understand, in the view of the teacher, how disruptive children became well-behaved and how students learned to persist on academic tasks. I also asked teachers to explain their academic lessons: why they had chosen particular activities, problems, and topics. Occasionally I showed them videotapes of American classroom lessons as a further catalyst for discussions about teaching. As well, I interviewed more than 30 principals and vice-principals regarding school activities, philosophy, goals, disciplinary practices, and opportunities for teachers to learn. Interviews with teachers and principals often sparked additional visits to the schools to observe school-wide meetings, teachers' research groups, special events, and so forth.

The sample of teachers I observed and interviewed was not a representative or random sample, so I cannot generalize about Japanese education on the basis of these observations. Like their American counterparts, Japanese teachers are diverse. Yet some practices were so pervasive that they would be likely to emerge in any sample. For example, all of the more than 30 elementary schools that I studied, in three cities in observations that spanned 8 years, had *children* assume considerable responsibility for classroom leadership and discipline. Likewise, all used cooperative, familylike small groups of children as the basic units for many classroom activities. Surely we should know something about these practices – even from a convenience sample of schools – before we begin to draw conclusions about the context of Japanese educational achievement.

Several limitations of my observations should be noted. Compared with a long-term ethnography, in which the observer spends many months or years at a single site, my observations may give a more "model" view of educational practices: I saw less behind-the-scenes action and more of what teachers and principals wanted me to see. Further, my original preschool observations are now more than a decade old. Yet what I report is remarkably consistent with the more recent independent observations of long-term ethnographers like Lois Peak, Lauren Kotloff, and Nancy Sato.

Many of the practices at the core of my discussion – such as children's fixed small groups and their assumption of responsibility for much classroom management – are long-term practices that could not possibly have been marshaled for the visit of a foreign researcher. On the other hand, lesson content or disciplinary force could easily have been modified with my presence in mind. If, indeed, there was distortion toward "model" practices, then what's model is surprising. For example, even in the presence of a foreign researcher, teachers apparently did not feel compelled to stop children's fistfights or to give the correct answer at the end of a challenging mathematics class.

REINTERPRETING THE ROOTS OF JAPANESE EDUCATIONAL ACHIEVEMENT

As debate on American education rages, the voices of Japanese teachers reverberate in my head. But they don't talk about test scores or accountability or more hours of schooling. They talk about the importance of friendship in children's learning, about the need for children to play, about whole children whose intellectual development cannot be extricated from their social, emotional, and ethical development. These voices – like the voices of many American teachers – challenge basic assumptions that underlie the curriculum, organization, and management of many American schools.

As I studied Japanese preschool and first-grade classrooms, I found myself reawakened to the importance of certain core American values, such as appreciation of diversity, that I sometimes found lacking in Japanese settings. In the chapters that follow, I explore several shortcomings of Japanese education for young children: the occasionally dangerous lack of supervision; the emphasis on selected emotions (such as cheerfulness) rather than on children's own self-expression; the idea that there is a single, correct way to stow shoes or arrange desk contents. But in my view, the most profound shortcoming of Japanese education is its failure to live up to its own early promise. Why does child-centered early education give way, at junior high, to monotonous lectures and authoritarian control?[4] Why don't the educational principles that serve so well in elementary school – producing happy, caring, able learners – extend to the later years of Japanese education?

Although many observers credit Japan's high academic achievement to after-school "cram schools" and rigorous college entrance exams, I think we must credit preschool and elementary education. As chapter 2 recounts, Japan's achievement advantage emerges early in elementary school, before a substantial number of children attend supplementary schooling, and despite the fact that Japanese

6

mothers spend less time than do Americans teaching their young children.[5]

American research provides growing evidence that schools, to foster children's fullest intellectual and social development, must be "communities" where all children feel known and valued. School as community is an idea at the very heart of Japanese education for young children. Japanese preschools and elementary schools create community by:

- Minimizing competition and helping children develop the feeling that "we're all in it together."
- Involving all children – whatever their academic skills – in leadership of the school.
- Focusing discipline on what it means to be a kind, responsible member of the school community – not on rewards and punishments.
- Designing lessons so that they simultaneously promote children's belonging, understanding of one another, and academic learning.

Of course, none of these ideas is new. As chapter 8 explores, many successful schools in the United States are based on these very ideas. Countless Japanese teachers invoked John Dewey and other Westerners as they explained their classroom practices to me. Yet these ideas may have found extraordinarily fertile soil in Japan, where Confucian traditions have long emphasized the inherently ethical and social nature of all learning and where native theories of child development emphasize children's inherent goodness.[6] How do children become responsible citizens and eager learners? How does schooling promote – or undermine – this development? These are questions profitably viewed from the vantage point of another culture.

1

A BRIEF BACKGROUND ON JAPAN'S EDUCATIONAL SYSTEM

THE REMAINING CHAPTERS OF THIS BOOK TAKE US INTO Japanese classrooms. As a context for those visits, this chapter provides a brief background on Japan's educational system. Readers interested in more detail can choose from several excellent volumes on Japanese education.[1]

JAPANESE PRE-ELEMENTARY EDUCATION

Diverse, Nearly Universal

Although compulsory education begins at age 6 with elementary school, more than 90% of Japanese children attend at least 2 years of pre-elementary education.[2] Some researchers argue that pre-elementary schooling is the most diverse and lively sector of Japanese education.[3] Pre-elementary options include both full-day childcare centers geared to the needs of working parents (*hoikuen*) and half-day preschools (*yōchien*). Like the institutions of kindergarten and the day nursery in the West, the *yōchien* and *hoikuen* originated to serve two very different social classes. Reflecting this difference, *hoikuen* are administered by the Ministry of Welfare, and *yōchien* by the Ministry of Education. Yet contemporary observers find great similarity between the two settings.[4] *Yōchien* and *hoikuen* use the same basic curriculum and teaching approaches, but *hoikuen* offer longer hours and may place children in cross-age groupings. "*Hoikuen* is *yōchien* with a nap and snack added on," explained a Japanese mother when I was looking for care for my own preschooler.

8

Within both half-day and full-day settings, options are many: facilities run by private individuals and groups (including Catholic, Protestant, and Buddhist denominations and nonreligious organizations) and by public entities (including local, prefectural, and national governments). Educational philosophies, too, are diverse: Schools based on the writings of Montessori, Dewey, and Froebel share the preschool marketplace with recent and centuries-old Japanese pedagogies that emphasize everything from early musical training to vigorous naked outdoor play. That more than 90% of Japanese 4- and 5-year-olds attend licensed preschools or childcare centers is particularly striking in view of the cost of pre-elementary education; parents spend roughly $800 to $1,800 annually for tuition, fees, and school lunch.[5]

Education for 5-year-olds is part of preschool in Japan but typically part of elementary school (in a kindergarten program) in the USA. The pressure to extend academic skills downward to 5-year-olds may thus be greater in the USA than in Japan.

Large Class Size

Americans are often surprised by the large number of students per teacher in Japanese pre-elementary settings. Japanese childcare centers are permitted to have up to 30 3- to 5-year-olds per teacher; preschools are permitted 40 students per teacher. Actual class size is slightly below 30.[6] Japanese preschool teachers envy the "mother-like" role of teacher that is possible in the small classes of American preschools. Yet they see some advantages in large class size and use it to deemphasize adult authority and to build children's reliance on one another.[7] Nearly all caregivers in Japanese preschools are women (94%), and about half are under the age of 27. About half of preschool directors are women.[8]

National Regulation and Support

Japanese government regulations ensure a shared, and relatively high, level of basic facilities across all preschools and childcare centers. Regulations specify the amount of floor space and outdoor playground space per child as well as the minimum educational and play equipment. For example, all licensed preschools are required to provide, in addition to large classrooms and indoor and outdoor play space, a host of facilities and equipment, including a teachers' room, "slides, swing, and sand playing space, pianos or organs, simple musical instruments, record players, building blocks, toys, tools for picture-story shows, picture books and other books, and tools for breeding animals, drawing, and handicrafts."[9] Many Westerners are surprised to discover that national government funds subsidize private as well as public facilities; in addition, many prefectural and municipal governments subsidize pre-elementary education.[10]

JAPAN'S ELEMENTARY EDUCATION SYSTEM

Flying into Japan in the summer, one easily spots elementary schools from the air by their swimming pools. Swimming is part of the elementary curriculum, and nearly all Japanese elementary schools (but fewer secondary schools) have swimming pools.[11] Why elementary schools? William Cummings argues that elementary schools are the flagship institutions of Japanese education.[12] Compared with the USA, Japan invests proportionally more of its GNP in K-12 education and less in university education. For more than 100 years, Japanese policymakers have seen elementary education as critical to national development. Arinori Mori, an architect of Japan's modernization, wrote in 1885: "Our Country must move from its third-class position to second class, and from second class to first, and ultimately to the leading position among all countries of the world. The best way to do this is [by laying] the foundations of elementary education."[13]

Ninety-nine percent of Japan's elementary students attend local public elementary schools.[14] Education at these schools is free of charge and open to all local residents. Like American schools, Japanese elementary schools differ from one another in many ways: in the income and occupation of the families they serve, in school histories and traditions, and in physical facilities. Yet several factors reduce variability among Japanese schools.[15]

10

First, Japan's national Ministry of Education, Science, and Culture (Monbushō) prescribes national instructional goals and hours, approves textbooks, and strongly shapes many other aspects of educational policy. Every elementary student studies the same subjects for roughly the same number of hours per year, using similar or identical textbooks.

Second, the national government provides almost half of all expenditures on public education and gives special allocations to poorer prefectures and municipalities in order to make their facilities and programs comparable to those of more affluent areas. The government conducts campaigns to provide all elementary schools with certain levels of facilities and staff. So, for example, 95% of public elementary schools are now equipped with indoor gymnasiums, and class size has steadily decreased over the past 35 years as part of five successive multiyear plans implemented by the Ministry of Education.[16]

Third, Japanese teachers are typically required to rotate to demographically different schools during their careers. For example, teachers in Tokyo must spend a minimum of several years teaching in each of the city's three geographic regions, which roughly correspond to its major socioeconomic divisions. This means that teachers, during their careers, teach pupils from a variety of backgrounds.

Elementary teachers rotate in another way, too: They rarely teach the same grade year after year. American teachers often develop impressive expertise in teaching a particular grade level.[17] In contrast, Japanese schools emphasize the stability of the teacher-child unit – usually having teachers and children remain a unit for 2 years – and the benefits of having teachers accrue experience at various elementary grade levels. Rotation to all divisions of an enterprise, so that one can understand the issues faced by one's coworkers, is typical of Japanese corporate training as well. Japanese educators explain that teaching at various grade levels helps teachers appreciate the challenges faced by students and teachers at each level and the connections between early and later learning.

Commonly Japanese students and their teacher are a unit that stays together for lunch and for most or all subjects of the school day, including music, science, and physical education. As subsequent chapters explore, Japanese teachers devote a great deal of attention to developing a sense of community within the classroom, and they regard lunch, daily class meetings, music, art, and other "nonacademic" activities as valuable opportunities to build this sense of community. Elementary teachers are generalists who must often pass performance tests in areas such as piano and swimming, as well as written tests in academic subjects, in order to become certified. About 60% of Japanese elementary teachers are women. Only 5% of elementary principals and 13% of assistant principals are women.[18]

Academic Achievement

Japanese students consistently rank very high on international tests of science and mathematics.[19] Japanese students generally outperform their American counterparts from the earliest elementary grades, and the gap increases with age. Yet the similar performance of Japanese and American children on tests of basic cognitive abilities makes it unlikely that these achievement differences are genetically based.[20] Nor does extra after-school instruction seem to account for the Japanese performance advantage, since some of the achievement differences emerge well before any substantial number of children attend after-school academic instruction and show up in samples that include few attendees.[21]

Both Japanese and Americans have expressed concern about whether "creativity" is fostered by Japanese education, but careful studies are lacking. Originality is associated with academic achievement in the United States, whereas persistence predicts academic achievement in Japan, suggests one study that followed children from preschool through elementary school. However, some tests of science and math achievement suggest that Japanese students actually outperform their American counterparts by a greater margin on items tapping conceptual understanding than on items tapping basic skills.[22] E. Paul Torrance, developer of a widely used creativity assessment, writes glowingly about the creativity of Japanese children as assessed by tests and in classroom observations, and he has actually suggested that American preschool educators

12

could learn a great deal from their Japanese colleagues. Other Western observers, too, have been impressed with the achievements of Japanese elementary students in the areas of reading, art, and music.[23] As chapter 7 explores, creativity may flourish in some areas of instruction – such as math and science – but languish in others.

Shortcomings of Japanese Elementary Education

Japanese, as well as foreigners, find many faults in Japanese elementary education. Pressure for conformity, failure to integrate foreigners and Japanese returnees from foreign countries, and failure to build international awareness are frequently cited as problems.[24] These are discussed in the chapters that follow, and chapter 8 focuses on a number of problems – including bullying, refusal to attend school, and youth suicide.

ELEMENTARY THROUGH HIGH SCHOOL EDUCATION

Nearly Universal Education

International comparisons of student achievement are often misleading, because America educates a very high proportion of its young people. This caveat does not apply to comparisons with Japan. Virtually all Japanese youth complete junior high school, and 95% of junior high graduates go on to high school. Three years later, 94% of those who went on to high school have graduated.[25]

High Prestige and Compensation for Teachers

Japanese teachers enjoy considerable prestige. The U.S. Department of Education reports:

> According to the 1975 survey [of Japanese public opinion], elementary principals and teachers ranked 9th and 18th highest in public esteem, out of 82 occupations. Principals' prestige was higher than that of department heads of large corporations, pub-

lic accountants, and authors. Elementary teachers enjoyed higher prestige than civil and mechanical engineers, white collar employees in large firms, and municipal department heads. University professors were ranked third, below court judges and presidents of large companies, but above physicians.[26]

The U.S. Department of Education reported in 1987 that Japanese teachers' salaries were generally higher than those of other Japanese professionals (businessmen, engineers, pharmacists, etc.) at initial hiring, equal at mid-career, and higher, once again, beyond age 53. A sharp and continuing rise in teachers' salaries with age provides economic incentive for remaining in the profession. In 1981 (the last year for which data are available), American teachers (elementary and secondary) averaged 13 years' experience; Japanese elementary and lower secondary teachers averaged 16.8 years, and upper secondary teachers averaged 17.5 years. Perhaps because of relatively high prestige and compensation, competition for teaching jobs is keen in Japan. In a two-step process consisting of prefectural (statewide) examinations and interviews, five applicants compete for each teaching spot.[27]

National Control over Curriculum and Textbooks

Japan's national curriculum is often cited as an important influence on national achievement. As chapter 3 explores, Japan's national Course of Study not only includes goals related to skills (for example, learning to write designated Chinese characters) but also goals related to children's feelings and motivation: for example, "love of nature," "joy of self-expression," and "active attitude, as one family member, of wanting to improve family life."[28] Textbooks, written and published by commercial publishers, are reviewed by the Ministry of Education to ensure that they cover the prescribed material in an "appropriate" manner. Some Japanese educators argue that this review system systematically bars innovative approaches and controversial ideas and effectively amounts to a system of censorship. For example, a high school physics textbook written by a Nobel laureate was rejected on the ground that it did not present "correct knowledge . . . in a predetermined and exact style"; a sixth-grade textbook was rejected because the onomatopoetic sounds used by a poet to describe a rushing river departed from the river sounds officially recognized by the Ministry of Education.[29]

Large Class Size

Japanese elementary classes are large by the standards of many American states but are steadily being reduced. Decrying classrooms where children are packed in like "pressed sushi," the Ministry of Education limited class size to 50 in 1959, in the first of five successive campaigns to reduce class size. The legal maximum class size for elementary schools was reduced to 45 in the mid 1960s, and to 40 in 1991. The actual average class size in 1991 was 29.[30] As we will see in subsequent chapters, many Japanese teaching techniques are well adapted to large class size. Familylike small groups (chapter 4) are the basic units for much classroom activity, enabling even relatively large classes to function smoothly. Teachers need exercise little direct control because, as explored in chapters 5 and 6, students themselves manage many of the routines of classroom life.

Avoidance of Ability Grouping and Tracking

The politics of American knowledge about Japanese education are revealing. One is hard pressed to find an American who *hasn't* heard that Japanese students score high on international tests of mathematics and science achievement. Yet many Americans are surprised to learn that Japanese achieve these gains *without ability grouping or tracking* during the compulsory education years (Grades 1 through 9). The U.S. Department of Education study describes Japanese education during the elementary and junior high years:

> During the compulsory school years Japanese education assiduously avoids making distinctions between students on the basis of ability or achievement. There are no separate tracks, ability groupings, remedial programs, or student electives. Promotion from grade to grade is virtually automatic as long as the student is attending classes. Students are almost never retained in grade or skipped ahead.[31]

Role of the Teachers' Union

Even more surprising to many Americans are the substantial role played by the Japan Teachers' Union (Nikkyōso) in shaping Japanese education over the past 40 years and the union's strongly adversarial relationship with the Ministry of Education. Socialist in ideology and political ties, Nikkyōso has strongly advocated student-centered education and opposed tracking and achievement testing of students.[32] For example, through their collective refusal to administer achievement tests, members of Nikkyōso have since the 1960s successfully prevented the Ministry of Education from ever implementing a planned system of nationwide student achievement testing. Such tests are regarded by many Japanese teachers as a first step toward tracking students by achievement and hence as an infringement of students' educational opportunity.[33]

University Entrance Examinations

Even a book devoted to preschool and early elementary education cannot ignore Japan's university entrance examinations, the force Thomas Rohlen has called "a dark engine powering the entire school system."[34] In Japan, the most prestigious jobs in industry and government go almost exclusively to graduates of a few elite universities. Universities are finely ranked according to their ability to place graduates in prestigious jobs; high schools, in turn, are ranked according to their graduates' success in entering the most prestigious universities.[35]

For entrance to elite universities, connections, recommendations, and extracurricular activities are largely irrelevant; the university entrance examination is critical. College entrance examinations require students to memorize and apply large bodies of information. The examinations exert downward pressure: 40% of fourth- to sixth-graders attend private *gakushūjuku* – after-school schools – designed to supplement their regular schooling by providing remedial help, review of regular schoolwork, or, less often, examination preparation. Half of junior high students attend such *gakushūjuku*.[36] The examination system may exert downward pressure even on some preschoolers, whose parents have them take entrance examinations for "escalator" preschools attached to selected private or national universities. But, as the next chapter explores, preschool entrance examinations are still a very limited phenomenon, affecting perhaps 1% of preschool children – ironically, often children whose parents want to spare them the trauma of later college entrance competition.[37] With so much media attention devoted to children on the elite track, it's important to remember that 99% of Japanese elementary students and 95% of junior high students attend public elementary schools that accept all local residents.

SUMMARY

The Japanese educational landscape contains many familiar features – such as a lengthy period of compulsory education, high rate of high school attendance, and diverse preschool options – but many features that differ sharply from the American educational landscape. These include, for example, the Ministry of Education's control over textbooks and instructional hours, the avoidance of ability grouping and tracking during the compulsory education years, and the downward pressure of college entrance examinations on elementary and even pre-elementary education.

2

THE PRESCHOOL
EXPERIENCE: PLAY,
COMMUNITY, REFLECTION

Preschoolers' spontaneous activity – that is, their play –
provides the learning that is essential for harmonious
growth of the mind and body. All the aims [of preschool
education] can be achieved fully through education in
which play is central.

Japanese Ministry of Education Preschool
Guidelines, Article One[1]

W HEN I BEGAN MY RESEARCH IN JAPANESE PRESCHOOLS,
I expected to find regimented, orderly classrooms and
teacher-led activities. My expectation was far from the mark. What I
found, instead, was that Japanese preschoolers spent long periods
in noisy, active free play. Free play was punctuated by a few activities that the whole class shared: activities such as singing, daily
meetings, and snacktime. The central role of free play in Japanese
preschool life has been confirmed by other researchers, in both
ethnographic and large-sample studies.[2] The first section of this
chapter takes us to a local public preschool in Tokyo to experience
free play. The next sections explore the connection between free
play and two central goals of Japanese preschool education: building a sense of community within the school and promoting children's growth as responsible, considerate members of that school
community. The final section of the chapter explores connections
between free play and children's intellectual development. It exam-
ines colliding images of Japanese preschools: settings for free play
versus examination preparation.

THE PRESCHOOL CURRICULUM: PLAY AS CENTRAL

In the 15 Japanese preschools I studied, 5-year-olds spent about half of their time in free play and half in whole-class activities. By "free play," I mean that children were completely free to choose what to do; they were not choosing among a limited set of teacher-designated activities. In the 15 preschools, the 5-year-olds spent their time as follows:

50% in free play (see examples below)

14% in an art or craft activity

8% in singing, dancing, or exercises to music

7% in ceremonies or meetings (such as class meetings or school assemblies)

7% in lunchtime or snacktime

5% in listening to a story

5% in clean-up

1% in academic activities (such as re-creating a pattern with blocks)

The half of the average preschool day spent in free play was unregimented and often even unsupervised (see chapter 5) – a noisy, exuberant time during which children ran freely from classroom to classroom and outdoors to the playground. My field notes from a Tokyo local public preschool illustrate the breadth and open-endedness of activities during a typical free-play period.

After brief morning greetings and a song, free-play period begins. Ms. Ishida[3] tells her class of 36 5-year-olds that empty boxes for making "empty-box creations" and colored cellophane are available today in addition to the usual play materials. Five minutes later, only nine children remain in the classroom. The rest have scattered to the playground, corridors, inside stairwell, and a big room with tumbling mats that serves as a gym. A teacher from another class is on the playground, but no teachers are in the gym room, stairwell, or corridors; teachers look in on these areas occasionally. One corner of the classroom is piled with empty boxes of all sizes and descriptions. Scissors, razor blades inserted in knife handles, and tape are available nearby. Sheets of colored cellophane are laid out on another table. Spot observations at 20-minute intervals over the nearly 2 hours of free play find children in the following activities: donning skirts from the dress-up box; trying to hit the ceiling with balls made from crumpled colored cellophane; playing tag outside; playing with water in dishpans inside the classroom; squirting hoses in the play yard; bringing large wooden blocks from the gym to the classroom (these blocks are 3 to 5 feet long and very heavy, requiring children to work together to carry them); building playhouses in the classroom from the large wooden blocks; playing with and feeding guinea pigs and rabbits; making an "irrigation project" with sand, water, and big plastic pipes in the sand play area outside; making airplanes, dollhouses, robots, etc., out of the empty boxes; making "candy" from the cellophane and "selling" it to classmates; making "juice" by filling cups of crumpled cellophane with water; playing on the trampoline, slide, swings, and other sports equipment; pulling one another in a wagon; throwing hula hoops up the indoor staircase and trying to catch them as they come down; writing or drawing on blank paper; running and playing tag and ball games; and carrying water and plastic dishes to the stairwell in order to play house. Some children move from activity to activity; others pursue a single activity for most of the morning.

The children sustain three activities over the entire morning: building playhouses with the huge wooden blocks, playing with the colored cellophane, and building objects out of the empty boxes. Together these activities involve one quarter to one half of the class members at the six spot observations. At various points, these strands of play merge, as the block houses become "stores" for selling cellophane "juice" and children add empty-box "furniture" to the block houses. During the 2 hours of free play, Ms.

Ishida spends most of her time responding to requests from children (mostly for help tying, taping, and using razor knives). On six occasions she helps integrate various children who are isolated – three times in response to requests by the children that they want to join in an ongoing game, and three times on her own initiative when she sees children sitting or wandering alone and unoccupied.

At 11:15 Ms. Ishida remarks to a few children near her that it's time to clean up for story time and lunch. Children scream in protest: "Look what we built. We don't want to put away the houses we built from blocks." Ms. Ishida surveys the elaborate configuration of "houses," "castles," and "stores" that cover nearly half the classroom floor and accedes to the children's wishes: "Okay, each group can find a lunch spot in a house or castle or wherever you want."

Often, as I sat in a Japanese preschool watching children make mud pies, build block houses, and chase one another, I wondered why I'd come halfway around the world to watch activities that I could see in my own backyard. But sometime during each preschool day, I'd suddenly be reminded that free play was not just a pleasant way to pass time: It provided the crucial raw material for what I came to see as the two major goals of Japanese preschool education: nurturing children's connections to one another and building their willingness and capacity to live in a group. The next two sections explore these two goals and how free play contributed to them.

USING FREE PLAY TO BUILD COMMUNITY

Children naturally come to know one another as they play together; Japanese preschool teachers use these natural contacts as the scaffolding for a class-wide community. For example, when several 5-year-olds at Western Japan Public Preschool made a construction-paper clock during free play, their teacher noticed it and asked them to show it to classmates during the daily class meeting. The following day, clockmakers proliferated, and during class meeting children suggested that they "sell" their burgeoning supply of clocks. The next day found many class members selling or buying at the "clock store" and making plans during class meeting for "clock store day" – a day of dramatic play in which the 5-year-olds would invite the younger classes to be "customers" at the clock stores. Over the next few days, the children made dozens of clocks and watches, storefronts, jewelers' headpieces, and money and purses for the "customers." Although this activity had its origin in the free play of a few children, it quickly became a group activity that involved first the whole class and then both classes of 5-year-olds, eventually culminating in a "clock-selling festival" that involved the whole school. Similarly, I saw puppet shows, dramatic performances, and "market days" that began in the spontaneous play of a few children and grew to involve the whole class or even the whole school in shared dramatic pursuits. Teachers supported the transformation from small-scale play to large-scale enterprise in many ways: by asking children to share their activities with the whole class, by telling about the kinds of free-play activities they had noticed, and by asking questions designed to encourage children's elaboration and involvement ("What could we do with these watches so many classmates are making?").

In a progressive Japanese preschool studied by Lauren Kotloff, the spontaneous play of three children sparked a 3-week class project:

> One morning during Free Play [three children] built a twelve foot long airplane out of large wooden blocks. In this school, activities that were initiated by an individual or a small group of children were often turned into whole class projects, and by the next day almost all of the children in the class were busy making various things for the airplane. . . . When it was finished the airplane ran the whole length of the classroom. The passenger section held six seats, each seat was numbered and fitted with a seatbelt. A TV made out of a large cardboard box was mounted in the passenger section. . . . There was a kitchen section, with child-made menus and food available for the passengers. The cockpit was equipped with maps, a steering wheel, and a panel of dials and buttons, all drawn with pencil and paper and taped into place. The plane could be refueled with a cardboard gas tank. Plastic curtains made out of trash bags were hung as sides to the plane. Below

22

their cut-out windows, each curtain was decorated with a mural made up of many children's drawings of "things you can see from the plane." A red stripe and the logos of All Japan Airlines decorated the wings and body of the plane. The wings had landing lights made out of styrofoam cups and tiny flashlights that really worked.[4]

Children's spontaneous play added some features to the airplane; daily class meetings sparked ideas for the airplane, too. Lauren Kotloff describes the interplay between free play and class meeting in the preschool she studied:

> Even when the children were involved in totally individualistic pursuits during Free Play, they always brought their accomplishments back to the group in the Class Meeting that followed. In the discussions that surrounded each child's presentation of his Free Play project, the teacher sometimes asked the peer group to offer advice and suggestions to a child who was encountering difficulties with his or her project. . . . The teachers . . . pointed out the unique features of each child's work, not simply to praise the child and build his or her self-confidence, but in the hopes that that child's accomplishment would spark the imagination of the others and motivate them to try out new ideas in their own projects as well.[5]

This preschool's low student-teacher ratio (only 18 students per adult) and Christian progressive origins may set it apart from some other Japanese preschools. But it shares with most preschools I observed a focus on free play, class meetings, and the use of each to foster the other.

OTHER STRATEGIES TO BUILD COMMUNITY

In many ways, Japanese preschool is inescapably *about* community. Students are often referred to collectively by their class name: "I hope all of us Cherry Blossoms can remember not to throw stones now that we're the big sisters and brothers in the school." The word for classmates is "friends" (*tomodachi*) . When teachers say, "The monitors will say grace when all friends are sitting quietly" or

23

"Don't forget to draw your friends when you draw the class field trip," they aren't referring to personal friends; they're referring to all class members. In fact, I was stymied in my attempts to ask about children's friendships until a Japanese researcher instructed me to ask about children's *personal* friendships (*kojinteki na tomodachi*) – a phrase that is amusingly redundant in English.

Part of being a community is having shared rituals, and all classes had rituals of singing, dancing, greetings, or discussion that began and ended each day. These rituals varied greatly. Some were very brief, like the song, greetings, and introduction of the daily monitors that began each day at Western Tokyo Preschool. Others were longer and more elaborate – like the school-wide calisthenics, songfest, and comments from the principal that covered the first hour of each day at a Buddhist-affiliated preschool. These diverse daily ceremonies underlined the connection between student and class, or students and school, and provided a shared ritual – most often a fun, noisy one. Children might ask, in unison, for God's help in being *genki* (energetic, enthusiastic) that day, followed by a noisy dance. Or they might sing and fall to the ground of the dusty playyard in a comical dance – followed by the opportunity to brush off each other's backsides. In addition to the daily and weekly rituals, dramatic school ceremonies and festivals punctuate the Japanese preschool year.[6] All students and teachers – and often mothers and fathers as well – gather for these ceremonies and festivals, including school entrance and graduation ceremonies; sports day; ceremonies to open and close each trimester; and, often, recitals or other cultural events, collective birthday parties, carnivals, and celebrations of various holidays. Children may spend weeks rehearsing dances or songs to perform for parents, for new students, or for local citizens.

Preschool events emphasize fun, participation by all members of the school community, and recognition of the *whole group's* growth or accomplishments. For example, the birthday parties I saw at three preschools were collective celebrations that recognized all children with birthdays during the preceding month or two. In one school, the whole student body and staff gathered in a large hall to eat cake, sing songs, watch the principal crown and congratulate

24

each birthday child, and learn about the favorite foods of each birthday child. To close the ceremony, all 200 children in the school made a "birthday train" by placing hands on the shoulders of the child in front and "chug-chugging" gleefully through the assembly hall and back to their classrooms. At another school, the mothers of the birthday children made brief speeches before the entire student body, telling what their children were like as babies and thanking all the students and teachers of the school for helping their children to grow up happy and healthy. A British anthropologist wrote of sports day at a Japanese preschool:

> Typically, in the West, sports day is an occasion for the recognition of individual achievement and competitive spirit. . . . Not so the Japanese version. Races are held, to be sure, but they almost all involve some kind of co-operation as an integral part of the event, and individuals represent a larger group such as their class or residential district. All the children wear reversible red or white caps, and most of the races are between reds and whites. At the end of the day every single child receives a prize.[7]

Songs, dances, ceremonies, and art projects all provided opportunities to strengthen the students' sense of themselves as a community of "friends" (tomodachi) – or "as a family" (kazoku mitai ni). All the preschoolers at Trinity Preschool began each day by singing and acting out a song that symbolically took the preschool "family" together through all the hours they had been apart. They sang and acted out this song: "We went home, we played, we ate, we brushed our teeth, we slept, and [as the children jumped up] we woke up to begin a new day at preschool." ("Some children are still sleeping? Let's tickle them awake," said the preschool director laughingly, as some children lingered "sleeping" on the floor.) In several other preschools, morning meeting was a time for the monitors or the class as a whole to report what they'd done since leaving preschool the preceding day. Morning meeting was also a time for students to note which "friends" were missing and to plan get-well cards, gifts, or visits for classmates who had been absent for several days.

Like class meetings and ceremonies, art projects, too, often underlined connections among children. Children frequently worked in small groups or as a class to create a shared art project: a mural of

25

ocean life that covered a whole classroom wall, a class "birthday train" whose passengers were self-portraits by the 40 class members, a poster to welcome incoming 3-year-olds. Even activities that children pursued individually – such as painting pictures – might be used to underline children's connections to one another. For example, in several preschools, children regularly painted pictures of school field trips and special events – enough, by the end of the school year, for each child to receive an album that included pictures made by every class member, commemorating the year's shared experiences. "Children have a hard time giving away something they've made, but these albums give them a chance to experience the joy of giving *and* receiving," said one teacher. "I want each child to have a way to remember every classmate," explained another teacher.

LEARNING TO BECOME A RESPONSIBLE CLASS MEMBER: THE ROLE OF FREE PLAY

In addition to connecting children in shared pleasurable activities, free play provided the grist for a second central goal of Japanese preschool life: learning to be a responsible, kind member of the class. Let's return to Tokyo Public Preschool to hear Ms. Ishida's comments during the end-of-day meeting:

> I'd like to tell you two things that made me very happy today. The first is that our class played with the Chrysanthemums [the 4-year-olds]. When I saw Chrysanthemums and Cherry Blossoms [her class] all head for the playground equipment, I was very worried, but then our class members began to play and share with the Chrysanthemums, and I felt so relieved. How was it to play with them? Was it fun? [At this, several boys who played with the younger class tell what they played and affirm that it was fun.]
>
> The second thing I'd like to talk about is a problem we had today. Toshiko wanted to take home all the pieces of colored cellophane. Kanako said, "You can't do that" and took them away. Toshiko started crying, and Mariko and Chie kindly asked her what was wrong. When they heard

26

the problem, they asked the other three children using the cellophane if it was all right for Toshiko to take some home. The other children said it was all right to take home a few pieces, but not all. Toshiko said she wanted to take home 20, but the other children said, "No, just 3." Toshiko started to cry again. Then Mariko said, "What about 5?" and Toshiko and all the other children agreed. Let's clap for all these children who helped solve this problem.

All preschools I studied had at least one daily class meeting, and it always included time to reflect on the day's activities. Incidents of fighting, crying, or dangerous behavior inevitably resurfaced in teachers' comments during these meetings. Teachers made community property out of incidents that I might regard as private – for example, Toshiko's selfish attempt to take home the class's craft materials or two boys' fistfight over a wrecked sand castle. In case anyone had missed the actual incident, the teacher reconstructed it in vivid detail – how it started, who fought and who helped along the way, and how it was eventually settled. The point of the discussions did not seem to be humiliation – in fact, teachers bent over backward to describe sympathetically each child's reasons for fighting. As they explored the feelings that led to conflict and the attempts of classmates to help solve problems, teachers made clear that the problems, and the responsibility for solving them, belonged to the entire class.

Class meetings provided a time for children and teacher to reflect on the events and problems of the day. Too, they underlined teachers' values and aspirations for class members. For example, like Ms. Ishida, many teachers commented on whether children had been "playing without excluding other children from play." The single most common topic of discussion at preschool daily meetings was group chores. In many preschools, groups of children reported daily on how well they had accomplished their chores. Their candor was appealing. "We probably overfed the rabbit, because everyone wanted to give him some food, and we couldn't agree on just one person," reported the rabbit feeders in one classroom. "We didn't do a good job cleaning up the dramatic play corner, because we started playing in the middle," reported chore-group members in another preschool. "Don't bring the guinea pig onto the classroom floor – it makes droppings everywhere," requested the sweepers in yet another school.

Teachers often used these comments to spark class discussion. Students discussed, for example, what it means to care for animals well; what to do when fellow group members shirk chores; what to do when you see another child doing something dangerous. Some of these discussions continued for as long as 20 or 30 minutes. Teachers worked hard to capture all children's interest. They described problems vividly ("Our poor rabbit, his stomach might burst from too much food"), made bridges among children's comments ("Taro thinks we should get angry at people who goof off during chores, and Ko thinks we should just forget about the shirkers and do the chores ourselves; what do other people think?"), and asked students to applaud classmates who had worked hard to solve the "class's problems."

Teachers were not heavyhanded in these discussions. They rarely supplied answers. Rather, they tried to provoke children to come up with solutions to problems – even when this took many minutes of class time. Because of the time and care devoted to these discussions, I came to see them as the real curriculum of the Japanese preschools I visited. Free play, with its conflicts and kindnesses, provided the grist for this curriculum. Whatever the planned activities for the day, problems – like Toshiko's appropriation of the cellophane – could always take precedence.

Research on a nationally representative sample of Japanese preschools underlines the importance of community building and responsibility as goals of Japanese preschool education. A 1984 survey assessed educational practices in a nationally representative random sample of 800 Japanese preschools. Preschools responded anonymously – a provision designed to reduce pressure to respond "correctly." A total of 653 preschools, or 82% of those surveyed, responded. Virtually all preschools reported either frequent (59%) or occasional (35%) whole-school activities and experiences.[8] In the same survey, preschools were given a list of 31 activities and asked to choose the 7 they most emphasized. The top two choices involved the class or school community. "Chore groups/monitors" was chosen most frequently (it was strongly emphasized by 56% of preschools); "Sports Day" was next, strongly emphasized by 46% of preschools. The survey also reveals twin emphases on free play (reported as a "frequent" activity by 70% of preschools) and on themes pursued by all class members in groups or as a whole class (reported as frequent by 73% of preschools).

PLAY AND LEARNING

Although I did not set out to study intellectual development, I couldn't help noticing how much children seemed to learn in the course of selling watches, constructing a massive "irrigation project" that brought water across a wide playground, or composing a puppet show to perform for another class. They made paper coins and shared their collective wisdom about how to add and subtract them; they tried to make water flow uphill; they discussed whether a plot made sense. Teachers often extended children's involvement by posing interesting or challenging questions or by bringing in supplementary materials. For example, the teacher observed by Lauren Kotloff brought in books with pictures of airplanes to give children ideas for improving their plane. My field notes record the teacher's comments at the end of a day spent making items for the "clock store" dramatic enactment later in the week:

> The teacher is looking around at the great array of clocks made from construction paper and old food boxes: wristwatches, mantel clocks, wall clocks, even grandfather clocks. "I'm disappointed because some of the clocks aren't finished yet." She moves on to some other clocks and says, "These are some of the clocks I'd like to buy if I were shopping." Holding up several clocks in turn, she says, "I think they're really good because they have hands that move and pendulums that swing. I'd consider buying a clock if it had just one improvement. All of the clocks that you made are good, but they need to be better if you're going to be able to sell them."

29

What was the improvement the teacher wanted? Oddly, she never told the students. Perhaps the children, like me, are still wondering what improvements would have "sold" their clocks to the teacher – and perhaps that's the point. Although direct teaching was rare, children seemed to be learning a great deal as they pursued a variety of challenging open-ended activities that grew from free play.

THE NATIONAL GUIDELINES FOR PRESCHOOL EDUCATION

My observations fit remarkably well with Japan's official guidelines for preschool education. The Japanese Ministry of Education sets forth five objectives for preschool education:

1. To foster the basic habits of daily life and the attitudes needed for a healthy, safe, and happy life and to build the foundation for a sound mind and body.

2. To foster affection and trust toward others and to cultivate attitudes of autonomy and cooperation and the awakening of morality.

3. To foster interest and concern about nature and other things close at hand and to cultivate the awakening of a wealth of feelings and the power to think about these things.

4. To foster, in daily life, interest and concern about language and to cultivate enjoyment in talking and listening and a sense of language.

5. To foster a richness of emotion through diverse experiences and to foster creativity.[9]

The Ministry of Education defines specific goals for each of these five areas. These goals focus on fostering particular emotional states – "interest," "concern," "desire" – not achievements. In fact, the guidelines explicitly criticize achievement-focused education, noting that "children's natural expression of their own feelings and ideas should be valued, and unbalanced education designed to teach particular skills separate from daily activities should be avoided." The guidelines specifically forbid direct instruction in writing: "Systematic instruction about the alphabet begins in elementary school; so at preschool, direct instruction in this area should not be conducted. Rather, each individual child's interest, concern, and feeling about the alphabet should be fostered naturally."[10]

COLLIDING IMAGES: FREE PLAY OR EXAMINATION PREPARATION?

American media have featured heart-rending stories about Japanese preschoolers preparing for kindergarten entrance examinations.[11] Americans are surprised, consequently, to hear that most Japanese preschool education centers on free play. How common is academically focused preschool education in Japan? The 1984 survey described earlier in this chapter found that most preschools center on free play (35%) or on "establishing themes adapted to children's lives and choosing activities and experiences related to those" (33%).[12] Only 2% of Japanese preschools described their emphasis as "development of children's ability through special activities (such as education in music, art, athletics, or the alphabet)." The same survey found that about 13% of preschools systematically instructed 5-year-olds in the alphabet, and 8% in numbers. Public and private preschools showed striking differences: 21% of private schools but only 1% of public schools reported instruction of 5-year-olds in the alphabet; 14% of private schools but fewer than 1% of public schools reported instruction in numbers. As the number of preschoolers declines in many parts of Japan, private preschools must compete for parent tuition dollars. Often they attract students by adding special academic or extracurricular programs.[13] For example, I visited several preschools that taught after-school subjects such as English conversation, swimming, and art and provided training with geometric puzzles and other materials that might appear on the entrance examinations of prestigious elementary schools. A public preschool teacher told me: "Public preschools do not have to add academic programs even if parents demand them, but private preschools have to respond by teaching skills required for first grade, like the alphabet or harmonica."

The only large-scale comparison of American and Japanese preschools, conducted by Harold Stevenson and colleagues, suggests that the heart-rending images of young children's study should feature American children, not their Japanese counterparts. American 5-year-olds spend 30% of their school day in direct academic instruction, whereas Japanese students spend only 5% of the day in such instruction. Relative to their American peers, Japanese 5-year-olds spend nearly four times as much of the school day in free play.[14] Surveys of more than 500 parents and preschool educators by Joseph Tobin and colleagues further underline the deemphasis of academic instruction and the focus on social development in Japanese preschools. More than half of the Americans cited "To give children a good start academically" among the top three reasons for a society to have preschools, but fewer than 1% of Japanese respondents chose this among their top three reasons. In contrast, 80% of Japanese respondents, but only 39% of Americans, chose "Sympathy, empathy, and concern for others" among the three most important things for children to learn in preschool.[15] A similar pattern emerges from the parents in Japan and the United States surveyed by Harold Stevenson. Only 2% of the Japanese mothers, but nearly half of the American mothers, thought they could best help their children do well in kindergarten by working with them on educational activities. Japanese mothers thought they could best help their children by keeping them healthy and by expressing interest in school activities.[16]

Lois Peak studied the prior educational experiences of more than 1,000 first-graders in a geographically diverse sample of 11 Japanese elementary schools.[17] These included rural, urban, and suburban public elementary schools and 2 highly selective "elite" elementary schools (1 private and 1 national). Approximately half of the first-graders at the 2 elite schools had attended exam-preparatory classes during their preschool years. Almost none of the first-graders at the 9 public elementary schools had attended such classes; the percentages ranged from zero at 3 rural schools to 6 at a downtown Tokyo school and averaged 1.5 across schools. Elite-school students are a very unusual sample, statistically speaking, because 99% of Japan's elementary students attend local public elementary schools. Lois Peak's data suggest that they are also unusual in having had exam-preparatory classes. The fact that such classes are very rare at the preschool level is, unfortunately, overlooked in many media portrayals of Japanese education. When they do occur, exam-preparatory classes for preschoolers teach not reading, writing, or arithmetic but "a cheerful, confident self-presentation, care and precision in following directions, familiarity with typical test items, and experience with the testing routine."[18] Out of deference to the ministry's position against preschool instruction in reading and arithmetic, reading and number skills required on elite elementary entrance exams are minimal, but children need to understand and remember complex instructions.

Let's once again examine Japanese preschool education, keeping in mind Lois Peak's descriptions of the skills tested by kindergarten entrance examinations. Few Japanese preschools appear to be "examination focused" if what we mean by this is drill in the academic skills of reading, writing, and arithmetic. If we look at whether children are systematically taught to follow directions, however, a different picture might emerge. Gary DeCoker found substantial differences among Japanese preschools in what he termed the "formality and intensity" of their practices.[19] For example, what happens to children who do not follow directions carefully or who do not wish to participate in assemblies or other group activities? If the examination system is exerting downward pressure on preschool education, as many observers suggest, it may be more likely to show up in behavioral demands than in academic demands, given the Ministry of Education's clear policy against academic training for preschoolers.

Chapter 3 describes several studies that document an emphasis on child-initiated compliance (rather than teacher-imposed punishments and rewards) and an indulgent attitude toward much of what Americans might consider misbehavior. To detect the impact of the examination system on preschool education, however, studies are needed that are more recent and larger in scale.

My observations – and the work of other researchers – suggest that Japanese preschool education focuses on free play and social development, not on academic development. Americans find this surprising. Why? First, Americans learn mostly about the bizarre fringes of Japanese preschool education: the cram schools for pre-schoolers, attended by a very small percentage of the population, or the off-beat preschool that encourages children to play naked in order to "build strength." We hear little about mainstream preschools.

Second, Americans may assume that Japanese preschool educa-tion must be highly academic because, although Japanese mothers do *less* teaching of their preschoolers than American mothers do, Japanese students show superior achievement in some subjects in early elementary school.[20] It may be hard for Americans to imagine a preschool system other than academic drill that gives children an academic advantage in elementary school. Yet, in fact, a child-centered preschool curriculum fosters greater motivation to learn and greater ultimate academic achievement than does direct in-struction, according to some American research.[21]

Why would a child-centered environment be more advan-tageous than direct instruction? Young children may learn best when they pursue activities they find meaningful – activities of their own or shared invention, pursued in an environment rich in friendship and built up through the thoughtful comments of other children and adults. As we've just explored, free play in Japanese preschools sometimes sparked passionate class-wide pursuits. This was no accident. Teachers actively worked to connect individual children to the larger group – to help them experience the pleasures and difficulties of group life and its richness as a source of ideas and inspiration for play.

CONCLUSION

My sons are fond of watching the Japanese television show *Hirake Ponkikki*. This Japanese counterpart to *Sesame Street* sometimes fea-tures 30 or more preschoolers who gather in an on-the-air preschool where they dance, sing, play games, and collaborate on art projects. My 9-year-old puzzles over why the show crowds 30 children onto the stage, rather than just a few, and why it features "real 3-year-olds who can't dance very well and who get distracted," rather than actors who "could really dance and behave themselves." My sons love the chaos of 30 real children on the screen and beg to watch over and over again one sequence in which children paint cardboard boxes, tape them together, affix decorations and ropes, and – surprise – pull to standing position a 20-foot robot. As the children and teachers work together, we hear their "preschool" song:

> We're all friends.
> We'll be friends forever, forever.
> Even when we go to elementary school, we'll be friends.
> Even when we become adults, we'll be friends.
> We've played together, we've fought together, we've laughed
>   together, we've cried together. We'll be friends forever.

Hirake Ponkikki's themes are themes that I encountered again and again as I interviewed Japanese preschool teachers: the importance of all children having fun together; of building a shared sense of purpose; of helping children share each other's fights and sadness as well as good times; of building friendship. Far from occurring "despite" this social emphasis, I think academic development occurs, at least in part, *because of* this emphasis on friendship, connection, and collaboration. In the chapters that follow, we'll explore why.

3

THE WHOLE CHILD GOES TO ELEMENTARY SCHOOL

Children don't come to school because they want to learn. Children come to school because they want to see their friends. So I put the most effort into getting friends for each child. Particularly when a child is slow, I try to get that child to enjoy friendships.

A Japanese elementary teacher

Japanese teachers believe in "whole-person" education. . . . They feel that their most important task is to develop well-rounded "whole people," not just intellects.

William Cummings, *Education and Equality in Japan*[1]

My job is to create happy memories.

A Japanese elementary teacher

EACH YEAR, THE JAPANESE MINISTRY OF EDUCATION PUBlishes a thick statistical profile of Japanese education. It includes extensive information on enrollment, class size, students' health and fitness, and students' access to cultural institutions and social welfare, but it provides no test scores or other indices of academic achievement. For example, 1992's summary of national educational statistics documents student-teacher ratios, the number of students with untreated cavities, and how far students can broad jump and throw a handball; academic achievement is addressed only by school attendance and completion rates.[2]

Westerners hear a great deal about the high academic achievement of Japanese children. But, as the statistics hint, Japanese educators are concerned with many aspects of children's development. Children's intellectual development is taken seriously – but so is their need for friendship, for connection to a caring classroom community, for wholehearted involvement in sports, music, and art. In the first part of this chapter, we spend a day with a first-grade class to see the ways that concern for children's social, academic, and civic development is interwoven throughout the lessons and activities of the school day. Next, we explore the goals found in 19 Japanese first-grade classrooms and in Japan's national Course of Study. Finally, we explore how the "whole child" approach may connect children to schooling and create arenas where all children are successful.

A Day at Downtown Elementary

It's almost 9 a.m. The large banner over the blackboard in Ms. Ishii's first-grade classroom says, *"Tomodachi ni narō. Saigo made gambarō"* ("Let's be friends. Let's persist until the end"). The blackboard shows the agenda for the morning meeting and the subjects to be studied that day. Students play and talk noisily until the two student monitors for the day come to the front of the classroom and ask their 34 classmates to be seated. Most students take their seats and quiet down quickly, but the monitors must quiet several children by calling their names. All students are seated and quiet when, a few moments later, Ms. Ishii enters the room. On a cue from the monitors, all students rise, bow, and chorus, "Teacher, good morning." Ms. Ishii bows and greets them in return. Students take their seats, except for the monitors, who announce, in unison, the beginning of morning meeting and the first item on the agenda: attendance. Ms. Ishii calls the roll. Children shout, "Present" when their names are called, trying to outdo one another with the loudness of their shouts. "Great – you've got lots of *genki* (energy) today," responds Ms. Ishii to the loud shouts.

The two monitors announce, from the board, the next item for the morning meeting: "Things to tell the class." A child raises his hand and one student monitor calls on him. "My tooth fell out last night," the boy volunteers. At that, a number of children begin shouting out how many teeth they've lost. The monitors ask children to raise their hands if they want to talk. It takes 2 minutes for the monitors to quiet the class, and Ms. Ishii sits silent during this time. Finally, the class settles down and the monitors call on several more students, who share some personal news with the class. The monitors then announce the next item: news from the teacher. Ms. Ishii speaks: "I want to praise something today. Every morning you pass by the 'aunties' who work in the kitchen and I know you say good morning in your hearts. But today you said, 'Good morning' with your voices. I was very happy and I know they were very happy." Ms. Ishii nods to the monitors, who announce, "Morning meeting is over. Take out your notebooks for social studies." Checking to see that all children have accomplished this, the monitors then announce, "Social studies will begin. Let's greet the teacher." Once again led by the monitors, the children stand, chorus, "Teacher, please (teach us),"and bow.

Social studies begins. As homework, children have visited local parks and copied in their notebooks the rules posted at the parks. Ms. Ishii asks students to report the rules they found and explain the reasons for them. One student reports, "I found the rule 'Don't play with balls here.' I think it's because balls might hit people." This student calls on another student, who adds, "Especially, balls might hit mothers with babies." This student, in turn, calls on another child whose hand is raised. For about 20 minutes, discussion continues in this manner, with each child calling on another child.

The students' comments build on one another remarkably well, with many students making reference to their classmates' comments: "This is similar to the rule found by Ishikawa-san . . . " or "In addition to the reason Kojima-kun mentioned, another reason might be . . ." Sometimes a number of children want to comment, and they wave their hands furiously at the child who is speaking. Ms. Ishii writes each new rule on the board. Occasionally Ms. Ishii too raises her hand and is called on by a student. Usually she plays devil's advocate: "Why shouldn't we take leaves off a tree? That doesn't hurt anyone" or "It's OK to play in phone booths, isn't it?"

After the children have listed and discussed all the rules they found, Ms. Ishii asks them to select three rules they found especially new, important, or interesting and write them in their notebooks along with their reasons. "Then read over what you've written to make sure I can understand it too, and bring your notebooks to me." Students spend the remaining 20 minutes of the lesson writing rules and their reasons in their notebooks while Ms. Ishii walks through the classroom, stopping to help individual children. As children finish, they bring their work to be checked by Ms. Ishii; she circles grammatical and writing errors, calling them "strange places" (*okashii tokoro*) and suggests that children figure out why they are strange and correct them. When the chime sounds, the monitors come to the front of the class and ask the class to bow and thank Ms. Ishii. The class stands, thanks her in unison, and bows.

Each of the subsequent lessons begins in the same way: The student monitors quiet and seat the class, remind students to take out the appropriate materials, and lead the class in formally greeting Ms. Ishii and bowing to her. The 10- or 20-minute breaks between classes are, however, bedlam, as students noisily visit, play tag, and even mount each other's shoulders for "chicken fights" in the classroom. Ms. Ishii leaves the classroom during some of these breaks; even when she's present, though, she makes no move to stop the shouting and games.

Second period is Japanese composition. Children spend the first 15 minutes recalling their recent class trip to dig sweet potatoes. "What was most fun?" begins Ms. Ishii. "Pulling hard," "Finding that my potato was huge," "Having my potato slip right out of the ground when I pulled it," come the enthusiastic responses. Hearing the last response, Ms. Ishii asks: "Did anyone have a different experience?" and several children shout out that their potatoes wouldn't come out even when they tugged and tugged. "Why?" asks Ms. Ishii, and several children volunteer their ideas: that the potato had deep roots, that several potatoes attached to the stem all pointed in different directions. Ms. Ishii illustrates these ideas on the board and asks children to think about whether their potatoes looked like her sketches or looked different.

The remaining 30 minutes are devoted to writing. Ms. Ishii circles the room looking at what children are writing. She occasionally addresses questions or comments to the class: "What was the place like where we dug the potatoes?"; "What was the day like?"; "What were you thinking as you were digging, and how did you feel?"; "Write what you felt when the potato came out"; "Write so that someone who's never been to dig potatoes will know just what it's like." Interspersed are occasional practical instructions, such as "Don't mix up the two ways of writing o." Ms. Ishii concludes the lesson: "Some children were able to write many lines, some just one or two. If you couldn't write much, practice at home tomorrow so everyone can write many lines on Monday."

Today's third-period lesson, mathematics, is canceled in order to devote a double period to physical education; the class needs to practice the lively jazz dance routine that will be performed the next day as part of Sports Day. I am surprised to see boys and girls strip down to their underwear and change into gym clothes in the classroom, but the children show no embarrassment. Once outside on the playground, the class assembles into its fixed small groups (see chapter 4), each group in a circle, and the class practices its dance to a jazz tape. Ms. Ishii is pleased with the dancing except for the timing of one step in which children are supposed to jump backward to the center of their small circles, bump backsides, and jump up in mock surprise. Ms. Ishii explains that the step's humor depends upon good timing – that the jump in mock surprise must appear to be the result of the backside bump. As she has the class practice this sequence for the third time, Ms. Ishii says,

"Watch yourself and others and see if everyone's starting at the right time. We'll have *hansei* (reflection) on this point later." Twenty minutes before the end of the double period, the students return to the classroom and assemble in their small groups. Each small group talks about whether it has the correct timing for the backside bump and devises strategies for helping children who are off (such as signaling them when it's time to start jumping).

The monitors announce the end of physical education and the beginning of lunch. Without a word of instruction from the teacher, children suddenly move in many directions. Some push desks together into dining areas for each group; others don hairnets and white aprons and fetch carts of food from the kitchen; others pass out straws and milk and set places for the classmates who are serving food. Children eat lunch with their fixed groups. On the wall, a richly decorated poster made by sixth-graders says, "Let's enjoy school lunch"; under it, a handmade sign lists this month's goal for school lunch: "To learn to eat a variety of foods without leaving any." A few minutes into lunch, the vice-principal's voice comes over the public address system: "Are you enjoying your lunch?" He goes on to give a brief talk, thanking by name several children who, on their own initiative after school, picked up litter on the school grounds and in a local park.

The fifth and final period of the day is devoted to the once-weekly class meeting. Sometimes class meeting features a class skit, a splashfest in the pool, or some similarly playful activity selected by the students. But sometimes, like today, students discuss an issue facing the class. "Who knows what *saikō* (utmost) means?" Ms. Ishii begins the meeting. "What does *saikō* mean when we're talking about Sports Day?" Children raise their hands and volunteer various responses: "Running your hardest"; "Pulling your hardest in tug-of-war"; "Doing your best." Ms. Ishii continues: "What about our class dance – what's doing your utmost mean for it?" Again, children raise their hands and volunteer responses: "Energetically"; "Smiling"; "Your very best dancing." "On Sports Day, we also have an opening ceremony and closing ceremony. What does *saikō* mean with respect to these ceremonies?" Children again volunteer responses: "Not playing with your hands"; "Listening to speeches quietly." Ms. Ishii goes on through each event of Sports Day and asks students to talk about what "doing your utmost" means. She then asks them to think about one way they're going to do their utmost the next day and calls on several children to share their ideas with the class. Most of the children volunteer that they want to run fast or dance beautifully, but one child says, "I want to sit still when the important people give their speeches. I want to sit so still that even my mother will think I did a good job." Ms. Ishii singles this student out for praise: "Ms. Takeda is so praiseworthy. She's chosen her most difficult thing to try hard at. We all know she's often cautioned for fidgeting when we're supposed to sit still. Tomorrow, when everyone's watching her, she wants to do her best to sit still. I hope you'll all think, like Ms. Takeda, about what is most difficult for you and vow to try hard at it tomorrow."

Ms. Ishii nods to the monitors, who come to the front of the class and announce, "Class meeting is over. End-of-day meeting will begin." The monitors ask each group to report on its goal for the week and whether the group accomplished it. Several of the groups chose "No forgotten things" as a goal. Others chose "Being ready at the start of every lesson" or "Not fighting." After several minutes of discussion within the groups, each group reports to the class briefly: "The members of our group remembered all their belongings this week"; "We were ready most of the time, but on Tuesday we had a hard time settling down for lessons."

The students then talk within their groups once again, to choose group goals for the following week. A few minutes later, a representative from each group announces its goal; about half the groups have chosen new goals, and the other half have decided to try again at the preceding

42

Fourth-graders' signed self-portraits and goals. For example, one student's goals are: "To write Japanese neatly. To volunteer my ideas a lot. To create lots of (happy) memories this year too." (Photo courtesy Ineko Tsuchida)

Fourth graders' self-portraits under their class goal: "Let's help each other in a friendly way." (Photo courtesy Ineko Tsuchida)

week's goal. The monitors then call on chore groups to make any needed announcements. Only the Flower group has an announcement today: They thank children for bringing in flowers and ask them to bring flowers next week so they can again have flowers for each group's dining area. The monitors choose a song – a rousing song that will be sung at the athletics festival the next day – and lead the class in singing it. Finally, they ask the class to stand and to bow and thank the teacher. In turn, Ms. Ishii asks the class to bow to the monitors and to thank them for their service to the class that day. "Enjoy tomorrow! Goodbye!" says Ms. Ishii, and school is over.

CENTRAL GOALS OF FIRST-GRADE LIFE: FRIENDLINESS, PERSISTENCE, ENERGY, SELF-MANAGEMENT

Elementary school? It often seemed more like Sunday School or a scout meeting. To enter a Japanese elementary classroom is to confront many clear, explicit values. Under signs that said, "Let's be friends and help each other," children spoke earnestly of what they had done during the previous school week to help others – or of ways they had fallen short of this goal. Teachers led the class in learning Japanese, mathematics, and seven other subject areas. But, like Ms. Ishii, they also led the class in thinking about social and ethical issues – the importance of friendly greetings to the kitchen staff, the reasons for rules in local parks, or what it means to do your utmost in a variety of situations.

Like Ms. Ishii's first-graders, students in other Japanese classrooms studied beneath banners and posters proclaiming their school, class, or group goals – a total of 94 goals in the 19 first-grade classrooms where I recorded them! All were written in the hiragana alphabet, in order to be readable by first-graders. They included goals for the trimester, month, and week; goals selected by the student council, the faculty, the class, or the small groups within the class. Table 1 summarizes the 94 goals. Note that nearly half of the

Table 1. *Goals Posted in 19 Japanese First-Grade Classrooms*

Socioemotional	44
Friendship, cooperation, consideration	24
Listen well; keep promises	9
Responsibility for self	2
Greetings	6
Other personal qualities, e.g., "calm," "beautiful heart"	3
Health and Nutrition	12
School lunch: "Enjoy eating"; "Eat a variety of foods"; "Eat in the allotted time"; etc.	6
Fix cavities	2
Wash hands; other general hygiene	4
Physical Energy and Exercise	10
"Be energetic"; "Play energetically"	9
Use horizontal bars	1
Neatness and Punctuality	9
Clean up around us; Keep desk contents neat; etc.	4
Keep to time schedule	2
Miscellaneous; Don't forget belongings; Get up early; Use blackboard neatly	3
Persistence	9
"Children who persist"; "Children who persist until the end"; etc.	
Academic	8
Become children who "Take the initiative in learning"; "Learn well"; "Think carefully"	7
"Try hard at Japanese"	1
Total goals	92

Note: Only goals intended to be read by children (i.e., written in hiragana) were recorded. The introduction describes the 19 classrooms studied.

goals focus on friendship, cooperation, and other aspects of social and emotional development: "Let's become friends"; "Let's be children who get along well with each other and help each other"; "Let's be kind children who easily say, 'I'm sorry' and 'Thank you'." The goals evidence concern with diverse dimensions of child

Table 2. *Content of Moral Education for Grades 1 and 2*

1. *Things Primarily Related to Oneself*
   (1) Leading an ordered life by being attentive to health and safety, treating objects and money carefully, keeping the area around oneself organized, and avoiding thinking only of oneself
   (2) Fully carrying out the study and work that are one's own responsibility
   (3) Taking the initiative in doing things one thinks to be good
   (4) Leading a life that is relaxed and ingenuous, not dishonest or deceptive

2. *Things Primarily Related to Relationships with Others*
   (1) Being cheerful with others by endeavoring to use greetings, language, and actions that are pleasant
   (2) Being warmhearted in contacts with younger children and older perons near oneself and showing them kindness
   (3) Getting along with friends and helping them
   (4) Thanking the people in daily life who care for one

3. *Things Primarily Related to Relationships with Nature and the Sublime*
   (1) Feeling intimate with the nature that's near oneself; being kindhearted in treatment of plants and animals
   (2) Having a heart that values life
   (3) Having contact with beautiful things and feeling ennobled by them

4. *Things Primarily Related to Relationships with Groups and Society*
   (1) Treating carefully things that are used by everyone and upholding promises and rules
   (2) Feeling love and respect for one's parents and grandparents and actively helping at home
   (3) Feeling love and respect for one's teachers, feeling intimate with the people at school, and enjoying classroom life

Source: Monbushō [Ministry of Education, Science, and Culture], 1989b, pp. 105–106 (my translation).

development: social, moral, personal, physical, academic. Note the relative deemphasis of academic goals (8% of goals).[3]

Across the 19 schools, goals seemed to derive from the same core materials: the Ministry of Education's guidelines for moral education (Table 2). But since principals, teachers, or students chose goals after discussion, the wording and nuance of goals varied from school to school. Each school developed a plan specifying how the goals could be pursued as part of each academic subject area, through class and school-wide special events, and through regular daily activities such as class meetings, lunch, and cleaning. Some goals – such as those related to health and hygiene – are self-explanatory, but others make sense only when we see how they were discussed and pursued by students and teachers. This section provides background on four goals that were central to first-grade classroom life: friendliness, persistence, energy, and self-management.

Friendliness (*Tomodachi, Shinsetsu, Yasashii, Nakayoku*)

Under banners that said, "Let's get along well with each other" or "Let's be kind," students reflected, for example, on whether they had done something kind for fellow students during the past week or how the members of a small group could show kindness while working together on a social studies project. What they talked about – helping others, not excluding others from play, listening respectfully to others' ideas, not teasing – encompasses what American researchers call "community" or "social climate." Teachers and students themselves, however, described their goal as a friendly school, sometimes even using the English loan word *furendori* (friendly).

Greeting others was the centerpiece of the *furendori undō* (friendliness campaign) waged by the student council at one elementary school I studied, and greetings were prominent goals at several other schools as well, in the form of goals such as "Always greeting others" or "Greeting others with a smile." As one first-grade class discussed at length their goal for the trimester – "To greet others with a smile" – their teacher raised questions such as "What makes you smile?," "How do you feel when you're smiling?," and "How do you feel when other people smile at you?"

Although I initially viewed the emphasis on greetings as concern with etiquette, teachers explained to me that greetings are the most basic way to recognize other members of the school community. They explained that children naturally greeted their friends with smiles; to smile and greet other children and adults created bridges that could be built upon and the scaffolding for a community. I was skeptical about the importance of greetings until my 5-year-old attended Japanese preschool. Loud, smiling shouts of "Good morning" and "Good-bye" were a favorite ritual in his Japanese preschool, despite the din of 350 children greeting and taking leave of each classmate. My son, typically rather shy, took this custom home with him to his American preschool. He cheerfully sought out each of his classmates and teachers to say good morning and good-bye each day, provoking several teachers and parents to comment on my son's "many friends." What I had thought a rather superficial custom did indeed seem to make classmates and teachers feel important and cared about.

Persistence (*Gambaru, Doryoku, Konki*)

Many scholars of Japanese education and culture have noted the central value placed on *gambaru* – persistence, trying hard, or doing one's best.[4] Japanese students regard effort as more important for academic achievement than do American students. In contrast, American students regard innate ability as more important than do Japanese students.[5] These assumptions may have potent consequences for achievement: Faced with failure, a student can choose to give up (a sensible course if innate ability is seen as important) or to try even harder (a sensible course if effort is seen as important).

In the goals I recorded, persistence was often a pure goal, an end in itself: "Let's become children who persist"; "Let's be children who persist until the end." But when children discussed persistence, they chose specific personal goals. In the months that I spent in Japanese elementary schools, I heard dozens of discussions in which children talked about persistence and identified personal goals for persistence. My first experience of such a discussion occurred near Tanabata, a holiday that celebrates the reunion, in the July sky, of two constellations said to be separated lovers. Linking their goal of *gambaru* to the Tanabata holiday's theme of making what is longed for come true, children decorated bamboo branches with white "wish" streamers on which they had written the things they wanted to try hard at.

48

Children spent most of a class period discussing and selecting their goals for self-improvement. Their choices were delightfully varied: "I want to stop punching my younger sister"; "I want to eat my whole lunch"; "I want to write the alphabet more neatly." Later in the year, they would revisit these goals and reflect on their personal progress. In another school, I saw a nearly identical lesson just after the New Year holiday. This time, students wrote New Year's resolutions, to be revisited in future lessons. Once again, students identified a wide range of goals: "To run around the whole track without stopping"; "To stop fighting on the playground"; "To brush my teeth every morning." Subsequently I saw the same basic lesson in several other schools as students selected goals for the "new trimester," for the "new season," and for the "second half of the trimester." Anytime seemed to be a good time to discuss persistence and to set goals!

Energy, Enthusiasm (*Genki*)

I found surprising the emphasis on *genki* – physical energy or exuberance. How could any first-grade teacher in her right mind display a huge banner exhorting students to "Play energetically" or to "Be energetic"? I reflected on this question during a 10-minute break between lessons, when under the banner "Let's play energetically" students ran at full speed around a first-grade classroom, hitting each other over the head with gym bags and climbing out the ground floor classroom windows. But both preschool and elementary teachers frequently urged children to show *genki*: When children answered roll call, sang, responded in unison, or danced, a teacher's comment "There's not much *genki* today" would result in loud voices and vigorous gestures.

Noisy exuberance meant several things to the teachers I interviewed. First, it meant children were "acting like children" – a phrase that seems to have much more complimentary connotations in Japanese than in English. Like the teachers interviewed by Merry White (1987a) and by Joseph Tobin and colleagues (1989), many teachers mentioned the importance of children's being "*kodomorashii*" (childlike) and complained that extracurricular lessons and examination preparation threatened to rob Japanese children of

49

their childhood. As one principal commented, "We devote the school's optional instructional time to outdoor games, because children's after-school lives allow so little play. But it's an odd state of affairs when schools have to make sure that children play enough."

Second, exuberant, enthusiastic participation demonstrated children's connection to the group. Japanese teachers worry greatly about children who won't participate wholeheartedly in group activities.[6] Finally, uncontained enthusiasm is the flip side of self-discipline – the more children let go, the greater the self-discipline they need to return to order. In both Japanese preschools and elementary schools, the alternation between exuberance and control is extraordinary, resulting in accounts of Japanese education as both freer and more regimented than American education.[7] As we saw in Ms. Ishii's class, the elementary school day in Japan is a series of 40- to 45-minute lessons, each followed by a 10- or 20-minute break during which children play rambunctiously. Intentionally or not, wild free play preceding each academic lesson provides a stringent proving ground for children's self-management, the final goal to be discussed.

Self-management

Self-management included general goals such as "Taking care of your responsibilities" (*jibun no koto o jibun de suru*) and specific tasks – keeping to the time schedule, keeping one's desk contents neat, keeping the area around oneself neat (*jikan o mamorimashō, tsukue no naka no seiton, mi no mawari o kirei ni shimashō*). All of the 19 first-grade classrooms where I recorded the wall contents had charts designed to help children self-manage. For example, just as Ms. Ishii had written the day's schedule on the board, all teachers I observed posted lesson schedules that enabled students to prepare for each lesson during the preceding break by laying out the right notebooks, textbooks, and materials or changing into gym clothes. These schedules also showed the length of the break between lessons (usually 10 or 20 minutes) and reminded children of options for that time: Use the bathroom, play outside, and so forth. Charts showed what should be brought to school each day (how many pencils, handkerchiefs, packages of tissue) and how desk contents should be arranged. Charts illustrated the proper posture for writing, reading, and standing to speak and showed the agendas for the opening and closing meetings. Chore charts made by the children listed the members and tasks for each chore group. Although the particular chores and responsibilities varied from class to class, responsibility itself was ubiquitous. In most classes, at least once a day students reflected on some responsibility: Had they watered the class garden and fed the animals? Remembered to bring from home all required items? Kept their desks neat? Laid out the correct notebooks and textbooks before each class?

GOALS AND VALUES COME TO LIFE

Goals festooned the walls; but they also made their way off the walls and into classroom life. Daily, children discussed goals and reflected on their progress. Sometimes the discussions were brief. For example, in many first grades I visited, "Our Goals" was a daily agenda item for the morning meeting, and "Reflecting on Our Goals" a daily agenda item for the closing meeting. The week that I visited Ms. Motoyama's first grade, the weekly class goal was "To play outside energetically." At the end of the day, most hands shot up when the two student monitors leading the class said, "Raise your hands if you played outside energetically today."

But often goals occasioned much lengthier discussion. The huge banner above the blackboard in Ms. Yoshimura's first-grade classroom proclaimed, "Let's become friends." Children had selected this as their goal for the month from a questionnaire developed by the teacher entitled "Our Hopes for Our Class." Ms. Yoshimura began the weekly class meeting by asking children to read the goal and think about friendly actions they had taken or witnessed that week. Children volunteered their experiences (the unfriendly along with the friendly); for example: "I helped Yamaguchi-kun when he spilled his crayons"; "At recess, I played with classmates I've never played with before"; "The boys hogged the dodge ball and didn't let the girls use it"; "We all made get-well cards for Ishikawa-san, and that was friendly." The teacher repeated each comment to the class and gave the class a chance to respond. The 30-minute discussion touched on how friends greet one another, how they work together, and how they play. Students identified ways they had made progress in "becoming friends" and areas that needed more work. I was touched by how freely students volunteered their ideas about friendship and their experiences at school.

The goals found their way not only into class meetings but also into academic lessons. Under a banner that read, "Let's become children who put their strength together," Ms. Ueda introduced a first-grade social studies lesson by talking about her own brother and two sisters. She made a chart on the blackboard that showed her own vocation, hobbies, strengths, and weaknesses and those of her brother and sisters. For example, her brother was an accountant who could cook well but could not get up in the morning. The teacher noted that she herself could not draw well and had a hard time remembering Japanese ideographs but could sing well. She ended by explaining how they put their strength together to make a happy family: "My sister corrects my writing, my brother cooks gourmet meals, I help everyone sing. . . . We are lucky to have each other, but in this class, we're even luckier because we have the strengths of 36 people that we can put together." She went on to read a story about a family whose members helped one another. Students then met in their small groups to brainstorm ways that family members helped one another and ways that class members helped one another.

Social and ethical goals consistently shaped class meetings and lessons in social studies and moral education, and they often found their way into other subject areas as well. Goals of "Helping one another" and "Pooling strength" were fundamental to many lessons in science, mathematics, music, art, and physical education. Children reflected on helpfulness at the same time as they investigated water volume (see chapter 4); they pursued a social studies project with the twin goals of "Building a three-dimensional model of the neighborhood and making sure all children in the group get a chance to say their ideas"; they played music together and then discussed both their musical performance and the strengths and weaknesses of the cooperation that shaped it. Judging from the attention and discussion it received, skillful collaboration was often as important as academic mastery itself. And sometimes the social and academic goals of a lesson were so intertwined that I couldn't distinguish them, as in the following social studies lesson in a middle-class Tokyo elementary school.

Studying Mothers' Work

The large banner over the blackboard in Ms. Yoshida's first grade exhorted, "Let's pool our strength" (*chikara o awasete*). The social studies lesson began with students' reports of their homework: to find out the kinds of work their mothers did at home. Ms. Yoshida wrote on the board the major categories of work children reported. Children were surprised to find, when they estimated the time each task took, that their mothers' work took more than 11 hours a day. One boy insisted, "My mother just reads magazines when I'm at school," but the other children urged him to notice how much time it took to do laundry, cooking, cleaning, childcare, and shopping.

The teacher posed a hypothetical problem: "What would happen if your mother was sick and couldn't cook dinner, and your father had to stay late at work?" Children volunteered responses: that they would ask older siblings, grandparents, or neighbors to cook or that they would cook themselves. The teacher then asked, "How many of you can fix dinner yourself? What would you fix?" Several of the children named dishes they could fix themselves.

Then the teacher asked the children to break into their fixed small groups of four children and to think of as many ways they could to help their mothers. Children talked for about 5 minutes within their groups, and then a representative from each group reported the group's ideas to the whole class. As she noted the items on the board, Ms. Yoshida frequently polled the class. "How many of you get up the first time your mother calls you?," "How many of you clean up your toys?," "How many of you help clean the bathroom and kitchen?," and so forth. After the class had listed and discussed all the ideas, the teacher asked each child to choose one way to ease the mother's work, to write and illustrate it, and to put it into practice starting that day. The teacher urged children to consider extra work they created for their mothers by needing reminders (to brush teeth, to do homework, and so forth). The teacher hung the children's illustrated goals on a bulletin board so that students could evaluate their progress during a subsequent social studies lesson.

BUILDING A COMMUNITY IN THE CLASSROOM

As we've just explored, Japanese early elementary classrooms present clear values and give students many opportunities to discuss these values and to apply them to daily life. But what leads students to care about these values? The teachers and principals I interviewed stressed that students' feelings of "unity" (*matomari*) and belonging lead children to accept school values – an idea supported by U.S. theory and research as well.[8] Japanese educators talked frequently about ways to create a sense of unity among the 600 or so individuals in a school community. Three themes emerged repeatedly. First, it was essential to build friendships among students. Second, students needed to be actively involved in shaping school norms. Finally, students needed to develop a sense of responsibility for one another. Children's involvement in shaping school norms and their sense of responsibility for one another are central themes of chapters 5 and 6, on discipline. The remainder of this section explores class and school activities designed to build a sense of belonging.

At the beginning of the school year, Japanese teachers' magazines are filled with articles on *gakkyūzukuri* – "building classhood." These articles urge teachers to provide chances for students to get to know one another as individuals, to have fun together, and to work together to shape classroom values and practices. For example, they recommend cooperative art projects and games, activities that help children find out about one another's families and hobbies, humorous songs and dances, and class discussions of "what kind of class we want to be." I was surprised that none of the 19 first-grade

54

teachers I interviewed mentioned academic skills among the skills and attitudes that children need to learn during the first month of first grade. Two thirds of the teachers mentioned children's friendships or sense of connection to one another. For example, here are three teachers' goals for the beginning of the year:

> The first thing children need is friends. Friends help make children at ease. What children like most about school is playing with friends, so I give them opportunities to play with everyone in the class.

> At the beginning of the year, I use music to help build our sense of classhood. I use music because I happened to be a music major in college, but you could use any subject – whatever happens to be your favorite. Using music, I give children the opportunity to create something bigger than any one child could create alone. The children share pleasure. They share the satisfaction of creating something together.

> At the beginning of the school year, I often have the members of each group name, each day, the things they like about each member of their group. Children naturally notice each other's bad points, but I tell them to find the good points of their groupmates. As they do this, their whole way of looking at one another begins to change.

Teachers also talked about the importance of building a "thread" – a connection – between the teacher and each individual child. This thread would invisibly connect teacher and child and allow each to know what the other was feeling. Most elementary teachers visited the homes of all their students early in the school year. These visits lasted just 20 minutes or so – since teachers had to visit as many as 40 homes – but teachers reported that the visits gave children a special sense of connection to the teacher.

In some elementary classrooms, "one-minute speeches" began each day. A typical format was for the daily monitors to tell the class what they had done after school the previous day, followed by a time for classmates to ask questions. Often the speeches and questions focused on favorite TV shows, hobbies, and after-school activities, providing rich connections to classmates.

55

Diaries provided another arena for building personal connections. Many elementary teachers had students write daily or weekly diaries, which teachers read and commented on, responding to the substance of children's experience, not to their writing skill. Daily lessons also wove in children's personal experiences and preferences, as children wrote or told the class what their most precious possession was, what their grandparents were like, what chores each family member did at home, what equipment their ideal playground would have, or what they had liked most and least about school during the preceding week. As a result, teachers had an amazing array of information about their students, and they often used it to personalize lessons. Teachers drew individual children into lessons with comments such as "Your grandmother lives with you, so has she told you about what our neighborhood was like when she was young?"; "You love fishing, so I bet you can tell us about where to find fish"; "Writing is your least favorite subject, so what did you think about today's lesson?"

Nobuo Shimahara and Akira Sakai, who studied on-the-job training for new Japanese elementary teachers, noted that *kizuna* – the bond or tie between students and teacher – is seen as the central principle of good education. In training new teachers, establishment of this bond takes precedence over technical competence. New teachers are urged to "mingle with students without disguise and pretense." They are coached on how to build enduring relationships with children and how to see things from a child's point of view. Here's the kind of advice experienced teachers gave their new colleagues:

Teaching is a kind of art. Emphasis should be placed on the relationship of hearts, the nurturing of bonding between the teacher's and children's hearts.

It is important to understand children as human beings whose characteristics are expressed in their activities. It is my belief that all children can do their best and concentrate on work. But it depends on the teacher's approach and desire. I am not concerned with how to teach children; rather I try to understand them first by developing personal relations, *kakawari*. When I get a new class I do not teach subject matter immediately. Instead I play with children intensely for a week to gain a good understanding of them. Then I will begin to know what kinds of children they are and gradually direct them toward the goals of learning on the basis of happy and trustful *kakawari* with them.[9]

The researchers contrast this with the experience of American teachers in training, who are told, "Don't make the mistake of trying to be friends with the kids." Relationships that foster empathy and "touching of the hearts" are stressed in many arenas of Japanese life.[10]

Other researchers have noted that Japanese teachers of young children personalize learning. In the communication game described in chapter 7, Japanese mothers and teachers were asked to describe pictures in such a way that preschool-age children would choose the correct target picture among four candidates. Whereas 75% of Japanese mothers and teachers personalized messages by referring to the child or the child's experience, only 35% of the American mothers and teachers personalized their teaching in this way.[11] Teachers' interest in personalizing lessons and their attention to the "thread" with each individual child seem paradoxical in a society known for groupism and conformity. Yet, as teachers explained to me, "To nurture the group, you must nurture each individual."

As the lessons and goals illustrate, Japanese teachers concerned themselves not only with students' intellectual development but also with their personal development. But the distinction between intellectual development and personal development may be one that is more Western than Japanese. Compared with the concept of the "intelligent person" held by Americans, the Japanese concept more strongly emphasizes qualities Hiroshi Azuma and Keiko Kashiwagi call "receptive social competence": sympathy, capacity to take another's viewpoint, good grace in admitting mistakes, modesty, and related qualities.[12] Research on many kinds of learning in Japan suggests that character development and learning are re-

garded as inseparable.[13] The famed Suzuki violin method, regarded by Westerners as a means to produce early musical vir-
tuosity, is regarded by its founder as a means to help children
develop a very different kind of virtue – "pure hearts."[14]

Large-scale survey research on the educational beliefs and practices of Japanese, Australian, and Korean elementary teachers lends
weight to the idea that Japanese teachers are particularly concerned
with children's personal and social development. Japanese
teachers, compared to their Australian counterparts, more strongly
emphasize the importance of the teacher-child relationship: of stay-
ing with children for more than one year; eating lunch together;
visiting children's homes; and taking responsibility for problem
children. Japanese teachers also emphasized, more strongly than
their Australian counterparts, the importance of relationships
among children: of avoiding ability grouping, not scolding students
in front of others, and so forth.[15] (Korean teachers fell in between
Japanese and Australian teachers but were closer to the Japanese
teachers on most of these items.)

Lois Peak's ethnography of a Japanese preschool notes that Japanese parents and teachers believe it is the responsibility of the
school, not the parents, to instill the discipline and motivation
needed to succeed at school. The cross-national survey provides
further evidence on this point. Whereas Australian teachers believed the family was responsible for developing children's basic
habits and attitudes related to schooling, Japanese teachers regarded this as the responsibility of the school. Researcher Tadahiko
Abiko characterizes Japanese education as concerned with "totality
of character" and U.S. education with "individual excellence." He
argues that Japanese place the ultimate responsibility for motivation with the school, Americans with the family.[16]

Japanese elementary teachers work hard to build a sense of community that extends beyond the classroom to the school as a whole.
Recall that Ms. Ishii's class spent three of five class periods preparing for Sports Day – two periods dancing and another period reflecting on what it would mean to do their utmost. At Downtown
Elementary and at other elementary schools, the weeks preceding

Sports Day were consumed in increasingly intensive preparations for the big event. Younger students spent art class crafting colorful invitations to send to local senior citizens. Older students organized brigades to escort and greet the senior citizens. All students practiced for the performances and contests and helped decorate and groom the school and its grounds. On many days, academic class time was so limited that students and teachers wore their gym clothes all day long. A kind of de facto interdisciplinary curriculum emerged. Art, music, writing, moral education, and social studies all focused on the need to prepare materials and activities – and students – for the upcoming events. Several other school-wide activities – such as Arts Day, Tanabata Festival, and overnight field trips – galvanized schools in much the same way.

The schools I studied typically had a school-wide event each month. At one school, for example, the school year began with a day of games planned by the second- to sixth-graders to welcome the new first-graders. The months that followed featured an arts festival in which each class presented a song, drama, or cooperative artwork to the whole school; an overnight trip to a local historical site; a school day carnival prepared by the older children for the younger grades; an overnight backpacking trip (day hike for the younger grades); a day of water play and swimming; spring and fall athletics festivals; and, finally, a day of skits and presentations in which the first- to fifth-graders honored the departing sixth-graders. Each school had a plan that connected these activities to the school goals for students – goals such as friendliness, persistence, initiative, and cooperation – and faculty and students alike reflected on the success of each activity in contributing to each goal. Major school-wide events might be evaluated not just by faculty discussion but also by teacher-student discussion, by questionnaires for the entire student body, and by having students draw or write their memories and feelings about the event. Events might be reshaped the following year in order to better serve the goals for children. For example, in one school I studied, the faculty decided to create cross-age small groups that would meet weekly and be the units for planning the carnival, arts festival, and several other school activities; this grew out of the realization that, despite many school-wide events, cross-age friendships were still rare.

The 30 or so days per year devoted to Sports Day, Arts Day, outdoor education, and other special events often represented prized investments in a school identity. For example, the principal and faculty at Ms. Ishii's school were deeply concerned about the decreasing contact between children and senior citizens and wove this concern into the school's special events. Children invited local senior citizens to school festivals and other shared events. On Arts Day, seniors paired up with first-grade "buddies" for shared picnic lunches, and the elder buddies taught fourth-graders how to play gateball, a croquetlike game that was the number one sport among local senior citizens. When I visited elementary schools, principals and teachers often pulled out photograph albums of school festivals and trips and regaled me for many hours with lively and humorous tales. Across schools, these tales often had the same message: that disruptive children could be brought into the fold through their participation in special events; that shared nonacademic experiences helped students, faculty, and administrators see one another "as human beings"; and that the school had become more unified (*matomari ga aru*) as a result of the school event. Nancy Sato and Milbrey McLaughlin note that shared school events are an important means of building solidarity in Japanese schools:

> Participation in activities is every student's right, not a privilege to be manipulated for control or extended as a reward for achievement. No student is denied participation because of behavioral or academic problems, and – just as important – no student receives special attention or rewards because of excellent performance.[17]

In other words, Japanese teachers want *all* children to feel part of the group. Diverse observers agree that Japanese schools invest considerable time in "nonacademic" school-wide activities:

> Many "facts" [about Japanese education] long accepted by the Western press are misleading. For example, [Japanese] students may spend more time in school, but they don't necessarily spend that time studying. The three hours of classes students have on

Saturday morning make up for the three nonacademic hours during the week that are spent on homeroom activities, teachers' meetings, club activities, and so on. In a typical school year some 65 to 70 days' worth of afternoons are either free time or given over to nonacademic activities. . . . Three or four school days per year are devoted to cleaning the school.[18]

Kitamaeno School, like most Japanese schools, frequently had activities involving . . . a whole grade level, or even the whole school, that took the whole day. These included sketching day, sports day, and an all day field trip. An arts and sciences festival (Gakugeikai) is held on one weekend in the fall when plays are put on by all grades and the faculty. There is singing, dancing, learning to make kites and woodwork, paper folding, cooking noodles, etc. It is a marvelous festival of fun, fellowship, learning, and accomplishment.[19]

Some commentators view these shared, nonacademic activities as an odd quirk, or even a shortcoming, of Japanese education, but I believe they undergird Japan's educational success. In the USA, researchers have measured "sense of community" within schools. At schools high in sense of community, students agree with items such as "My school is like a family," "My classmates care about my work just as much as their own," and "In my class the teacher and students decide together how to solve problems." They disagree with items such as "Students in my class try to do better than one another" and "Students in my class just look out for themselves." In schools with a high sense of community, students show greater respect for teachers, liking for school, academic achievement, and resistance to delinquency.[20] Chapter 8 explores why sense of community within a school may support such a wide range of positive student outcomes.

As Japanese children noticed each other's good points, discussed the ways family members and class members help one another, and identified goals for self-improvement, they seemed to grow not only in knowledge but also in their understanding of self and others and in their appreciation of hard work. How do these goals square with Japan's national curriculum?

JAPAN'S NATIONAL ELEMENTARY CURRICULUM

Western researchers often cite Japan's national curriculum as an influence on achievement. Two things about the national curriculum are striking. First, it sets goals related to the development of the whole child and allocates instructional time accordingly. Table 3, taken from the Course of Study for Elementary Schools in Japan, shows the number of 45-minute classroom periods per school year required for each subject. One surprising aspect of the schedule is the amount of time devoted to what many Westerners would regard as "enrichment" subjects. For first-graders, art, music, physical education, and special class activities together total 268 periods, or nearly one third of total instructional time. Together, art and music account for as much time as mathematics. For sixth-graders, art, music, physical education, and homemaking account for more than one third of total instructional time.

The school year begins in early April and goes through about mid-March of the following year, with approximately a 6-week summer vacation and a 2-week winter vacation. Students attend school for a half day three Saturdays per month, although reduction of Saturday schooling is planned. Table 3 raises questions about the much-publicized longer Japanese school year, variously estimated at between 195 and 240 days, compared with an average school year of 180 days in the United States.[21] Interestingly, Japan's total required instructional hours translate to only about 185 to 189 U.S. school days a year (if we assume 4½ hours of instruction for U.S. first-graders, gradually increasing to 5½ hours by sixth grade).

By focusing on how much time Japanese children attend school – rather than how much time they spend in instruction – existing accounts may overestimate Japanese instructional time. As shown in Table 4, approximately 2 hours of the Japanese elementary school day is devoted to lunch, cleaning, and recesses. The national goal of "energetic play" is reflected in the 10- or 20-minute recess that follows each 45-minute academic lesson, giving children opportunities to relax or play vigorously throughout the school day. The daily schedules from the more than 30 elementary schools I have

Table 3. *Required Elementary Instructional Periods*

Subject	Grade					
	1	2	3	4	5	8
Japanese	306	315	280	280	210	210
Social Studies	—	—	105	105	105	105
Mathematics	136	175	175	175	175	175
Science	—	—	105	105	105	105
Daily Living[a]	102	105	—	—	—	—
Music	68	70	70	70	70	70
Art & Crafts	68	70	70	70	70	70
Home Economics	—	—	—	—	70	70
Physical Education	102	105	105	105	105	105
Moral Education	34	35	35	35	35	35
Special Activities	34	35	35	70	70	70
Total	850	910	980	1,015	1,015	1,015

[a]Daily Living replaces science and social studies for primary grade students and is designed as a more experiential approach to the two subjects. *Source:* Monbushō, 1989b (my translation).

visited generally vary in only minor ways from Table 4. Table 4 does, however, mask some seasonal variation in the school year. For example, first-graders generally attend school only in the morning for the first month or so of the school year, with the length of their school day gradually increasing after that. During the 3 weeks of July that precede summer vacation, half days are common for all students.

Japanese students attend school for a number of extra days each year beyond those needed to fulfill national instruction requirements. Yet it's unlikely that they receive academic instruction during these extra days. School-wide special activities and ceremonies such as Sports Day, Arts Day, school trips, festivals, graduation, and so forth consume about 30 days per year, according to the U.S. Department of Education estimate. My own experience conducting observations during the final 2 months of the Japanese school year is that teachers are often struggling to fit in enough academic classes to meet the national requirements for instructional hours in

Table 4. *Daily Schedule from a Japanese Elementary School*[a]

Time	Monday	Tuesday	Wednesday	Thursday	Friday	Saturday
8:30–8:45	Whole-school meeting, followed by class morning meeting	Class morning meeting	School-wide children's meeting, followed by class morning meeting	Class morning meeting	School-wide exercises, followed by class morning meeting	Class morning meeting
8:45–9:30	Period 1	Period 1	Period 1	Period 1	Period 1	Period
9:30–9:40	Recess	Recess	Recess	Recess	Recess	Recess
9:40–10:25	Period 2	Period 2	Period 2	Period 2	Period 2	Period 2
10:25–10:45	Recess	Recess	Recess	Recess	Recess	Recess
10:45–11:30	Period 3	Period 3	Period 3	Period 3	Period 3	Period 3
11:30–11:40	Recess	Recess	Recess	Recess	Recess	Flexible; students go home at 12:00
11:40–12:25	Period 4	Period 4	Period 4	Period 4	Period 4	
12:25–1:05	Lunch	Lunch	Lunch	Lunch	Lunch	
1:05–1:30	Cleaning	Cleaning	Cleaning	Cleaning	Cleaning	
1:30–1:45	End-of-day class meeting	Recess	Recess	Recess	Recess	

| 1:45–2:30 | 10-min recess, then club activities | Period 5 | Period 5 (Grades 3–6 only) | Period 5 (Grades 2–6 only) | Period 5 |
| 2:30 on (students return home at 1:45–3:30, depending on age and day) | Club activities continue | End-of-day class meeting (15 min), then student committee activities until 3:30 | 10-min recess, then Period 6 (art, library, gym, or class special activities, Grades 4–6 only, 45 min), then 10-min end-of-day class meeting | End-of-day class meeting (10 min) | End-of-day class meeting (10 min), then Period 6 (art, library, gym, or class special activities, Grades 3–6 only) |

[a]From the 1992–93 school year in a Nagoya public elementary school. The 15 daily schedules I reviewed from elementary schools in four Japanese cities differed in minor ways from that shown above. Some schools had 5-minute breaks between most lessons and a longer recess after lunch. The morning schoolwide activities differed from school to school in frequency and content (e.g., songfests, jogging, student-choreographed exercises). Schools also differed in the day of the week that was shorter than others and the time of day for cleaning.

each subject. I would be surprised to find that instruction routinely goes beyond the required hours.

The Course of Study is striking in its focus not just on academic development but on social, emotional, and ethical development as well. Table 5, excerpted from the Course of Study, shows the overall goal for each subject for the elementary years. These goals emphasize how children are to feel about the subject matter as well as what they know about it. "Interest in language," "affection for our country and its history," "love of nature," "love of music," "richness of sentiment," "fondness for exercise" and "reverence for life" are among the goals. Emphasized, too, are the connections between learning and daily life. Students are expected to develop, for example "a habit of actively applying [mathematical processes] in their own daily lives" and to be "provoked to reflect on oneself and one's daily life." The Course of Study explicitly targets children's social development, seeking to develop children who have "autonomy," "an active attitude, as one family member, of wanting to improve family life," and "an approach to life that is happy and pleasant."

Survey research suggests that Japanese elementary teachers take seriously the focus on social development advocated by the ministry. When asked to rank the importance of eight goals of education, Japanese elementary teachers ranked students' "personal growth, fulfillment, and self-understanding" and "human relations skills" first and second, and "academic excellence" and "specific occupational skills" seventh and eighth.[22]

I have been puzzled by reports that Japanese teachers spend fewer hours teaching than their American colleagues, because the teachers that I observed, in more than 30 elementary schools, spent all or most of every school day with their students, teaching them most or all subjects (including art, music, and physical education) and eating lunch with them. Schedules collected from elementary schools in four cities suggest that first- and second-grade teachers generally teach all subjects (a total of 25 or 26 45-minute periods per week); third- and fourth-grade teachers teach all subjects but one (for a total of about 27 or 28 45-minute periods per week); and fifth- and sixth-grade teachers teach all subjects but two (for a total of about 27 45-minute periods per week). The subjects not taught by

Table 5. *Subject Area Objectives for the Elementary Grades*

Japanese Language
While fostering the abilities to correctly understand and appropriately express oneself in Japanese, nurturing thinking, imagination, and a feeling for language; deepening interest in Japanese; and nurturing an attitude of respect for the language

Social Studies
Striving for an understanding of life in society, building an understanding and affection for our country and its history, and nurturing the foundation for the qualities of citizenship needed as constituents of a democratic, peaceful country and society that exists within the international community

Mathematics
To acquire the basic knowledge and skills related to quantity and geometry, to foster the thinking ability to make predictions about everyday phenomena and reason logically about them, and at the same time to foster an understanding of the merits of mathematical processes and a habit of actively applying those in their own daily lives

Science
Developing familiarity with nature and conducting observations and experiments; fostering problem-solving ability and a love of nature; at the same time, attempting to understand natural things and phenomena and fostering a scientific viewpoint and way of thinking

Life Environment Studies
Through concrete activities and experiences, gaining interest in the connection between oneself and the aspects of nature and human society that are close at hand; being provoked to think about the connection between oneself and one's daily life; in that process, acquiring the habits and skills needed for daily life and nurturing the foundations for autonomy

Music
While building the foundations of musicality through activities of expression and appreciation, building a love of music and sensitivity toward music and nurturing a richness of sentiment

Art
Through activities of expression and appreciation, fostering the abilities fundamental to creative artistic activity, allowing [students] to taste the joy of self-expression, and nurturing a richness of sentiment

67

Table 5. *continued*

Home Economics
Through actual activities related to food, clothing, shelter, and so forth, to acquire the basic knowledge and skills needed in daily life; at the same time deepening understanding of family life and fostering an active attitude, as one family member, of wanting to improve family life

Physical Education
Through appropriate exercise and through understanding of health and safety as they relate to the immediate experiences of daily life, to develop a fondness for exercise, to seek improvement of health and increase of bodily strength, and to foster an approach to life that is happy and pleasant

Moral Education
The objective of moral education is in accordance with the basic spirit of education set forth in the Fundamental Law of Education and the School Education Law. It is to foster morality that provides a foundation for keeping alive, in concrete daily activities in the home, school, and other parts of society, a desire to respect human beings and a reverence for life; to work for the creation of a culture rich in individuality and the development of a democratic society and nation; and to raise autonomous Japanese who can actively contribute to a peaceful international society

Source: Monbushō, 1989b (my translation).

the classroom teacher are often taught by the principal or assistant principal (or by a nonclassroom teacher, if one is available), with the purpose of equalizing the teaching load of lower-grade and upper-grade teachers.

In addition to their teaching time, teachers are with their students daily during morning and going-home meetings, lunch, and, often, recesses and school-based extracurricular activities. Technically, teachers' *instructional* time may be relatively short (the 25 to 27 periods amount to about 20 to 21 hours per week). These calculations ignore, however, the noninstructional time that teacher and students spend together, which Japanese teachers see as central to the role of the teacher, as noted above. In practice, the students and teacher in a Japanese elementary class are very much a unit, spending all or almost all of each day together.

PARENTS' ROLE

When my son attended a Japanese elementary school, I looked forward to the days, about once every 6 weeks, when I could crowd into the back of his classroom with other parents and watch an actual classroom lesson. It was revealing to see my son and his classmates in action, grappling with subject matter and with one another. Similarly, the preschool attended by my younger son held parent observation days at about 4- to 6-week intervals, when parents could observe their children in their usual preschool activities. These open lessons provided a fascinating window on my children's progress and on the curriculum. Informal opportunities to volunteer at school – as a tutor, classroom helper, library aide, or in the other roles familiar to American parents – are rare in Japan.

Japanese educators may see important reasons to exclude parents from the classroom. Children need to establish independence from the close, indulgent parent-child relationship. Inequities among children are introduced when some (but not all) parents volunteer in the classroom. Parents, with their diverse ways of relating to children, may be regarded as a threat to the classroom culture so carefully created by teachers. Just as Japanese schools often seem remarkably tolerant in their treatment of children, they often seem remarkably *intolerant* of parents' needs.[23] For example, even working parents are asked to prepare elaborate lunches and handmade items for their preschoolers. A Japanese colleague of mine, who sent her child to a childcare center for full-time working parents, was chided for covering her child's craft box with self-stick paper instead of fabric and paste, on the ground that such a slapdash product communicated "lack of affection" to her child. Lois Peak relates the following comments by a Tokyo preschool director:

> *Obentō* [boxed lunches] are very important. By taking the trouble to make a nice lunch each morning, the mother communicates her feelings for her child. It's only during preschool that the mother

will have this chance to get up a little early and do something nice for her child. . . . It's also important the *obentō* be made especially for the child, not food left over from dinner or the adults' *obentō*. . . . The *obentō* is her chance to make something especially for that child and encourage his appetite. We ask mothers to prepare small quantities of three or four different cooked foods, plus fruit and rice, each day. . . . It should be nutritious, be the kind of food children enjoy, look colorful, and be cutely prepared.[24]

At PTA meetings, it was common for school officials to lay out guidelines for children's bedtimes, hygiene, and possessions brought to school. Some of these guidelines were meant to help build a sense of unity among students. For example, parents at one preschool were asked to send only plain white tissues with their children. Tissues with cartoon characters had become a fad the preceding year, creating a "competitive and materialistic" climate among the children, according to the end-of-year *hansei* (reflection) by the teachers. "Please pack in your child's lunch only foods that all families can afford," requested the director of another preschool. "It's natural to want to surprise your child with the first – expensive – watermelon that arrives in the stores, but please wait until watermelon is fully in season, at a price that every family can afford. Think of your child and friends, all opening up their lunches together, and be sure you've packed things every child can afford." Guidelines published by elementary schools urge that children rise before 7 a.m. every day during summer vacation to do calisthenics.

Rather than welcoming parents' concerns and ideas, teachers in Japanese childcare centers may, early on, establish that *teachers* are the authorities on what children need and that *teachers' concerns* should set the agenda for parent-teacher conversation.[25] Parents may be reluctant to express their concerns to the teacher or principal, even when a child is quite upset. Some disturbing accounts of bullying in secondary schools suggest that parents' complaints about abuse may not be taken seriously by teachers.[26]

Underlying parents' reticence may be a widely shared belief that parents' strong emotional ties to their children make it impossible for them to judge their children's needs objectively. The need for outsiders to socialize children is expressed in Japanese proverbs that urge parents to "Send a beloved child on a journey" and have children "Eat others' rice."[27] Too, Japanese parents may be intimidated by teachers' power to place unfavorable comments in their students' school records in a society where negative recommendations may be insurmountable.[28]

To what extent is Japanese educational success built on a foundation of parental reticence? The job of Japanese teachers is no doubt eased by parents' ready compliance with requests. How many American teachers could ask parents to label more than 100 items in first-graders' math sets, confident that they would all appear, properly labeled with the child's first and last name, on the appointed day? It may be relatively easy for Japanese teachers to create a cohesive classroom community and a consistent approach to discipline because parent volunteers are not bringing in their own styles of interaction with children.

Yet I see nothing inherently incompatible between the strengths of the Japanese system and the more extensive parental involvement in children's classrooms found in many American schools. In fact, I think it's likely that Japanese education would be strengthened – at least at the preschool and early elementary level – by greater involvement of parents in schools. It should be noted, however, that parents might well exert pressure for less humanistic, more examination-focused education; such parental pressure has been noted in Japanese private preschools and in public elementary schools serving relatively advantaged populations.[29]

SUMMARY

We've explored a number of ways in which Japanese early elementary education goes beyond intellectual development. Classroom values stress friendliness, helpfulness, persistence, and responsibility, and children have daily opportunities to reflect on these values and to apply them during academic lessons and nonacademic pursuits. Values strongly emphasize a friendly, inclusive school community. Special school events join children in fun, collaborative pursuits. Nearly one third of the nationally required instructional time is devoted to "nonacademic" activities: art, music, physical education, and special class activities. Values emphasize doing one's best, not academic achievement per se.

These values create a system that is likely to connect all children positively to schooling. In a diverse curriculum that includes many enrichment subjects, children are likely to find activities they excel at and enjoy. School events such as Sports Day and school trips provide further opportunities for all students – whatever their academic skills – to contribute to a shared endeavor. And if my Japanese friends in their 40s and 50s are indicative, students carry lifelong memories of the real torches that opened Sports Day's races, the hilarious skits concocted by teachers, and the outings and projects that added a decidedly informal dimension to the student-teacher relationship. Classroom values – focusing as they do on community and basic character – provide a counterweight to academic achievement: an additional, and very important, set of standards by which children judge themselves. These values exclude no one. Everyone can try harder. Everyone can be friendly. And because they include goals such as "Be energetic" and "Play vigorously outside," they extend recognition even to children whose strong suit may not be sit-down academic work.

American researchers recognize belonging as a fundamental human need that must be met if children are to develop an attachment to the family or the school.[30] As chapter 8 describes, American schools that meet children's needs for belonging are richly rewarded. Students in such schools develop motivation to learn and to uphold school values. Yet American teachers must often function in schools where the measures of their "success" – quiet classrooms, high achievement test scores, students' "time on task" – are irrelevant or inimical to their efforts to build friendships and a sense of community among children.

Backed by a national curriculum that strongly emphasizes children's social and ethical development, Japanese educators are not embarrassed to say that helping children to "Enjoy friendships," "Notice one another's good points," and "Create happy memories" are central goals of schooling. How many American teachers and administrators – even those who believe deeply in the power of

72

belonging and sense of community – feel free to describe their goals in this way? In our rush to study Japanese educational achievements, we should not miss what Japanese educators themselves consider central goals: caring, committed children in a school community where all feel valued.

4

THE SMALL GROUP:
A HOME BASE FOR CHILDREN

I try to place distractible children with children who like to take care of others, shy children with generous children. A good group is one whose members help one another.

A Japanese first-grade teacher

I want groups to become like families, where people live life daily thinking about one another.

A Japanese first-grade teacher

A friendly group is one that helps.
Always ask!
Always tell!

Sign posted in a Japanese third-grade classroom

UNASSISTED BY AIDES OR PARENT VOLUNTEERS, JAPA-nese elementary teachers manage 30–40 students. How do they keep large classrooms running smoothly? How do they deal with the disparate levels of children's skills without tracking or ability grouping? How do they help children develop a sense of belonging? This chapter explores a shared answer to all three questions: the fixed small groups that are the basic units for much of Japanese classroom life. These small groups provide effective units for classroom management, a familylike emotional home base for children, and ready help with children's academic and social needs.

All the first-grade classrooms I studied, and nearly all preschool classrooms, had fixed groups of 4–8 children. Colorful murals designed and created by the children proclaimed group names and membership. Preschool "*gurūpu*" – they were known by the English loan word – might be same-sex or mixed-sex groups and often sported names chosen by the children: the Prehistoric Monsters, the Superheroes, the Candies. First-grade groups, called *han*, included both boys and girls; their members sat in adjoining seats and could quickly meet as a group just by turning in their seats.

Children ate, played, worked, and planned in these fixed small groups several times a day, dozens of times a week, for weeks or months (in the case of elementary students) or even years (in the case of preschoolers). In several senses, these groups were like families. First, the members of a fixed group together pursued a wide range of activities, from math to lunch to physical education. Groups were not casual, nor were they specific to a single subject such as reading.

Second, groups included diverse children. Putting together children who could learn from one another academically and socially was often the central principle Japanese teachers used to organize groups. Like the teacher quoted at the outset, teachers might place a shy child with a nurturant child, an obstreperous child with a well-adjusted leader.

Finally, the groups, like families, embraced all aspects of development; groups were expected to help children develop socially, emotionally, and intellectually.

As we visit group activities in a preschool and a first-grade classroom, let's keep in mind several questions: How do the teachers get children to collaborate with one another? How do the activities meld academic and social goals? Why do the children actively pursue these activities without any external reward, such as grades?

PRESCHOOLERS MAKE PICTURE DRAMAS

Midway through a morning of free play, Ms. Mikami called together her 40 5-year-olds: "Look, everyone can draw a picture that becomes part of a picture drama (*ka-mishibai*). Here's how." One at a time, she showed five pictures, telling a story that continued across them. She asked children to assemble in their groups. Noise and movement filled the classroom as children roamed and shouted, trying to locate fellow group members. When the five children of each group had found one another, they sat down in a circle, put their feet together, lay back on the floor in the shape of a pinwheel, and sat up again. This maneuver left the children of each group facing one another in a circle. "Talk within your group about what kind of a picture drama you want to make. You need to decide what happened and then what happened next, and who's going to draw each part," Ms. Mikami instructed. Over the next 30 minutes, as children planned and drew their pictures, Ms. Mikami circled the room, listening to each group's deliberations. "Will you be able to make a good story if everyone in your group draws the same scene?" she asked the class after listening to one group's discussion. When she established a listening post outside another group, the students started to tell her what they wanted to make. "It doesn't do any good to tell me. Tell your groupmates what story you want to make," Ms. Mikami said, physically reorienting two girls so that they were facing in toward the group, not outward toward her. Ms. Mikami moved on to listen to another group, where three children were silent and two talked nonstop. "What have you decided?" she asked. When the children replied that they had not yet decided, Ms. Mikami replied, "Then talk about it some more." Once again, only two children talked. Ms. Mikami asked one of the quiet children, "What would you like to draw?" The child described a scene, and Ms. Mikami said to the group, "That's what she's thinking, so listen to her." In the same way, Ms. Mikami encouraged a second quiet child to tell the others what she wanted to draw. Then she engaged the third quiet child: "Everyone's saying this and that, but do you really understand what they mean? If not, you need to ask questions." Finally, the children began to explain to one another what they wanted to draw, and Ms. Mikami went on to observe other groups.

The children worked in their groups for about a half hour altogether, planning, drawing pictures, putting the pictures in sequence, and telling Ms. Mikami their stories. When all groups had finished, Ms. Mikami played a few chords on the piano and announced with a flourish: "It's show time." Students gathered around, and she asked all members of the Apple group to raise their hands so that the rest of the class could see who they were. In dramatic tones, she began to tell their story to the class, mentioning the name of each child in turn as his or her drawing was shown. Story finished, Ms. Mikami asked the Apple group to stand for a round of applause. "Thank you for creating a wonderful picture drama for the class," she said, as the Apple group members stood, beaming at the class's applause. Ms. Mikami went on to present each group's picture play in the same way, followed by thanks and applause.

FIRST-GRADERS INVESTIGATE WATER VOLUME

When the student monitors announced, "Science class will begin," each four-person *han* was seated around a laboratory table – rather precariously, it seemed to me, on tall stools. Mr. Yanagi introduced the lesson to his first-grade class: "I have some worries about this lesson. First, I have a feeling that about three people will fall over during today's lesson. You will hit your heads and say, 'Ouch.' I think it would be lovely if no one fell over today. Second, I'm worried that water will spray everywhere and get everyone wet. Please try not to get everyone wet. Finally, if we do have water spills, let's help each other clean up without saying things like "It's not my fault" or "You did it."

For the first 10 minutes, the first-graders "introduced" the empty plastic bottles they had brought from home, explaining that they were bottles from juice, soy sauce, oil, or whatever. Encouraged by questions from Mr. Yanagi or their classmates, some students eagerly added details about the favorite beverages or foods that had recently inhabited the bottles. Then Mr. Yanagi filled two glasses – one short and wide, one tall and narrow – with water.

"Our first problem is to decide which has more. Can we figure out the correct answer by looking at them? Talk within your groups about how to figure out which has more." As the small groups talked, Mr. Yanagi circulated, listening to each group and occasionally making comments such as "Two groups seem to be talking together well." After several minutes of discussion within the groups, Mr. Yanagi asked each to report, saying, "It's all right to mention more than one way of comparing them. It's also all right to say you couldn't figure out the problem." Several groups reported that they could figure out which glass had more just by looking. Several groups suggested pouring the water into identical cups to compare the amounts. One group suggested weighing the water. Mr. Yanagi said, "Well, we have a disagreement. Groups One and Two disagree with the groups that said you can tell just by looking; tell each other your ideas." For several minutes, proponents of the two viewpoints debated, without comment by the teacher. Mr. Yanagi then said, "This is an interesting debate, and we'll be finding out more about it. Now, let's all give a round of applause to Group Four; they were the only group that thought of investigating by weight."

With great drama, Mr. Yanagi announced that the time had come to see which glass actually contained more. A class member came up to pour the contents of the glasses into identical containers. As the child poured the water, other children shouted their predictions. When the amounts appeared to be exactly equal, a roar of excitement came up from the class, and many students rushed up front to inspect more closely. Mr. Yanagi allowed the students to inspect the glasses and talk and then proceeded to the next activity. He filled two identical pitchers with tap water, adjusting the amount several times until all students agreed that the pitchers held equal amounts. Then he poured the contents into two glasses of different widths and said matter-of-factly, "See, now this one has more because it's higher." Children shouted out, "You're wrong, you're wrong" and "The lower container is wider." In mock defeat, Mr. Yanagi moaned, "You're too smart for me. I thought I could trick you." Then he explained the final problem: to work within each group and decide whose bottle had the greatest volume and then to announce the results and explain how they were obtained. Each group received two measuring cups. Some students searched cabinets to find pitchers of the kind used by Mr. Yanagi; one enterprising group delved into a closet to find a scale. Students worked for about 10 minutes in their groups, pouring, measuring, and talking. When all groups but one seemed to have finished, Mr. Yanagi announced, "We'll hear from each han as soon as Han One is finished. Please make a decision in your group about who will announce your results."

When Han One finished, Mr. Yanagi began his wrap-up: "As I was thinking about this lesson yesterday, I was thinking about who would make a mess with the water. I imagined Han One and Han Four would. Han Four was neat, but Han One caused a major flood. Now, I'd like a representative from each han to tell us which bottle you predicted was biggest, which you found was biggest, and how you investigated." As each group reported, Mr. Yanagi asked the whole class to predict what the result would be. Students shouted their predictions and eagerly watched the results. Mr. Yanagi recalled children's introductions of the bottles: "Aha, Yamaguchi-kun's juice bottle looks very tall and would make the juice he loves so much look delicious, but it turns out it doesn't hold much."

HOW TEACHERS BUILD AND MAINTAIN GROUPS

The picture dramas pushed at the frontiers of 5-year-olds' development – both socially and intellectually. Could young children imagine a story in five-part sequence? Agree on which child would draw each part? Negotiate problems? Ms. Mikami modeled,

Daily, children eat lunch – and pursue many lessons and other activities – in their familylike small groups.

to groups having difficulty, some essential skills: how to ask group members what they wanted to draw and ascertain whether a quiet group member actually understood the plan. But Ms. Mikami made clear that group members needed to talk to one another, not to her. She provided techniques – such as sitting up from the pinwheel – that "naturally" oriented children toward one another.

Likewise, Mr. Yanagi's first-graders faced a challenging task, both socially and intellectually. To compare the volumes of four bottles, they had to share observations, reasoning, and equipment. Mr. Yanagi made clear from the outset that the goals were social as well as academic: to cooperate in ways that would avoid accidents and water spills and to show helpfulness when spills did occur. Both teachers set up tasks that demanded communication and co-operation among members. How did they help children build these skills? The answer goes well beyond the day's lesson, into the way teachers chose and trained groups and the goals they held for them.

80

Building Groups

On the same day they investigated water volume, the groups in Mr. Yanagi's class rehearsed group disco dance routines, shared lunch at desks pushed together to make a small dining table for each group, worked cooperatively within groups to make maps of the school, and reflected, during end-of-day meeting, on the strengths and weaknesses of their cooperation that day. Across the many daily activities they shared, the children of a small group came to know one another very well. They learned that members who excelled at mathematics might need help on the parallel bars, that the child who was too shy to speak in front of the whole class had interesting things to say within the group, that the child who was slow to finish academic work was a thoughtful and conscientious partner in group chores. But children did not just happen to find these things out. Teachers carefully designed groups and group activities in ways that would help children discover one another's strengths and help one another with weaknesses.

When teachers formed groups, they placed together friends or children who had a natural basis for interdependence. For example, two preschool teachers and a first-grade teacher explained how they formed groups:

> I don't form groups. The children form groups naturally. The friendships formed by children are the core of the groups, and then I ask them to choose group names.

> You try to choose the groups so that the children teach each other, rather than having the teacher teach.

> I put good speakers with poor speakers, children who like to help others with children who are slow. You need a mix of abilities and a mix of outgoing and more inward children.

As shown in Table 6, most preschool teachers grouped friends together; about half the preschool teachers also distributed across groups various abilities and personal qualities, ranging from leadership, sociability, and concern for others to drawing skill and athletic ability. All of the teachers who considered children's personal

81

Table 6. *Teachers' Strategies for Building Small Groups*

	Preschool Teachers (N = 11)	First-Grade Teachers (N = 20)
Neighborhood	3/11	1/20
Height/Seating Chart	0/11	8/20
Lottery	0/11	3/20
Personality[a]	4/11	10/20
Friends Together	8/11	2/20
Friends Apart	1/11	1/20
Spread Abilities Across Groups	5/11	7/20

Note: Teachers were asked the open-ended question "How do you decide which children go in each group?" All responses were tabulated.

[a]All 14 teachers mentioned that they grouped children with different personalities (e.g., a leader with a shy child). Several teachers also mentioned grouping children with similar personality characteristics (e.g., grouping followers so their leadership skills would emerge).

qualities in forming groups placed together children with complementary qualities: for example, "distractible children with children who like to take care of others, generous children with shy children." At the beginning of the school year, however, teachers lacked information about their students. Preschool teachers often postponed grouping children until they had had a chance to observe children's natural play patterns. First-grade teachers often started with arbitrary groupings (for example, by the seating chart, which placed the smallest children at the front of the classroom) until they had had a chance to observe the students.

Researcher Susan Holloway suggests that when students in a classroom are grouped by ability it may focus their attention on ability as a determinant of achievement.[1] She argues that Japanese students may assign little importance to ability and much to effort, in part because of their classroom experience in mixed-ability groups. Typically, group members share a wide range of experiences – from cleaning halls to conducting science experiments to music making – and can discover the diverse strengths of group members. If children have never been ranked into a "top" reading group or a "bottom" math group, ability may not become a salient category for them.

Maintaining Groups for a Long Time

Most preschools kept the same groups for at least 1 year. First-grade groups lasted an average of 2 months. What is the effect of working in the same group for weeks, months, or even years? How does it compare with the effect of changing groups frequently or using different groups for different purposes? An experimental study suggests an interesting answer. American researchers asked groups of four preschoolers to build block towers, giving each child a point for each block of his or her own that was in the completed tower.[2] Because the block tower would topple – and no child would receive points – if children shoved or tried to put on too many blocks, the children needed to cooperate. Children were trained under one of two circumstances: with the same four children or with changing groups of four children. After the training was complete, all children were put in new groups. The researchers found that the children trained in a single group showed more cooperation – measured by the height of the block towers they built – than children trained in changing groups.

This finding was surprising to the researchers, who expected that exposure to many different children would help children learn to cooperate. Why did the children trained in fixed groups show more cooperation? The researchers noticed that children in the fixed groups seemed to learn more about one another and devise strategies based on what they had learned. For example, one group whose members toppled the tower by putting on too many blocks decided to build the tower to a certain height and then hold hands, in a group self-control maneuver that helped members resist the urge to add extra blocks.

More than the casual group where members come and go at will, the enduring group may provide a place where children experience the natural consequences of their actions. Domineering children may be more likely to get their comeuppance, shy children to assert their rights. And, as we'll see, Japanese teachers explicitly design group activities so these events will occur.

Tasks That Demand Cooperation

Students didn't just work *in* groups; they worked *as* groups. Sometimes collaboration was as simple as the need to share paints, science equipment, or wooden building blocks too large for one child to lift alone (such massive blocks were found in three quarters of preschools). Teachers planned activities so that children had to share and even, as children got older, so that conflicts would emerge. As one preschool teacher said: "For the 3-year-olds we put out plenty of toys; as children get older, we put out fewer toys. Teachers plan things so that there will be more fighting as children get older." Another preschool teacher explained that she began the school year by putting out enough paintbrushes for all the children but gradually reduced the number so that children within each group would have to coordinate their use of each color. She had introduced the day's art project by saying, "Today we'll be putting drops of paint on the paper and then blowing them with straws to spatter them. So think about what you want it to look like after you blow on it. Also, each group has just one bottle of each color paint. Do you think we can share without grabbing? If not, we're sure to spill paints."

Sharing materials was only one form of interdependence in group tasks. For preschoolers, many simple gestures of daily life built in helpfulness. The humorous dance that began each day at Buddhist Preschool ended with children falling in the dirt playyard, followed by each child's wiping off the dusty backside of a partner. At Our Shepherd Preschool, group members cleaned *each other's* seats after art projects. By first grade, interdependence was often much more complex, as han members jointly built a three-dimensional model of their ideal playground, coordinated the many actions needed to serve lunch to classmates, cooperatively drew a map that showed each member's route to school, and blended four instruments to play a song.

As Ms. Mikami's preschoolers concocted the plots for their picture dramas, their efforts had the quality of an epic struggle. Life as a 5-year-old means, after all, that one's own needs are urgent, that it is difficult to understand the perspectives of others, that it is hard to think several steps ahead. Yet this struggle was precisely what teachers seemed to want. As one preschool teacher noted: "Bumping up against others (*butsukariai*) is important. Children must learn both to form their own ideas and to understand the ideas of others." As we explore the goals for groups, we'll see why teachers sometimes sought conflict, as well as cooperation, within groups.

GOALS FOR THE GROUPS

Self-management

Everything's easier if you have groups, because each group provides order.

In autumn [four months into the school year] group cooperation peaks; and the teacher's life becomes leisurely afterwards.
                    Japanese elementary teachers

When Americans visit Japanese elementary schools, I always suggest that they watch lunch preparations. Here's how lunch began in a first-grade classroom typical of many that I studied.

The two daily monitors in Ms. Harigaya's first-grade class announced that mathematics was over and lunch period would begin. Suddenly students were moving in many directions at once, as if following some orchestral score audible only to them. One student from each han left the classroom; these students made their way to the cafeteria and returned several minutes later pushing heavy carts piled with food and utensils. Meanwhile, another student from each han had donned a white chef's hat and apron, ready to serve food. The two remaining members of each han rearranged desks to create a mini-dining table for their han; they spread it with cloth napkins brought from home by each child and laid out straws, milk, and utensils for each han member. Then they lined up to be served stew and rice. Less than 10 minutes after mathematics ended, the servers had folded and stowed away their hats and aprons, and students in each han sat facing one another, ready to eat. The daily student monitors rose, waited until all groups were quiet, and gave the class permission to eat. Lunch began, all preparations executed without a single word from the teacher.

The smooth lunch preparations executed by Ms. Harigaya's students illustrate one goal teachers held for groups: that self-management by each group will add up to a smoothly functioning classroom where teachers need spend little time giving instructions. But it takes many months to achieve this smooth functioning – months in which children learn to coordinate their actions, help difficult or forgetful classmates, and solve conflicts that arise. Spills, squabbles over who will serve what, and long waits only gradually give way to smooth cooperation, as students confer daily about what they need to improve. But, in the view of the teachers I interviewed, the investment of time was well worth it, for once the children in each group learned to work as a unit, many new things were possible. Children could eat lunch in a new place, go on a field trip, play a new sport, or try a complicated science experiment. Even teachers at the two preschools that did not use groups recognized the ways small groups eased the teacher's job as manager: "We don't use groups because children at age 5 don't have a sense of belonging to a group. Groups at this age are just for the teacher's convenience." Yet most teachers held goals for the groups that went well beyond ease of classroom management.

Belonging

Groups helped children make connections to one another and to the experience of schooling: "It's easier for children to have ideas in a small group than in a big class, especially at the beginning of the year," in the words of one first-grade teacher. "Even children afraid to speak to the whole class are able to speak up in a group of four," said another.

When I asked teachers what a "good" group was, they often answered, "One that plays well together," "One whose members help one another," or "One that has *matomari* (unity, cohesiveness, or a sense of belonging)." The first-grade teacher who had group members mention each other's good points at the end of each day explained she continued this practice until she saw clear signs of group *matomari:* "Students' whole way of looking at each other changes, and they begin to help each other spontaneously – for example, lending gym shoes when classmates have forgotten them. Then I know that the group is beginning to become a real group."

Many pleasurable activities of the school day – meals, snacks, art or drama projects, games, trips around the neighborhood or farther afield – were conducted by group. Like the Apple group, who stood and beamed as the class applauded their picture drama, students often received recognition by group for some shared pleasurable activity. Children were often referred to by group name rather than individual name: "Let's clap for the Apple group to thank them for the wonderful picture drama"; "Let's clap for Han Four because they had the magnificent idea of weighing the jars to compare them." Among the dozens of techniques teachers used to build *matomari* within groups, one public preschool even had monthly meetings of mothers' groups that paralleled the membership of each small group of children. These mothers' groups, the teachers explained, would deepen bonds among children in a group because their mothers would know each other.

Children's activities in their small groups often connected them to something much larger. The "backside bump" jazz dance learned in the fixed small groups became part of a coordinated dance for the athletics festival that involved more than 100 children. At one public preschool, the 4-year-old and 5-year-old *gurūpu* prepared for school "market day." Each 4-year-old group made play money and wallets, and each 5-year-old group chose what kind of "shopkeepers" to be and set about producing crepe paper "vegetables," "fruits," and "bread" to sell in their shops. When market day came, the whole school gathered in a large double classroom where 4-year-olds strolled arm in arm and "shopped" at the stores set up by each group of 5-year-olds.

So small groups connected children to the larger class and to the school. In the words of one elementary teacher, "At first, it's easier for children to feel relaxed in a small group than in a large class." This comment may shed light on why fixed groups were maintained for a longer time at preschool than in first grade. As children became more relaxed in the school environment, teachers could reconstitute groups more often, in order to help children get to know a wider range of students in the class. As mentioned, most preschool teachers maintained the same groups for at least a year; the shortest tenure was 2 months. Young children need a lengthy period, I was told, to "feel unity" as a group and to collaborate with fellow group members in a sustained way. First-grade teachers maintained groups for a shorter period. According to Masami Kajita and colleagues, 47% of elementary teachers maintain the same groups for a trimester (3 to 4 months); 24% change them "as needed"; 13% change them once a month; and 4% keep them for 6 months.[3]

In discussing how often groups should be changed, teachers repeatedly mentioned their efforts to balance two kinds of benefits: the relaxed familiarity and smooth collaboration of an old group, and the chance to meet new people and learn to work with them offered by a new group. Commented one first-grade teacher, "Maybe we can change groups more often in first grade because our preschool colleagues have done such a good job of introducing children to daily life in small groups."

What about competition between groups? Teachers or students sometimes compared the behavior of the various han or *gurūpu*. For example, the two daily monitors in one first-grade classroom announced at the beginning of each class period: "We're now looking to see whether each han is ready." On a chart, they noted whether each han was ready to begin each lesson and announced each group's record at end-of-day meeting. Just as Mr. Yanagi announced which han had created "a major flood" and which han had come up with an unusual way to study water volume, teachers often publicly acknowledged group successes and failures. Although students and teachers might reward the first han ready to study (or swim or sing) with the opportunity to go first, groups did not generally compete for rewards such as points or honors. Teachers pointed out the dangers of intergroup competition: Groups that lost might not enjoy working together in the future; less able children would be disliked by groupmates; other groups would be seen as adversaries, detracting from a sense of "class-hood." As one first-grade teacher said: "I don't have competition among groups. I particularly avoid wins and losses around school-work, because if one person in a group can't do something, they feel bad that they've lowered the group's average." The absence of group rewards (other than the natural reward of going first if you're ready first) may also reflect teachers' general distaste for rewards as a way to motivate children's behavior, a topic addressed in chapter 6.

Groups Foster Children's Social and Academic Development

As groups transformed the classroom to lunchroom or gleefully painted a cooperative mural, their potential to ease classroom management and to give a sense of belonging was impressive. But I found even more impressive the idea – frequently mentioned by teachers – that groups would shape children's development as friends, learners, citizens of the classroom. Let's visit Western Tokyo Preschool for end-of-day meeting.

After nearly two hours of free play and a 20-minute chore time, students seated themselves, each *gurūpu* at its own table. "Think about whether you did your chores well," instructed Ms. Shiba. She called on each group in turn, asking members to stand and report to the class on their chores. The first group reported that they had completed their chores; Ms. Shiba thanked them for their hard work. When Ms. Shiba called on the second group, some students were play fighting and didn't hear her. She waited for several minutes, not saying anything, until a classmate nudged the group members to stand. The group members reported that they had completed their chores, and Ms. Shiba thanked them for their hard work. The third group was similarly slow to stand, and again Ms. Shiba waited quietly without repeating her request. Several members of the group urged the distracted members to stand, and after several minutes they did. "Did you clean the guinea pig cage?" asked Ms. Shiba. "No, we didn't finish," shouted several group members. "Why not?" asked Ms. Shiba. "Because we started playing in the middle," answered one group member.

"What can we do if only a few group members are doing a chore and the rest are off playing?" Ms. Shiba asked the class. "The people who get there first should do it all," suggested one class member. "Do you think that's all right?" Ms. Shiba asked, receiving a chorus of protests in response. Another classmate volunteered, "We could get angry at the other people or make them stand in the hall." "Is it a good situation if people work because they are forced to?" asked Ms. Shiba. After several students volunteered their experiences with delinquent chore mates, one student suggested, "The people who are working could get together and call the other people in a big voice." Ms. Shiba nodded approvingly at this pragmatic suggestion, repeated it to the class, and called on the next group to report.

The delinquent cleaners of the guinea pig cage remind us that placing children together in a group and giving them a shared task does not ensure that they will work together smoothly. Japanese teachers regard being part of a group as natural, pleasurable, and even essential to being "fully human."[4] Yet teachers also regard it as something that needs to be taught. Teachers explicitly taught many basic skills for working with others – how to "listen with your eyes," ask before reaching for paints, face others while talking.

But the primary means for learning to work with others was, I think, _hansei_ (reflection). It's hard to spend even a few hours in an elementary classroom without experiencing _hansei_. After group activities, group members often reflected on the quality of their cooperation. For example, during a first-grade music lesson, the four members of each han held different musical instruments: tambourine, pianica (a harmonica with a keyboard), castanets, triangle. The children played a lively song, interrupted occasionally by the teacher's instruction "Switch," the cue to exchange instruments quickly within the han and resume playing without missing the next phrase of the song. In their reflection time at the end of the music class, each han evaluated not only the musical quality of its playing but also how well its members shared and exchanged instruments. As each han shared its self-evaluation with the class, the teacher picked up on problems in cooperation and posed them to the whole class, asking, for example, what hanmates could do if one member wanted to keep a single instrument for the whole period and what to do if exchanges were so frantic that instruments might be damaged or dropped. She raised these issues and encouraged discussion but did not offer solutions. In this lesson, as in many I witnessed, getting children to reflect on cooperation seemed to be as much a goal as was cooperation itself.

During reflection, children had opportunities to think and to hear others' thoughts about what it meant to be a considerate, responsible participant in the activity at hand – be that painting, a science experiment, or cleaning a guinea pig cage. The aim of reflection went well beyond social skills, to the very values children brought to group life and the strength of children's bonds to one another. As one teacher said, children's "whole way of looking at one another changed" as they reflected on help and kindness offered by classmates. As children reflected on whether they had cleaned up spilled water without recrimination and whether they'd done their "utmost" on group projects or chores, they were building an appreciation of certain values of group life: kindness, responsibility, doing one's best. Too, they were learning – through their own thinking and the comments of groupmates – how well they approximated these ideals.

Students in some first-grade classrooms wrote good-bye letters to fellow group members at the end of their months together. In these letters, students were asked to write each groupmate about his or her strengths and shortcomings. Before students wrote, the teacher led a discussion of what kinds of comments would be helpful or unhelpful to groupmates. One class agreed, for example, that it would be unkind to comment on qualities a groupmate could not change, such as height or facial features. Ms. Nishimura, their teacher, regarded the small group as an important force shaping children's social development and helping children to recognize how their actions affected others. Like many teachers, she wanted group life to be pleasurable. But she also viewed group life as an opportunity for students to gain honest feedback about their shortcomings from friends they had worked with closely.

Because groups mixed students with diverse abilities and personal qualities, they gave students ready access to needed expertise – social or academic. Disruptive children were often grouped with very nurturant children or with charismatic and responsible leaders. Many elementary teachers tried to see that each group included at least one student who was skilled at reading and writing and could help slower students. A fourth-grade teacher interviewed by Ineko Tsuchida described her strategies for forming groups:

TEACHER: These are the third groups this year. At the beginning of the year, I needed to learn the students' names, so I had them sitting in order of the attendance list and formed the groups that way. Then next I chose as group leaders students who had not had a chance to be group leaders in earlier grades. The students formed groups around those leaders, in a mutual process in which the leaders and members chose each other. I told them five children per group, three boys, and two girls but let them work out group membership unless they asked my advice on problems. . . . Then for the current set of groups I chose the leaders.

TSUCHIDA: So this time you chose the leaders yourself and asked students to go into the groups they wished but to keep groups balanced by sex. How did you choose the leaders?

TEACHER: Well, I've had a chance to observe the students for 2 months now. This month, I'd like to make mathematics central. I haven't said anything to the students, but I've been thinking that this month I'd like to help the students who are having difficulty in mathematics. So for each han I tried to select a leader who's kind, takes care of others, and who is fairly good at mathematics.

TSUCHIDA: Why did you choose mathematics?

TEACHER: I think mathematics may be the area of greatest ability differences. For a mathematics problem, some chil-

92

dren may be able to do it in 30 seconds; others try and try and can't solve it even after thinking for 30 minutes. The gaps are big. I think it's because mathematics builds on previous learning. Social studies and science don't build so much on themselves – students' life experiences or personal interests still contribute quite a bit. Sometimes fourth-graders change dramatically in their achievement in science or social studies, depending on the curriculum materials or whatever. But mathematics depends so much on what's been learned previously, so the gap widens with age. So, to shrink the gap, I thought it would be fun for them not to learn just from me but from their friends as well.

TSUCHIDA: You've thought quite a lot about this, haven't you?

TEACHER: (Laughing) No, no, it's just that I'm getting the children to help me out.[5]

Like the teacher interviewed by Ineko Tsuchida, teachers mentioned a variety of different strategies – sometimes opposing ones – for selecting group members. Early in the 2 years that most classes spent together, teachers might form groups primarily to strengthen students' sense of attachment to the class. Once children had learned to "see each other's good points" and work well together, teachers might target a particular social or academic need – math, in the example above. For example, several teachers mentioned that, well into the school year, they sometimes grouped together similar children: "First I try building groups around natural leaders. But, during the year, if the followers are not themselves developing the confidence to be leaders, I might group all the followers together, to see if their leadership qualities will emerge." Most elementary teachers surveyed by Masami Kajita and colleagues tried to balance groups by ability and achievement (64%); yet many used other strategies, too, such as building groups around leaders (56%), putting friends together (16%), and basing groups on sociometric data about who would like to work with whom (14%).[6]

93

COOPERATIVE LEARNING AND JAPANESE PRACTICES

> Pay attention to similarity rather than to difference. . . . Think . . .
> of coexistence rather than . . . exclusion.[7]
>> Yoshihisa Shiota, founder of the "Bazu Method" of
>> cooperative learning

The group activities of Japanese students will make many readers think of "cooperative learning." Cooperative learning – an instructional approach familiar to many American educators – has children work together interdependently in small mixed-ability groups. Indeed, cooperative learning has a long history in Japan; the earliest Japanese studies of small cooperative groups in education were published more than 75 years ago.[8] Table 7 shows that Japanese elementary teachers frequently use small groups, typically in combination with whole-class and individual work in the course of a single lesson. Surveys and observational studies suggest that Japanese small-group instruction typically meets the definition of cooperative learning: It brings together children of various skill levels in a collaborative task.[9]

In several ways, Japanese small-group learning appears to differ from some American versions. First, Japanese students are rarely grouped by ability. Second, when Japanese children work in a group they typically work *as a group:* Their work is interdependent. (In contrast, American students sometimes work in groups on individual assignments that require little shared planning, execution, or sense of purpose, such as individual worksheets or round-robin reading.)[10] Third, Japanese teachers typically choose group activities that are inherently interesting or challenging, whereas some American approaches to cooperative learning use point systems, group grades, or some other form of extrinsic reward to keep children on task.[11] Recall the challenges faced by Ms. Mikami's preschoolers as they created a five-part picture drama, and by Mr. Yanagi's first-graders as they devised ways to compare water volumes. These teachers relied on the intrinsic interest of the task and the gradual cumulative effect of the reflection (*hansei*) that followed group activities to keep children on task.

Table 7. *Teachers' Most Frequently Used Instructional Patterns During 40-Minute Class Periods*

Grade	Pattern	%
1–2	Class-group-class	43
	Class-individual-class	34
	Class-individual-group-class	30
	Class-group-individual-class	18
	Class-individual	18
	Class	18
3–4	Class-individual-class	48
	Class-group-class	46
	Class	27
	Class-individual-group-class	26
	Class-group-individual-class	20
5–6	Class-individual-group-class	49
	Class-group-class	47
	Class-individual-class	42
	Class-group-individual-class	21
	Class	17

Note: Teachers were asked to describe the instructional pattern they used most frequently; up to three responses were coded. Multiple responses are included in the percentages.
Source: Data from Kajita et al., 1980: random sample of 216 Aichi prefecture public elementary teachers.

The Japanese "Bazu Method" of cooperative learning derives its name from the buzz (*bazu*) of conversation that accompanies cooperative work. Japanese teachers – with their school-wide goals promoting "energetic" children – may find much more acceptance of noisy classroom activity than do American teachers (see chapter 3).

Finally, Japanese teachers and students explicitly define and reflect on the *social* goals of group work – helping, friendship, responsibility, and so forth. Recall how the first-grade groups learned to "Find each other's good points" and to clean up spills without recrimination. Some American forms of cooperative learning embrace all these practices – use of inherently interesting tasks, focus on social as well as academic goals, and reflection – with impressive success in American classrooms. But other forms of American cooperative learning employ rewards such as grades or points, emphasize the product of cooperative work rather than how children work together, and have teachers evaluate student performance rather than emphasizing children's own reflection.[12]

THE BENEFITS AND DANGERS OF SMALL-GROUP TRAINING

In the many months I spent observing small groups in Japanese preschool and elementary classrooms, I generally felt comfortable with children's treatment of one another. Even the shiest class members spoke up when they worked in their small groups. Spontaneous affection and intimacy – hugs, smiles, arms around one another's shoulders – were common as group members huddled to plan a skit or observe a puzzling science experiment.

But do small groups also bring coercion?[13] Historically Japanese authorities have used small groups to control individual citizens through surveillance, threats of exclusion, and the specter of collective punishment for individual misdeeds.[14] Recent incidents of bullying in Japanese schools underline the group's psychological power. Teased or excluded by classmates, some Japanese students have resorted to desperate measures, including suicide.[15] Small groups play a central role in Japanese classroom life, and this may invest them with more emotional power than they would have in a more individualistic setting. One Japanese student who opted for an American college education over a Japanese one explained his choice to an *Oakland Tribune* reporter: "In Japan, it's like a group. We have to think about everybody else. Here, I don't have to think about anybody but myself."

American research suggests that small group participation can benefit or hinder children's development, depending on the values that govern small-group life. When students participate in groups

Third-graders decide how they will dramatize a short story for the class. Two students have their arms around one another – a common sight.

that are helpful, collaborative, and friendly, more frequent participation is associated with a host of positive outcomes for children, including increased academic motivation, liking for school, and concern for others. In contrast, when students participate in groups that are unfriendly and unhelpful, increased small-group experience is associated with negative academic and social outcomes. So the effect of small-group participation depends on the quality of interaction in the groups.[16]

Likewise, whether or not groups promote conformity depends upon the values that govern group life. American schools that take part in the Child Development Project give students many opportunities to work in cooperative small groups and to build strong friendships with their classmates; indeed, students in these schools report much less loneliness and twice as many friendships as do children in matched comparison schools. Yet children in Child Development Project schools report *greater* willingness to express their own opinions when these diverge from group opinion.[17]

97

Why should attachment to the group lead to greater willingness to express divergent views? Perhaps friendships and belonging give children a sense of security, so that they feel free to express their opinions. Perhaps the focus on personal responsibility that is also part of the Child Development Project increased children's desire to express their opinions. Whatever the reason, this research suggests that a strong sense of belonging need not undermine children's ability to dissent from the group – indeed, that it may support it.

Both Japanese and American children work in groups. So the question is not *whether* children will work in groups of some kind, but *what values* will govern children's work with one another. In their small groups, are children encouraged to treat each other with fairness and respect or simply pressed to "get the job done" as expeditiously as possible? Is the power of the small group used to humiliate dissenters or to provide a forum where all children can be heard? Is *hansei* a time for safe, genuine reflection or a kangaroo court?

Occasionally, I felt uncomfortable with the authority vested in children's groups in Japanese classrooms. In some classrooms, students checked to see whether classmates had remembered all required textbooks, cut their fingernails, and brought handkerchiefs and tissues to school. They tallied the number of delinquent class members and reported it to the class. Japanese teachers saw such peer management as less threatening to children than adult sanctions would have been. Yet I wondered why public enumeration of forgotten belongings was necessary at all.

SUMMARY

Like the teacher quoted at the outset, Japanese teachers often described the ideal small group, class, and school as a family, where students learned from one another and were concerned about each other's welfare. The metaphor of the school as a factory or workplace where children do "work," so common in American schools, was notably absent from the Japanese schools I studied.[18] Although it's dangerous to make too much out of metaphors, they may in fact suggest different concerns in Japanese and American schools. "Factory" or "workplace" implies a concern with product rather than process. So, for example, children are grouped by the quality of work they "produce" in a particular subject area rather than in ways that might promote their personal development or attachment to the group. In contrast, the metaphor of family implies enduring, intimate bonds. It signifies concern with all aspects of members' development, not just with the quality of the work members produce.

A Japanese teacher's expectations on any single day – that the children should share paints without grabbing or respond to spills with mutual help – may seem modest. Yet in time these expectations may weave a vivid tapestry for children of what group life means. Group life means helping one another. It means learning to share materials without fighting and to handle mishaps without recrimination. It means each member does his or her part. It means having a good time.

The teachers I observed and interviewed did not regard successful work in small groups as something that simply happens. They believed it required a careful choice of activities that would bring children into close collaboration and even conflict; daily opportunities to work together and to reflect on the strengths and weaknesses of that work; and then further opportunities to work on the difficulties identified through reflection. Likewise, children's social development was viewed as a process that needed careful support. Groups must nurture connections among children and place shy or difficult children near peers who would help them. Group activities must build a sense of belonging and help children to recognize one another's positive qualities. Children must have opportunities to hear feedback from groupmates.

The teacher quoted at the outset of this chapter who said that she tried to place "distractible children with children who like to take care of others, generous children with shy children," is, I think, speaking about all three goals of group life discussed in this chapter. She is building groups that will ease classroom management, because peers socialize their distractible or withdrawn members. She is building groups that will help each child, even one who is shy, develop friendships and a sense of belonging. And – by placing a nurturant child with one who is distractible – she is building groups in ways that may shape children's lifelong development.

5

THE ROOTS OF DISCIPLINE: COMMUNITY AND COMMITMENT

They have a great deal of freedom there. . . . The children were under no visible discipline, but were good as well as happy.

> John Dewey (1919), commenting on Japanese kindergarten and elementary education[1]

For Japanese teachers, it's a matter of pride that students do things without being told. The teacher shouldn't have to say a word.

> Shigefumi Nagano, Japanese educational researcher

Personal bonds with adults in the school have a greater capacity to motivate and engage than do traditional forms of social control that emphasize obedience to authority and conformity to rules.

> Educational researchers
> Milbrey McLaughlin, Joan Talbert,
> Joseph Kahne, and Judith Powell[2]

VISITORS TO JAPAN OFTEN REMARK UPON THE FREEDOM of young children. Parents seek harmony with their young children, not rules or "limits"; a close parent-child relationship, not obedience.[3] Yet somehow these "indulged," undisciplined toddlers become attentive, well-disciplined schoolchildren. By first grade, Japanese students are more attentive than American students and spend less time in inappropriate behavior.[4] Even more surprising, Japanese first-graders manage many aspects of classroom life: They seat and quiet the class before lessons, run class meetings, and manage the very transitions – from one lesson to another, from recess to study – that American *teachers* find most stressful.

How do Japan's undisciplined toddlers become disciplined schoolchildren? This chapter argues that Japanese children behave well not because of rewards or punishments but because they genuinely care about the school's rules and values. As children come to care about the school community – a topic explored in chapters 2 and 3 – they come to care about its values as well. And, as we'll explore in this chapter, Japanese teachers manage classrooms in ways that build children's personal commitment to good behavior.

As Japanese first-graders, without any direct management by an adult, serve lunch to 40 classmates or break into small groups to conduct and discuss science experiments, their discipline often seems effortless, seamless – a fact that prompts many casual American observers to assume that an authoritarian system "must" be behind children's good behavior. But I found just the opposite: that the smooth management of Japanese classrooms is achieved by muting adult authority, by strongly involving children in shaping class norms, and by giving children's own problem solving and reflection a central role in the classroom. Japanese classroom management is not always smooth or seamless. In fact, teachers treasure the problems that do arise – the forgotten chores, the fistfights, the failures to quiet down for lessons – as valuable teaching opportunities. These problems provide the grist for class discussion; they provide the concrete examples needed to deepen children's commitment to shared norms.

We'll begin exploring the roots of discipline with some examples of children's self-management in preschool and first-grade classrooms. Then we'll explore four cornerstones of discipline: (1) the rotating leadership system, (2) children's involvement in shaping classroom rules and norms, (3) teachers' low profile as authority figures, and (4) children's reflection on their own behavior.

GOING-HOME TIME AT NATIONAL UNIVERSITY PRESCHOOL

National University Preschool is affiliated with a prestigious public university. Like many preschools I studied, it devoted most of each morning to free play. Children waded knee-deep in mud puddles, ran freely from inside to outside, and moved at will among corners set up for dramatic play, crafts, and block building. Yet somehow at 11:45 each day, the 40 5-year-olds of Ms. Mishima's class began to shout to each other: "Time to clean up" and "Get your things ready to go home." When they heard these shouts, children began to wash their mud-covered arms and legs at outdoor spigots, put away play materials, and sweep the classroom. The teacher worked alongside the children. She wielded a full-size broom; they used miniature versions. Within 15 minutes, the classroom was clean and straightened up, and all 40 children had fetched their caps and bags, and pulled chairs into a circle and were sitting, ready for going-home time. Throughout all this, the teacher had given only one instruction. Her quiet remark "The big hand's on the nine" had precipitated children's clean-up. Why should one whispered remark initiate such a stream of activity? Could it be that some dire punishment or magnificent reward motivated the children's behavior? When I questioned the teacher, she was shocked by my suggestion, and she made clear that her aspirations were even more extravagant: "It's unfortunate that I have to remind them what time it is. Soon I hope they will be looking at the clock and initiating going-home preparations without even a single word from me."

TIME FOR A PUPPET SHOW

A group of children in a Tokyo public preschool created a puppet show during free-play period. Their teacher suggested that they perform it for the class, and they agreed. The teacher said quietly to several children near her: "It's time for the puppet show. Let's get the class together." The children had a hard time calling together classmates, who were scattered throughout the school and playground, until one resourceful boy borrowed a frying pan and metal spoon from the kitchen and went to the balcony overlooking the playground. There, joined by several friends, he banged on the frying pan and shouted to classmates. The teacher then asked assembled class members whether all 40 classmates were present. "Check and see if everyone in your small group is here," suggested the teacher. Children remembered several missing classmates and initiated another round of searches and frying-pan summonings. It took more than 10 minutes for the children to assemble; the teacher herself never raised her voice or named missing children.

FIRST-GRADERS RUN A DAILY MEETING

The end-of-day meeting that I saw in a suburban Kyoto elementary school was typical of dozens of daily meetings that I saw in Japanese elementary schools: It was led by students and provided a chance for students and teacher to review the day's activities. The two daily monitors stood at the front and quieted the class; they urged several slow children to hurry up. They referred to a handwritten poster that showed the following agenda for the meeting:

End-of-Day Meeting

Reflection on Goals

Things We Noticed

Announcements from the Chore Groups

Teacher's Comments

Say Farewell

In unison, the two monitors announced, "Raise your hand if today you accomplished our goal of 'Playing outside energetically.'" All hands shot up. "Raise your hand if you didn't." Children were motionless. The monitors called for a show of hands from children who had and hadn't accomplished the second goal: "Avoid dangerous activities." This time a few children signaled that they had not accomplished the goal. The monitors said, "Let's try even harder tomorrow," and then moved on to the next item: "Things We Noticed." Taking turns, the monitors called on six children who had raised their hands, each of whom reported some misdeed by another child: "Hayashi-kun climbed out the window"; "Moriwaki-kun was running in the hall"; "Kurita-kun stepped on the morning glories." When the teacher said, "Let's say good things too," several children named classmates who had helped them with academic

104

work or clean-up. The two monitors then called on chore groups for announcements. A student from the Flower group thanked, by name, two students who had brought flowers for the teacher's desk. A student from the Library group reported that books had been upset during the class's visit to the library, mentioned that it had taken a lot of time for the group to reshelve them, and asked students to be more careful on their next visit. Two members of the Forgotten Belongings group held up items at the front of the class, saying, "Who does this belong to?" Students claimed some items; others were left unclaimed. When all chore groups had reported, the monitors called on Ms. Noda, who commented, "I feel so happy that classmates are now remembering to water the flowers and to feed the goldfish," and then turned the floor back to the monitors, who asked the class to rise, bow, and say good-bye to the teacher. In turn, Ms. Noda asked the class to bow to the monitors and thank them for their hard work.

EVERY CHILD A LEADER: THE TŌBAN SYSTEM

In Japanese classrooms, leadership is not a privilege accorded to the well-behaved few. It's a regular responsibility of all students. In all first grades and nearly all preschools, daily rotating monitors, usually called *tōban*, shared leadership with teachers. All children became tōban in turn – not because they were well behaved or able but simply because they were members of the class. Yet often children were anointed monitor with great pomp and ceremony. In one preschool, a trumpet fanfare played as the previous day's tōban placed Olympic-style gold medals around the necks of the new tōban, and the entire class bowed, asking the new tōban to take care of them that day. Both teachers and students called monitors "san," a higher honorific than the "kun" or "chan" normally used to address preschoolers.

The monitors' particular jobs varied from classroom to classroom, but monitors always had a very visible role as leaders. In preschools, the monitors – sometimes as many as six per classroom – might mount a podium and lead the daily calisthenics, decide when the class was quiet enough to eat, pass out snacks, inspect children's lunchboxes, and dismiss individual children to play outside. By first grade, monitors – usually one boy and one girl – assembled and quieted the class before the teacher arrived for each lesson. In addition, they often led meetings, evaluated other students' behavior, and led the class in solving disputes or problems that arose. In fact, first-grade monitors – not teachers – managed much of the mechanics of classroom life, freeing teachers to teach.

Children's enthusiasm for the tōban system was evident. Often preschoolers checked the tōban chart – usually a flip chart made up of drawings by all the children – and talked excitedly about when their next turn would come up. Even the "problems" with the tōban system pointed to its popularity: When their turns came up, children were so eager to be monitors that they might arrive at school an hour early or refuse to stay home if they were ill.

Life as a monitor was prestigious but not always easy. Others depended on you. All the children in the class bowed to you in the morning; but they would be disappointed if you failed to get their snacks or art materials or to quiet the class for a meeting. And when the monitors failed to do their jobs, teachers were reluctant to bail them out. For example, in one preschool, monitors representing two groups punched each other while monitors from the other groups obtained snacks. The hungry groupmates complained bitterly, but the teacher simply commented, "Oh my goodness, if these two monitors keep fighting, the Tulips and the Morning Glories [their group names] will never get any snack." In a first-grade classroom, students missed the first few minutes of the weekly moral education program because the monitor – involved in playing with a neighbor – forgot to turn on the television. His angry seatmate slapped him on the back to remind him. The monitor protested to the teacher, who explained simply, "He hit you because you forgot your job."

The tōban system seemed to capitalize on children's natural interests for attention, prestige, and a chance to lead others and seemed to give children a chance to experience the pleasure – and

Elementary students clean the school daily: They sweep, wipe down floors and desks, scrub bathrooms, and care for the grounds.

<u>headaches</u> – of <u>responsibility.</u> Too, I think it built empathy for authority. The child standing at the front of the class struggling to quiet classmates could be you – and would be in a matter of days. As one preschool teacher said, the monitor system "teaches how hard people can make it for you and how much better it is to have help." And, as teachers pointed out, the tōban system extended the experience of leadership to all children: "The tōban system allows even a child who can't normally be a leader a chance to be a leader. The children who are least able to lead others in daily encounters are often the ones who work the most carefully when they are tōban."

In addition to chore groups – which performed tasks essential to classroom life – many elementary classes had students form committees, based on their ideas about how to enhance classroom life. Before school, during breaks and lunch, and sometimes during weekly class meetings and other periods set aside for the purpose, students earnestly pursued a host of activities they had concocted: They wrote class newspapers, posted new jokes and riddles daily, recycled household items, performed line-dance routines and science experiments to entertain classmates, and – my favorite – updated a bulletin board titled "News from the Committee on Recent Prehistoric Discoveries."

And students didn't just *do* chores and committee activities; they reflected on them. Had everyone helped? Were class animals and property being cared for well? What should children do when classmates shirked chores? Was it OK to change committees without finishing a project? Like the tōban system, chores and committee work provided a regular way for all children – even those "least able to lead others in daily encounters" – to contribute to the welfare of the class. And during reflection time, children themselves often recognized the quiet, slow workers who had plugged away at chores even as their more gregarious or charismatic groupmates became distracted. As students reflected on their classmates' contributions to classroom chores and activities, they seemed to be carving out a model of "good student" and "good person" that heavily emphasized contribution to the group and that could be attained by anyone who tried hard enough.

SELF-MANAGEMENT: CHILDREN HELP SHAPE CLASSROOM RULES

As a child, I remember plotting with my siblings to figure out how we could present an idea to my father in such a way that he'd think he thought it up himself. We intuitively recognized the importance of autonomy – the need to be the origin of one's actions.[5] When Japanese teachers talked about classroom rules and routines, their central concern seemed to be children's autonomy: how to introduce rules and norms without imposing them on children. Often teachers used the words *shizen ni* (naturally) and *muri naku* (without force, voluntarily, naturally). (These are favorite words, too, in the

Ministry of Education's writing on young children.) I found it amusing that – although all preschool and first-grade classes had chores and almost all had a daily monitor system – teachers took pains to explain that these systems had happened to emerge "naturally" because the children noticed the need for them. Two preschool teachers described how the system of responsibility for chores emerged in their classrooms:

> Several months into the year, everyone talked about the need for someone to do chores, so the idea emerged of taking turns. Now [4 months into the school year] the monitors come back to the classroom early from outside and do all the work without my saying a word. They open the windows, pass out the straws, and wipe the tables. At the end of the day, the children have a "baton touch" and transfer authority to the next day's monitors. The monitors are so excited they come to school early.

> In our school, children think up the jobs that need to be done in the classroom; then they decide who will do them. Usually they take responsibility to do them, since they've mentioned the job themselves. If they don't, the teacher may do the job for awhile.

Most preschool teachers avoided any discussion of rules or chores until the second or third month of preschool life, when all children had "bumped up against one another" and could understand the need for rules – "promises," as they were called, underlining the personal commitment they entailed. Some went to great lengths to have rules and chores emerge "naturally" from the children. For example, a preschool teacher recounted her ongoing 3-month effort to have the children adopt a new chore.

> Every day for the last few months a boy named Ken has closed the classroom door at the end of the school day. Every single day I've said thanks and mentioned to the class that the neighborhood cats would come in if Ken didn't close the door. But so far, the children have not picked up on my hint to add this to the regular chores. But I don't want to tell them.

The teacher justified her plan to keep hinting rather than openly request the new chore: "Children must learn through their own

109

activities. It should come from the children." Similarly, many first-grade teachers delayed chores until children noticed what needed to be done in the classroom – and even then, the initial chores were most often self-chosen, simple, and fun: turning the TV on and off (for moral education programs once or twice a week), arranging flowers, caring for animals, opening and shutting windows. In many elementary schools, sixth-graders did the hard work of sweeping and cleaning first-grade classrooms for the first few months of the school year, giving teachers a chance to wonder out loud whether "we'll soon be big and strong enough to clean the classroom ourselves."

Like rules, decisions often emerged "naturally" from the children. If even one child objected, a teacher might refrain from enforcing a new policy. For example, in Central Japan City Preschool, a teacher asked six boys to carry a box of blocks to another classroom. Several boys grumbled, as they worked, that they wanted to keep the blocks in their own classroom. The teacher said, "We've had them for a long time, so we'd like to lend them to the other class. Do you think that's a bad idea?" Most of the boys said, "It's okay"; one boy disagreed. Immediately the teacher responded, "Then please stop moving them. We need to ask how the whole class is feeling about this." During end-of-day meeting, the teacher recounted the incident and mentioned that the school owned only one set of these expensive wooden blocks and that the other 5-year-old class probably wanted to enjoy them too. "But we shouldn't give them the blocks unless we all agree," she added. Most of the class readily assented, but two boys expressed reluctance. After children shouted out their opinions for several minutes, one student suggested a compromise: that the class keep the blocks for 2 more days. The two reluctant boys brightened at this suggestion and readily assented.

By first grade, children decided more than chores and the occasional conflict over blocks: They shaped the very norms and values by which they would live in the classroom. At brief meetings once or twice a day and longer weekly meetings, children often discussed their hopes for the class: that it would be friendly, fun, considerate; that classmates would not keep one another waiting or leave messes for each other to clean up. They discussed problems raised by the children and teacher or submitted anonymously to class suggestion boxes. The goals for the day, week, month, or trimester, described in chapter 3, often emerged from these meetings. Daily and weekly goals bore children's marks most clearly: "Let's play Steal the Bacon without shoving today"; "This week, let's play dodgeball without the boys' hogging the ball." But even the goals inspired by national moral education objectives differed in wording from school to school, reflecting student and faculty opportunities to shape school culture. In the cross-cultural research conducted by Masami Kajita and colleagues, Japanese elementary teachers were significantly more likely than their Australian counterparts to view classroom rules as something that should be decided by the students.[6]

First-Graders Run a Weekly Class Meeting

I was astounded the first time I saw two 6-year-olds – the daily monitors in Ms. Mori's first grade – run a 45-minute class meeting. A poster provided the following guide:

How to Lead a Discussion

- "Class meeting begins now."
- "Today we have to decide X and Y."
- "First we'll talk about X." . . . X is decided.
- "Next we'll give our opinions about Y." . . . Y is decided.
- "Do we have anything else to decide?"
- "Now the class meeting is over."

The two daily monitors stood at the front of the class, looked at the poster, conferred, and announced in unison, "Today's topic for discussion is choosing our next special activity for the class." Students' hands shot up, and suggestions were plentiful: a talent show, a tug-of-war, a class play, clay projects. The monitors initially called on children in turn, but soon all children were shouting at once. The factions for a talent show and a tug-of-war shouted the most loudly. Ms. Mori did not speak. After several minutes of shouting, a boy sprang to the front of the class and shouted, "Let's take a vote between talent show and tug-of-war." One of the monitors pulled the teacher's chair over to the blackboard and stood on it to tally votes on the board. The class quieted to vote. One monitor counted the hands and the other recorded the tallies. "The talent show wins," they announced and then led the class in deciding the date for the show, which groups would perform, and which would be audience. The teacher sat quietly during most of this time, occasionally raising her hand to be called upon. Even when there was a short scuffle between two boys over which groups would perform, the teacher did not intervene. The monitors settled the scuffle by asking the two boys to abide by the results of the hand play "scissors-paper-stone." Referring again to the poster, the monitors asked, "Do we have anything else to decide?" With no responses, the monitors summarized what had been decided, and one monitor wrote each decision on the board: to have a talent show, its date, which groups would perform and which would be audience, and the dates for practice.

The monitors then introduced the teacher with the words "This is what the teacher has to say." The teacher addressed the class for several minutes about "Things I noticed this week." She mentioned how happy she was that children helped one another spontaneously when a big wastebasket was spilled at lunchtime earlier in the week; how happy she was that children were including all their classmates in playground games rather than leaving some children to feel lonely; and how sad they would all feel if the children who continued to run in the hall were to fall and hurt their heads. Ms. Mori turned the floor back to the monitors, who led the class in bowing and thanking her; in turn, the teacher asked the class to bow and thank the monitors for their leadership of the class meeting.

The student-led discussion in Ms. Mori's class typified many discussions in first-grade class meetings, moral education, and social studies. The teacher was not so much a leader as a resource. Often teachers challenged students to justify their comments, to reconcile them with what other students had said, or to relate them to ideals of friendship and community. Yet teachers shied away from authoritative statements that might short-circuit children's own problem solving. Discussions were designed to involve all children. As the national moral education guidelines specify,

> Great care must be taken to choose issues that provide, as much as possible, a shared problem of great interest to all the children. . . . Whatever the format, care must be taken to guide the discussion so that all children actively participate and so that it doesn't go off-track or become just a formality.[7]

The strong emphasis on class-wide participation was evident in the reflection questions teachers asked at the end of the school day. For example, teachers asked students to reflect privately on questions such as "Did today's class discussions involve all classmates or just a few classmates?" and "Did I volunteer my ideas sometime today?" I often had the feeling that teachers, as well as students, gauged their success by the answers.

In the short run, it would have been more efficient for teachers to make unilateral decisions about class activities, rules, or problems. Instead, teachers involved students in these decisions. Supported by a national curriculum that emphasizes social and ethical development, teachers regarded students' participation, sense of shared aspirations, and personal commitment to rules as important yardsticks of education's success.

TEACHERS' LOW PROFILE AS MANAGERS

Jack and Elizabeth Easley, who studied mathematics education in a Japanese elementary school, found several aspect of schooling "totally surprising":

> We noted in Kitamaeno School, as compared with U.S. schools we know, that children are, from the outset, given greater responsibil-

ity and treated with greater respect for their own person and their own learning. This is true during and between classes, where, for periods of up to 30 minutes, all the children in the school will be unattended by a teacher or anyone else who is legally responsible for them. . . . When a teacher is absent, other teachers, the assistant principal, or the principal, drop in from time to time to assign work to the class, as there are no substitute teachers. . . . A child who disrupts a lesson is rarely singled out for special treatment by the teacher, who usually waits for the disruption to cease or goes on in spite of it. In short, the children are treated more the way we treat adults.[8]

Like the Easleys, I was surprised that Japanese teachers seemed to downplay their own authority. Preschool teachers did not even keep all children within sight: During free play, preschoolers were free to roam the school or playground and to play in unsupervised areas. In only 53% of my spot observations could preschool teachers even see all their students; in 13% of the spot observations, they could see none. I repeatedly questioned preschool teachers about children's unsupervised play and was repeatedly told that students sometimes played unsupervised; they were expected to search out an adult if problems arose. Preschool teachers freely left their classrooms on errands and to check occasionally on areas where large numbers of their students played unsupervised – for example, a shared gym room where no adult was present. In first-grade classrooms, teachers often left the room during the 10-minute or 20-minute breaks between classes.

To my Western eye, the low profile of adult authority occasionally made Japanese preschools dangerous. In a "model preschool" featured in a Ministry of Education videotape, the 30-odd 5-year-olds of a preschool class gleefully construct towers and bridges by stacking and taping together huge wooden building blocks 3 to 6 feet in length. They play in these block structures for hours, crawling from one structure to another across the bridges they have constructed to avoid the "water" below. When it is lunchtime, they fetch their box lunches and eat them in the block structures they have built. Some children sit on the roofs of two-story structures they have built, with other children sitting directly below them. I can't think of another videotape or film that captures so well the sustained creative play that is a touchstone for so many educators, East and West. Yet I shuddered the entire time I watched the tape, for I could not get my mind off what would happen if the flimsily taped wooden blocks came crashing down, with some children falling 3 or more feet to the floor and others crushed under the heavy wooden building blocks.

Over half of the preschools I studied provided oversized wooden building blocks – so big and heavy that children had to work together to carry them – and play like that featured in the videotape was common. About two thirds of the preschools I studied had other dangerous objects available to children: sharpened leather punches, razor blades in knife handles, nails, or sharp scissors. I frequently saw children borrow and use these objects and once saw a 5-year-old gash her hand with a razor knife as she tried to cut a milk carton for a craft project. As the teacher bandaged her palm and kept pressure on it for many minutes to stop the bleeding, she quietly remarked, "Next time, don't you think you should ask my help to use the razor knife?" Yet the teacher returned the razor knife to its spot in an open bin, at children's eye level. At another preschool, I was surprised to see 3-year-olds freely use real hammers and nails. When I inquired about students' hurting themselves, a teacher explained that "children don't really cry when they hurt themselves in the course of doing something they've chosen to do; it's only when they're made to do something, or are hurt by others, that they really cry." When I asked whether children might use the nails aggressively – to poke other children – I received a quizzical look. No matter how many ways I asked about children's mischievous use of nails, I received the same reply: Children know, or can readily learn, that nails are to be hammered.

I found appealing the faith placed in preschoolers to use heavy blocks and real tools responsibly. Yet I would prefer to err on the side of safety. Children's freedom and their safety are often at odds with one another. Japanese friends of mine rejected an otherwise appealing childcare center because it had safety gates at the top of the stairs: "Gates treat children like animals; children should not be penned in." Some safety devices, such as stair gates and automobile car seats, that are commonly accepted by American parents are still relatively rare in Japan. My guess is that most Americans would prefer preschools where razor knives are safely out of reach of children and where aspiring architects are limited to one-story structures – even if this means some limitation on children's freedom.

Questions and Explanations, Not Demands

Even when teachers were physically present, they often took a low profile as authority figures, responding to children's misbehavior with questions or explanations – not demands. Take the following examples.

A 5-year-old boy at Private University Preschool is throwing sand and calling it snow. The teacher asks him to stop, but he continues. She asks him twice more, explaining how it could hurt others' eyes. But he continues to make it "snow." The teacher suggests that he make a racetrack from the sand and see how fast cars can travel, but he brings more sand to throw. The teacher says, "If you fill up the tunnel with snow you can't have a race." He continues to "snow" sand. Shrugging her shoulders, the teacher turns to a student teacher and says, "It's no use. They want to make it snow no matter what you do." The teacher walks away; but she later raises the incident as a topic of discussion during the going-home meeting.

Four boys at Tokyo Central Ward Preschool Number One are building a tower in a classroom doorway. The teacher says, "It's crowded here. I know a better spot." They ignore her and continue building. "Look, if you go over there, no one will bump into your tower and knock it down," the teacher continues. The boys continue building, ignoring the teacher. She walks away.

On the playground of Our Shepherd preschool, a teacher sees a 5-year-old boy throw a stone. Teacher: "What did you just do?" Boy: "I threw a stone." Teacher: "Why?"

Boy: "To surprise him." Teacher: "Can you think of any other ways of surprising him?" Boy is silent. Teacher: "How would you feel if I threw a stone at your eye? Do you think your friend is different?" The teacher pats the boy on the shoulder to send him off to play.

Students at a middle-class Tokyo elementary school have just returned to school after vacation. The daily monitors are trying to quiet the class, but students are noisily visiting and practicing karate moves on one another. It takes the daily monitors 17 minutes to quiet the class for the morning meeting, as various groups of children leave their seats to talk or play at karate. During this time, the teacher sits at the front of the classroom waiting but does not say a word. He later raises the incident during a class meeting and asks children to discuss why it took them so long to quiet down and what they were feeling during the 17 minutes.

In other words, teachers often responded to misbehavior with questions, explanations, or discussions – not with punishments or even direct requests for compliance. Research on Japanese and American mothers' disciplinary strategies underlines the importance of harmony in adult-child relations.[9] When asked how they would handle several different kinds of misbehavior by their children, many American mothers reported that they would assert their own authority or cite impersonal rules: "I told you not to do that" or "Blocks are not for throwing." Significantly more Japanese responses focused on feelings and on the human consequences of the child's act: "You wouldn't want to be hurt by a block like that"; "Vegetables will help you grow strong and healthy"; "The store owner has worked hard to arrange the shelves neatly." Japanese mothers reported more use of persuasion – and less use of external control – than did American mothers.

Japanese mothers' and teachers' reluctance to set and enforce demands flies in the face of conventional American wisdom. After all, aren't clear, consistent rules best for children? Findings in this area are hotly debated.[10] Some research suggests that children are

117

most likely to internalize rules if they see themselves as obeying willingly – that is, without external pressure or manipulation.[11] In this view, firm control can actually *undermine* children's obedience in the long run by leading children to obey *only* when under surveillance. An experiment illustrates this. The "forbidden toys" study placed a child alone in a room with some very desirable toys, telling the child that "it would be wrong to play with" these toys.[12] Additionally, children received either a strong prohibition (that the adult would be "very upset and very annoyed" if the child played with the desirable toys) or a mild prohibition (that the adult would be "a little bit annoyed" if the child played with the toys). Although children in both conditions resisted temptation immediately, children who received the mild prohibition were significantly more likely to resist temptation subsequently – even in a different situation as much as 6 weeks later. Why did the milder prohibition lead *more* children to internalize the request? The child who obeys in response to a mild request from an adult may think, "I'm a good child who behaves without any pressure from adults." Complying under only a mild prohibition may have led children to see themselves as good children who obeyed willingly.[13]

Even surveillance – without any kind of reward or punishment – may lead children or adults to conclude that they're doing something because they must, undermining their willingness to pursue the task for its own sake later. For example, young children who believe they're being watched through a videocamera as they work on puzzles are much less interested in the puzzles several weeks later than are children who initially played with the puzzles when the videocamera was "turned off."[14] Why should telling children they're under surveillance undermine their subsequent interest in a task? It's likely that children actively draw inferences from their own behavior. The child told her puzzle play is being monitored by videocamera so an adult can "see how well" she's doing may think of the puzzles as something she does for adult evaluation, not just for the fun of it.

A very surprising and troubling set of studies suggest that rewarding children for an activity they already enjoy can actually *undermine* their interest in the activity. Mark Lepper and David

Greene "turned play into work" in a preschool classroom, where they rewarded children for drawing pictures with magic markers – an activity the children already enjoyed and did willingly. Weeks later, when the magic markers were reintroduced as a free-choice activity, this time with no promise of rewards, the children who had previously been rewarded were much less likely to choose the activity than were children who had not been rewarded. Children's decrease in interest seemed to be related to their perception of doing it for the reward: Children who had received *unexpected* rewards for drawing continued to be interested.[15]

Why do rewards and surveillance diminish children's subsequent interest in a task? Several explanations are plausible. Perhaps an external reward or surveillance distracts children from the pleasures of the task itself. Instead of enjoying the drawing or puzzles, children may have their attention focused on the reward or surveillance. Perhaps children devalue a task that is rewarded: "It must not be much fun if they're offering me a reward for doing it." Perhaps children make inferences about themselves. They may come to see themselves as liking puzzles or drawing: "I must enjoy this task – no one's rewarding me for doing it." Or they may think, "I only work on puzzles when someone's checking to see how well I do."

Whatever the explanation, these studies suggest that one trick of effective socialization is to get children to behave responsibly without attributing their obedience to some external pressure such as surveillance or rewards. Japanese practices thus show an interesting fit with attribution theory. Teachers' reluctance to use direct control and their hard work to see that class norms emerge "naturally" from the children may create a classroom situation in which it is very hard for children to attribute their behavior to adult control – and very easy for children to think of themselves as responsible, good children committed to norms they've helped to shape.

Research suggests that Japanese teachers may well succeed in helping children make school values their own. For a variety of academic tasks and procedures – homework, classwork, tests, etc. – Japanese fifth-graders report that their effort is internally motivated (that is, motivated by a belief in what they are doing), whereas

119

American fifth-graders report that their actions are due to some external carrot or stick. For example, 70% of American students but only 32% of Japanese students give an external reason for doing homework ("You're supposed to"); 53% of Japanese students but only 29% of U.S. students give an internal reason ("It helps you learn"). Similarly, a majority of American students give an external reason for getting high test grades ("It means I'll get a good report card"), whereas a majority of Japanese students give an internal reason ("It means I've learned a lot"). The Japanese students, compared to their American counterparts, are also more likely to feel bad about their own violation of class norms.[16]

HANSEI

The preceding sections discuss three conditions that may foster children's personal commitment to classroom rules: regular opportunities to lead the class; involvement in shaping class rules and decisions; and teachers' low profile as authorities. A fourth factor is *hansei* – reflection. *Hansei* pervaded many nonacademic and academic activities. Chapter 2 describes how children identified their own weaknesses – and sought self-improvement – through *hansei*. Children's self-identified goals often related to discipline: "To stop punching other children on the playground"; "Not to talk when the teacher is talking"; "To remember all my things for school."

In most first-grade classrooms, children reflected on some goal or experience each day. Sometimes self-evaluation was private or informal. Children might be given a few minutes to think privately about their progress on self-identified goals or about questions such as "Did I do anything nice for others at school this week?"; "Did I do anything naughty?"; "Did I try my hardest?"; "Did I volunteer my ideas?" Or the teacher might begin a class discussion by asking these questions or others such as "What did you like most this week at school?" and "What did you like least?"

Other times, self-evaluation was more formal and public. At one central Tokyo elementary school, students formally evaluated themselves each Friday. The week I visited, their two goals were "Let's restore the rhythm of our daily life" (*seikatsu no rizumu o*

120

torimodosō) and "Let's have order in our daily life" (*kejime no aru seikatsu o shimashō*). Both were popular goals for the wiggly month following summer vacation, and the children had voted to retain the latter goal for a second week because they felt they had not adequately achieved it the first time around. Children self-rated each goal, using a three-symbol system: a circle if they achieved it, a triangle if they partially achieved it, an X if they failed. The teacher asked children to report their self-evaluations by a show of hands. For both goals, children's responses split approximately evenly among the three categories. "Oh, you were tough on yourselves," the teacher said, smiling approvingly. In another school, first-graders rated themselves each month on a list of 24 characteristics the class had chosen during the early months of the school year; these characteristics included qualities such as friendliness, helpfulness, responsibility, initiative, cooperation, and persistence.

Japanese children and parents consistently rate children's educational achievement less favorably than do American parents and children – an ironic fact, given the higher actual achievement of Japanese children.[17] Similarly, Japanese children report lower satisfaction with themselves than do American or European children. Faced with a list of seven qualities – popular, good at sports, friendly, diligent student, hard worker, courageous, honest – Japanese children are less than half as likely as American children to rate themselves as very high on each characteristic.[18]

These findings could have many interpretations, but I wonder if they relate in some measure to children's experience with *hansei*. *Hansei* may focus children's attention on their shortcomings – on the fact that there's always room for self-improvement. Much research suggests benefits from a self-critical attitude. It can motivate striving for improvement, lead one to notice and care about problems that might escape a less critical eye, and catalyze a search for creative solutions.[19] On the other hand, some Japanese commentators link a self-critical attitude to reticence and to a sense of inferiority or incompleteness, raising the interesting question of what's an "appropriate" level of self-criticism.[20]

Is it possible to maintain a habit of self-criticism and yet have the benefits of high self-esteem, such as willingness to undertake challenges? As practiced in the classrooms I studied, the answer would seem to be yes. Self-criticism and reflection seemed to make all sorts of endeavors more interesting. It provided a chance to think about one's own actions and a window on the thinking and feelings of others. Supported by a teacher and classmates who earnestly considered their own shortcomings and praised the "magnificent" self-criticisms of others, *hansei* often seemed pleasurable, just as it's pleasurable to reflect by keeping a journal or by reviewing the day's activities with a trusted friend or colleague. Though we currently know little about *hansei,* I think it's an important puzzle piece in our understanding of Japanese education. In the year that I spent as a student in a Japanese high school and in the months that I spent observing in Japanese elementary schools, I found myself powerfully shaped by the reflection going on around me. As students and teachers earnestly asked themselves, "What have I done to help others this week?" and "What are my goals for self-improvement?," I couldn't help asking myself the same questions.

SUMMARY

Let's revisit the question that began this chapter: How do children move from indulgence at home to self-discipline at school? We've found that all students – not just a select few – have daily opportunities to see themselves as good, responsible citizens. Students assume leadership. They help shape the rules and values that govern classroom life. They reflect on their own behavior and how it affects their classmates. At the foundation of Japanese children's self-discipline, then, are several practices:

- Children help shape classroom rules and norms. They feel committed to rules and norms they have helped shape.
- All children – whatever their behavior or abilities – regularly lead the class, an experience likely to build their identification with authority.
- Children contribute daily to the well-being of classmates through chores and other activities.

- Children frequently reflect on their behavior and discuss how it relates to such values as kindness and responsibility. Such reflection may build an enduring habit of self-evaluation.

By helping children build a personal commitment to rules, a strong connection to a classroom community, and a habit of reflection, Japanese teachers invest much effort in prevention of behavior problems. But what happens when misbehavior does occur? We'll see in the next chapter.

6

DISCIPLINE: HOW PEERS AND TEACHERS MANAGE MISBEHAVIOR

Punishment, in the form of extra work, isolation, ridicule, or physical pain, was never used. The faculty helped each other work out difficulties they were having with certain children. Although the principal or assistant principal chaired the faculty meetings in which some of these matters were discussed, and sometimes made inspirational talks to the children, they seemed to have none of the special disciplinary functions often associated with these roles in American schools.

Jack and Elizabeth Easley[1]

Reward children for good behavior? I think it's demeaning. In fact, I wouldn't even want to train animals that way. Even for a dog, it's humiliating to do tricks in the hopes of getting something for it.

A Japanese elementary teacher

Love me most when I deserve it least. That's when I need it most.

An American greeting card

AT THE HEART OF JAPANESE DISCIPLINE ARE THE EXPERI-ences, described in previous chapters, that foster children's positive attachment to the school. As children develop this attachment, they begin to identify with the school's values and to behave in ways consistent with the goals of kindness, cooperation, and responsibility that are so prominent in Japanese school life. But, in the meantime, what happens when students do misbehave?

124

HANDLING MISBEHAVIOR: AN OVERVIEW

This chapter explores four features of discipline in Japanese pre-school and early elementary settings. First, peers are extensively involved in managing misbehavior, and adult authority is muted. Second, teachers attribute positive motives to children, making it very hard for children to develop an identity as "bad" children. Third, teachers focus on children's understanding, not compliance, as the goal of disciplinary intervention. Finally, teachers tend to see misbehavior as a problem of inadequate attachment to the school community and choose disciplinary strategies designed to strengthen children's bonds to classmates and to the teacher. We will begin with an incident I observed that illustrates several of these themes.

Preschoolers "Bomb" Goldfish

Two hours into a morning of free play at National University Preschool, several 5-year-old boys began to roll small clay balls and drop them into the class's goldfish aquarium, shouting, "Bombs away." Ms. Nomura, standing nearby, looked over and commented softly, "That could hurt the fish." The boys continued dropping the "bombs," and Ms. Nomura explained in a matter-of-fact tone, "That clay looks like the food we give them, but it's not good for them like food. In fact, it could hurt them." The boys continued to drop clay balls into the aquarium, and Ms. Nomura said wistfully, "How sad the class will be if the fish get hurt." Several boys continued to drop clay balls into the aquarium, but Ms. Nomura said no more. An hour later, during going-home meeting, she described the incident to the whole class: "Today several of our classmates rolled clay into little balls and dropped it on the fish. They thought they were helping the fish, because the little balls of clay look like the food pellets we give the fish. But the clay doesn't help the fish. In fact, it might hurt them, even kill them. What does everybody think about this?" Children shouted out responses. Although a few children said,

125

"It sounds like fun to drop clay pellets," most children said they did not want the fish to be hurt. "What shall we do about this problem, then?" asked Ms. Nomura. Children volunteered suggestions for several minutes. Ms. Nomura summarized two common themes in these suggestions: "Well, then, classmates are saying that nobody should drop clay on the fish and that if you see somebody hurting the goldfish you should tell them to stop. And I have one more suggestion to add myself. Maybe people who are dropping clay on the fish would really like to feed the fish. So tomorrow let's think about rotating chore groups, so that more classmates have the fun of dropping food into the aquarium."

INVOLVING PEERS IN DISCIPLINE

Ms. Nomura treated the bombing of the goldfish as a problem for the whole class to solve. Similarly, teachers treated dozens of other problems – from fistfights to loneliness – as problems to be solved by the peer group, not by adult authority. For example, when a 5-year-old at Our Shepherd Preschool ran to tell the teacher, "The Tulip group is throwing stones out of the playhouse," the teacher did not investigate but simply responded, "Why, then, explain to them it's dangerous." Both preschool and elementary teachers often encouraged children to watch one another's behavior, so that they could conduct *hansei* (reflection) later. At dismissal time in a public preschool on Japan's Pacific coast, the teacher said, "As we've discussed, when you're dismissed, please don't drag your chairs. Let's all watch our classmates to see if they pick up their chairs." She then dismissed the children one by one.

When students had difficulty handling peers' misbehavior, teachers waited patiently, sometimes for 10 or 20 minutes. In one first grade, the custom was for the daily monitors to quiet the class before each lesson by saying, "We will look at the groups. We will count to 10." On the count of 10, the monitors judged whether each group was sitting quietly, ready to begin the lesson, and rated each group by writing a circle or X on a chart. On one of the days that I visited, the monitors had considerable difficulty quieting the class. "Groups One and Five are still not ready. Please do your best," cautioned one monitor when she had counted to 10 and the class was not quiet. The other monitor called a child by name to sit down but named the wrong child, unleashing a round of protests from classmates. By the time all groups were sitting quietly, the monitors had counted to 30, not 10. In their summary at the end of that day, the monitors noted that only two of the class's eight groups had been ready to begin all lessons that day. This finding was the grist for a brief discussion within each group about what they could do to improve.

In another first-grade classroom, the teacher had to wait for more than 15 minutes while the two monitors tried to quiet the class. I was struck by the fact that the teachers did not intervene to quiet children in either of these cases. "I don't want to create children who obey because I'm here. I want children who know what to do themselves, children who learn to judge things themselves," explained one first-grade teacher. Teachers often transformed individual misbehavior into a problem for the whole class to solve. For example, if a child failed to participate in greetings, the teacher might ask the whole class to say greetings again, "because Matsuda-kun missed it the first time." When two children were fighting as a preschool class assembled for singing, the teacher waited patiently at the piano, announcing, "We'll wait until those two are finished fighting. OK, now go ahead and fight." What struck me about these incidents was that teachers, if they were angry, did not reveal this to the children. "We're all in this together" was the attitude they projected. It was as if they confronted some powerful, inevitable act of nature – perhaps a thunderstorm – rather than rebellion within their own ranks.

Even fistfights were sometimes managed by children themselves. I was shocked to see two 5-year-old boys locked in combat, pulling each other's hair and crying, while their preschool teacher looked on. "*Gambare* " ("Do your best"), the teacher cheered on the smaller boy, adding, "Look, Taro's gotten strong; now he can fight without crying." Although the teacher did not intervene herself, she encouraged the children standing nearby to intervene, saying,

"Why don't you ask the fighters why they're fighting?" and then, "Tell us what you found out about the fighting" and "Ask them what would make them stop fighting." After the bystanders described each child's reason for fighting, the teacher responded, "You're the caretakers, so you should decide what to do" and then turned her back on the situation. The "caretakers" encouraged the fighters to apologize to each other but failed and gave up. Soon the boys were hitting again, and the teacher asked some other onlookers to intervene. After making this request, the teacher announced, "I am washing my hands of this" and walked away. The onlooker and another girl who had been watching the fight each began to question one fighter, saying, "Why are you fighting? Are you still mad? If not, say, 'I'm sorry.'"

The teacher, who had been keeping an eye on developments from a short distance away, returned to the fighters and drew a circle in the sand: "Inside this circle are the fighters and the children helping to solve the fight. Everyone outside the circle should begin cleaning up to go home." The two girls who had been questioning the fighters each brushed the sand off one fighter and encouraged him to apologize. After several minutes, the girls finally succeeded in eliciting apologies from both fighters. Each girl held hands with one fighter, and then the girls held hands with each other, forming a chain that linked the fighters. From a distance, the teacher announced, "Great! The problem has been solved, due to Misa and Rie's help." Noticing that one boy was still crying, the teacher said, "Now it's your problem alone, if you've already made up." Although it was already past dismissal time, the teacher discussed the fight with the whole class. She started with a blow-by-blow description, naming the fighters and describing how they had thrown sand, pulled hair, and hit. She also named all four mediators, described their failures and successes in trying to end the fight, and praised them all for helping solve the class's problem. Parents waited for 20 minutes beyond the normal dismissal time while the teacher discussed the fight, described in detail the words and strategies the mediators had used to find out about the fight and elicit apologies, and thanked by name the mediators who had helped solve "the class's problem."

Like the teacher just described, many preschool teachers told me that they handled most fights by allowing them to continue while watching carefully (*kenka o mimamoru*). Several teachers remarked that they valued fighting:

> When I see kids fighting, I tell them to go where there isn't concrete under them or to go where there are mats. Of course, if they're both completely out of control, I stop it. Fighting means recognizing others exist. Fighting is being equal in a sense.

> If children can solve fights on their own without people getting hurt, I let them do it themselves and ignore it. Kids start out rooting for the weak kid if the teacher stays out of it. If I can, I let them solve it.

> If I don't see a fight myself, I get witnesses to tell what happened. Unfortunately, children usually say that the last one to hit is bad. When I'm told about a fight, I get both sides to come, ask both what happened, and get both to agree. I don't try to suppress it, because it will come out somewhere. I also don't listen to tattletales, though. You have to gain the agreement [*nattoku*] of both sides. For 4-year-olds, though, often you can't take the time to do that; you just have to solve fights quickly because there may be fighting somewhere else. With 5-year-olds, you have to watch for days afterwards to see how they're treating each other.

> The fact that there isn't more fighting among children is considered a problem by many teachers and parents. Teachers plan things so that there will be more fighting – like decreasing the number of toys for 5-year-olds. We try to get kids to take responsibility for each other's quarrels. We encourage children to look when someone's crying and to talk about what the child is feeling, thinking, and so forth.

The comments suggest that teachers tried to foster children's own ability to stop aggression. Fighting was not a personal problem; it was a class problem – and an opportunity. Teachers' tolerance of fighting did not mean they approved of it. Their tolerance rested, I think, in the twin convictions that children can and must learn to manage one another's quarrels. It's important to note that teachers did not simply ignore fighting, crying, teasing, and other kinds of conflict. These incidents inevitably resurfaced in teachers' comments at the end of the day. For example, Ms. Ishida made the following comments to her class at the end of a day at Western Tokyo Preschool:

> I'd like to talk about some of the things that happened in our class today. [Teacher describes an incident of sharing she saw.] . . . There was an incident of crying, too. I told you to line up with your friends, and Akiko wanted to line up with some other girls: Mari, Chie, and Emiko. Akiko was crying. And what did you decide to do? [Several girls explain how they decided to hold hands with Akiko too, because they didn't want her to feel bad.] My heart was very happy to see all this kindness in our class today.

Another preschool teacher mentioned at the end of the day how pleased she was that children playing house that day had "included all the children who wanted to play." When I asked her about this remark, the teacher said:

> It's important to get children to take an interest in lonely children. It's important to get them to see that it's everyone's problem – not just the lonely child's problem. The teacher's role is to help children learn to take the initiative in integrating lonely children, newer children, and so forth.

Research conducted in other settings suggests that peer socialization can be harsh. When children are left to judge other children, they often choose more extreme punishments than adults would.[2] Yet the Japanese schools I studied seemed to escape this difficulty of peer socialization by strongly emphasizing values of friendship, kindness, and community.

PROTECTING THE "GOOD CHILD" IDENTITY

Although the boys in Ms. Nomura's class shouted, "Bombs away" as they dropped clay balls into the aquarium, she somehow surmised that the boys actually wanted to help the fish: "They thought they were helping the fish, because the little balls of clay look like

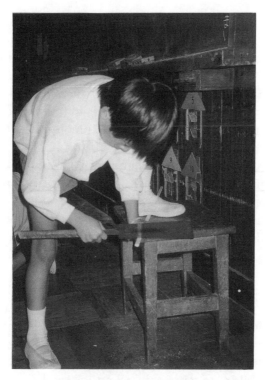

Third-grader using a saw.

the food pellets we give the fish." Teachers seemed oddly unwilling to attribute malicious motives to children. Children had not broken rules; they had simply "forgotten their promises" or "didn't understand." Misbehavior was called strange or odd (*okashii*) behavior.

In a half dozen preschools, I saw children hit their teachers or hang onto them with their whole weight. I was surprised that teachers showed no anger in response to these assaults. When I questioned teachers, they talked about hitting and hanging on as primitive, but well-intentioned, attempts to make contact with teachers: "There's no real hitting, and when they hang on it's to express their feelings. It's because they like you." When ethnographer Lois Peak was repeatedly kicked by one boy in the Japanese preschool she studied, teachers gently explained the problem as the ethnographer's failure to recognize the kicks as crude overtures of friendship.[3]

When a 5-year-old boy on the playground at National University Preschool cocked his arm to throw a large rock, a teacher standing nearby said casually, "Lend me the rock," and demonstrated, by touching the rock to the child's head, how the rock could hit a classmate's head. The teacher then returned the rock to the child, saying, "Carry it carefully." I was surprised that the teacher neither asked the child to put down the rock nor implied that the child intended to throw it.

The belief that children are inherently good is a dominant theme in accounts of Japanese childrearing, both historical and contemporary.[4] Research conducted in American laboratories suggests that when adults interpret children's misbehavior as well intentioned, it can help children develop positive qualities. Richard Dienstbier and colleagues asked young children to watch a toy train carefully to make sure it didn't go off the track and break – a task so tedious that children quickly tired of it. When the train fell off the track (which it did as soon as the child failed to watch it for 10 seconds), an adult made one of two suggestions to the child: that the child felt bad for being caught not watching the train or that the child felt bad because the train broke (i.e., because of a sense of responsibility). Later, when children were again asked to watch the train (without known surveillance), the two groups of children differed dramatically in the level of responsibility they showed. The children told they felt bad for being caught watched the train only half as carefully as the children whose feelings had been attributed to a sense of responsibility.[5]

The train-watching study suggests that a few words from an adult can dramatically shape children's interpretation of their own behavior. When the adult highlighted children's *discomfort about being caught*, children apparently felt little subsequent responsibility toward the task; when the adult focused on children's *discomfort at having done the wrong thing*, the children apparently felt considerable responsibility toward the task.

How might this study of adult interpretations apply to the boy on National University Preschool playground with his arm cocked to throw a rock? In that incident, the teacher asked to borrow the rock, explained its dangers, and returned it to the boy. The teacher's action implied that the problem was one of information – that the boy hadn't thought carefully about how the rock might hurt others. The teacher's action also implied that the boy was capable of self-control; after all, the teacher gave the rock back to the boy. In contrast, if the teacher had taken away the rock or imposed punishment, the boy might have inferred that he was untrustworthy or incapable of self-control; and he might well have focused on punishment as the reason not to throw rocks, rather than on the danger of injuring others.

At National University Preschool, the child who received the explanation and the rock may well have strengthened his sense of himself as a good, trustworthy child. In contrast, a child who was punished or asked to put down the rock might think of himself as untrustworthy or incapable of self-control. Of course, I've oversimplified the issues here. If the boy were an alienated 12-year-old who indeed intended to hurt a classmate, and the teacher returned the rock to him, he might simply figure the adult was a fool. But I don't think many 5-year-olds are so cynical. Their identity as good children is emerging – and fragile. They look to adults for judgments of their own moral worth.

UNDERSTANDING, NOT COMPLIANCE, AS THE GOAL OF DISCIPLINE

I interviewed Ms. Nomura after school and asked her about the boys who bombed the goldfish. Did she *really* think the boys were trying to help the fish? Our exchange was as follows:

AUTHOR: Did you really think the children were trying to help the fish by throwing the clay pellets?

TEACHER: Yes.

AUTHOR: Don't you think the boys understood they might hurt the fish by throwing the clay pellets?

TEACHER: If they understood it was wrong, they wouldn't do it.

In other words, when children "understand" what is right, they will do it. Teachers frequently told me that students didn't yet "under-

133

stand" rules. I came to realize that "understanding" rules didn't simply mean being able to repeat or explain them. It meant understanding why those rules were essential to humane life in a group – a kind of understanding that, teachers told me, would "naturally" – without force or coercion – result in proper behavior. Hence understanding, not compliance, became the goal of disciplinary efforts.

At what age should children understand they shouldn't drop clay on goldfish or monopolize the class's art materials? A great deal of American research suggests that preschoolers, and even 5- to 7-year-olds, can have considerable difficulty comprehending the needs and perspectives of others. Preschoolers' moral principles are often constrained by their own pressing needs. "It's fair for me to have more cookies because I want them more than he does" is a remarkably common kind of reasoning during the preschool and early elementary years.[6] Japanese practices make sense in light of this evidence on children's egocentrism. Like many developmentally focused American preschool teachers, Japanese teachers assume that children of preschool and early elementary age are still developing their understanding of rules, and they treat transgressions as opportunities to deepen understanding – not as causes for punishment.

MISBEHAVIOR: ITS IMPLICATIONS FOR THE CLASSROOM COMMUNITY

Six-year-old Shoji Itoh repeatedly jumped up from his seat during the reading lesson. Each time, he shouted, *"Baka yarō"* ("You're a jerk") at the teacher, so loud that it could be heard several classrooms away. Each time little Itoh yelled, Ms. Nakanishi went over to his seat, put her arm around his shoulder, and pointed out the sentence currently being read out loud. The class read aloud, with intermittent outbursts from Itoh, for about 15 minutes. Then they began an activity Ms. Nakanishi called "collecting words." Up and down the rows, each of the 35 students named a favorite object in a picture projected on the front wall; Ms. Nakanishi wrote each named object on the board so that students could later notice the different alphabets used for Japanese-origin and foreign-origin words. When Itoh's turn came, he named "electric rice cooker." Ms. Nakanishi asked him to come to the front of the class, put her arm around him, and praised him extravagantly: "You are very smart. Most second- and third-graders don't even know a word as difficult as 'electric rice cooker.' See how smart Itoh-kun is? Let's all clap for him. Today he's done so well." Itoh gave a theatrical bow to the class's applause and took his seat, beaming.

Why did Ms. Nakanishi single out for praise a child who had been so disruptive just moments earlier? I saw this strategy used by several other first-grade teachers as well. For example, one teacher repeatedly scolded a boy for leaving his seat and making noise during music class; at the end of class she called on him to show class members "how to put away your pianicas, since he is doing such an excellent job"; another teacher gave the honor of modeling sports poses in front of the entire class to a child who had repeatedly yelled out during much of the art class. Teachers explained that disruptive children needed to strengthen their bonds to other children. Ms. Nakanishi explained her strategy for handling Itoh: "I try to find something to praise him for during each period, in order to let him feel spiritually relaxed and to keep his classmates from giving up on him."

What I saw as issues of control and misbehavior, teachers talked about as issues of community; they transformed my questions about discipline to discussions of the teacher-child bond and the bonds among children. What interested the teachers seemed to be not so much the misbehavior itself as what it signified about the child's bonds with teacher and other children. For example, the teacher who waited 17 minutes for the student monitors to quiet the class for morning greetings told me, "I could have gotten the class to do morning greetings by saying one word, but I didn't. I wanted to know what the students were feeling."

Teachers often described their disciplinary choices as attempts to balance the need for order with the need to maintain the child's bonds to other children. Even as they scolded children, they often tried to help them preserve their identity as "good children" and save face with classmates. For example, when a first-grade boy

135

repeatedly left his seat and ran around the classroom during social studies, his teacher told the class: "Ichibashi-kun came to my house over summer vacation several times, and we had a very good time together, and he studied hard, but now he needs to act like a first-grader when he's with the whole class too." In another first grade, a boy repeatedly tried to distract classmates by dumping unwanted objects on their desks, and then he finally took his arms out of his sleeves and whipped his empty sleeves around, hitting nearby children. His teacher scolded him: "You have been inconveniencing us all since earlier today. You are good. You can do it." A first-grader who put a paper bag over his head and left his seat during social studies elicited the scolding, "You are really a good child. So you can understand what I'm saying. You can understand. You're in first grade now."

MISBEHAVIOR: AN APPEAL TO FEELINGS

Discipline appealed to feelings. Teachers made comments such as "If you break that hat, your mother will cry," "Your pencil-san will feel miserable if you peel it," "Your pianica is crying" (to a girl about to drop her pianica), and "Please behave properly on parents' day. If you don't, the parents won't laugh at you, they'll laugh at me." Like Ms. Nakanishi, who sought disciplinary strategies that would keep Itoh's classmates from "giving up on him," many teachers described discipline as a delicate balancing act: how to strengthen the child's bonds with teacher and fellow students and at the same time maintain an orderly environment for study. When teachers appealed on behalf of the "feelings" of objects or people, they were asking for children's help – and in a way that masked the conflict between the desires of child and teacher. In contrast, a direct request would have underlined this conflict.

This focus on feelings is reminiscent of the study, reported in the preceding chapter, of Japanese and American mothers' disciplinary strategies. Over half of the disciplinary responses of Japanese mothers appealed to children's feelings ("The farmer worked hard to grow these vegetables for you") or explained the problems created by children's behavior ("The store owners have lined things up neatly so that people will buy them"). In contrast, American mothers simply asserted their authority ("Do it!") or cited a rule ("Crayons are not for drawing on walls") in more than two thirds of their disciplinary responses.[7]

Of course, in a system that pays so much attention to building strong teacher-child and child-to-child relationships, the real trump card is those relationships – and the fear of losing them. I did see occasional – but only occasional – instances in which teachers threatened exclusion of children. One preschool teacher said to a child who repeatedly disrupted athletics festival practice: "We don't need children who act like that in this class. Please leave." (She did not follow up on this remark, and the boy made no move to leave.) A first-grade teacher asked – albeit in sweet, helpful tones – whether several children who repeatedly left their seats during class needed to leave their classmates and go back to preschool. Yet humiliation and threats of exclusion were much less frequent than I had expected from historical accounts of Japanese childrearing and education.[8] In fact, Japanese elementary teachers who viewed my videotapes of American lessons expressed concern about many disciplinary techniques commonly used in American classsrooms: writing the names of disruptive children on the blackboard, warning children that they might lose a privilege, and publicly calling attention to an individual's misbehavior. Japanese teachers worried that these techniques might humiliate and stigmatize the children most in need of deeper bonds to the group.

When misbehavior occurs, then, Japanese discipline tends to be emotional, not legalistic or mechanical. It appeals to feelings and to the child's bonds to teacher and other children. Often it tries to strengthen those bonds. The Japanese discipline I saw contrasted sharply with behavioral approaches such as "assertive discipline" that are found in many American schools. Behavioral approaches focus on controlling immediate behavior – through rewards and punishments – rather than on building the child's bonds to others or on promoting the child's long-term internalization of values. The stickers, "motivators," point systems, and rewards for behavior or achievement that are common in American schools were rare in the

Japanese schools I studied.[9] They were used widely only in one experimental "open school" consciously modeled on Western schools. In several other schools, students recorded their progress on various tasks (songs mastered on musical instruments, athletic feats mastered on the horizontal beam) using sticker charts. Even in these cases, effort was often as important as mastery: In one preschool, children affixed a blue sticker when they had mastered an athletic feat, a gold sticker when they had "tried hard but failed."

In the Japanese schools I studied, students often self-rated their performance, but teachers doled out neither rewards nor punishments. When I asked teachers whether they would consider using stickers or other rewards for good behavior, they expressed discomfort on two counts: They worried it would create competition among children and an "impersonal" (*mizukusai*) climate. From his study of Japanese high schools, anthropologist Thomas Rohlen suggests that systems of reward and punishment are used only as a last resort: in extreme cases in which trust has broken down and there is no other basis for motivating behavior.[10]

DISCIPLINE: A LONG-TERM VIEW

I was also struck by teachers' long-term view of discipline. For Shoji Itoh, who was shouting epithets during reading class, Ms. Nakanishi regarded first grade as an opportunity to try out various strategies for helping Itoh. Before I visited, she had already tried several strategies, such as giving him extra help with his schoolwork and inviting him to her home. "This year, in first grade, we'll experiment to see what works best, and next year, in second grade, we can implement the strategy." Ms. Nakanishi seemed under little pressure from colleagues or administrators to "cure" Itoh quickly. Perhaps, like the preschool teachers interviewed by Joseph Tobin and colleagues, Ms. Nakanishi felt Itoh's classmates were fortunate to have a difficult child as classmate: "By having to learn how to deal with a child like [him], they learn to be more complete human beings."[11]

The whole faculty and administration knew of Itoh's problems and seemed to regard them as an interesting challenge, not as evidence of any inadequacy on Ms. Nakanishi's part. Disruptive children like Itoh – whose reputations from preschool sometimes preceded their arrival at elementary school – were often placed with the most experienced and well-regarded teachers, making them symbolic of a teacher's success, not failure. Ms. Nakanishi gave brief reports, which amounted to an ongoing case study of Itoh's behavior, during daily staff updates and weekly staff meetings. Several of the strategies she tried had been suggested by other teachers, who were eager to find out how their suggestions had worked out in practice. Just as individual teachers made crying and fighting the "property" of the whole class, a school faculty often made difficult students like Shoji Itoh a shared concern of the whole faculty and staff – a topic for ongoing discussion, reflection, and intervention attempts.

DISCIPLINE BY PEERS VERSUS ADULTS: WHAT IS THE DIFFERENCE?

As we've seen, Japanese children are likely to find their classmates – not their teachers – managing many facets of classroom life. Children assemble and quiet their classmates, inspect lunch boxes to decide who can be dismissed for recess, run class meetings, and even settle fistfights. What difference does it make that classmates, rather than teachers, assume this kind of authority?

I'd like to speculate on three consequences. First, teachers can remain benevolent. Children assume much of the daily work of telling others to sit down and be quiet, so that teachers remain nurturant, warm figures. Peter Drucker, management expert and former president of Bennington College, commented on his leadership of that college's student-run disciplinary system: "My main function was to dispense mercy." Likewise, Japanese teachers dispense mercy. When preschoolers suggested punishing children who shirked chores, their teacher commented, "Is it a good situation if children work because they have to?" When students reported each other's transgressions, teachers urged students to men-

139

tion the good things fellow students had done. By having students assume so much day-to-day responsibility for management, teachers could remain warm, benevolent figures.

Second, children may experience sanctions from peers as the natural consequence of their behavior; sanctions from adults may seem more contrived. For example, when the daily monitor fails to notice it is time for lunch and is hit on the back by hungry groupmates, the child may experience this very differently from a teacher's reprimand. The slap may seem like a direct, natural consequence: "My classmates are hungry and I'm keeping them from eating." Such natural consequences may provide very clear, immediate feedback about one's shortcomings.

Finally, peer criticism, in comparison with adult criticism, may pose less of a threat to a child's identity as a "good child." Children's criticisms of other children can be brutally harsh; yet children's self-image as good children may depend much more heavily on how adults view them. As one first-grade teacher told me, "I don't do anything about checking whether children have forgotten to bring the required materials to school. If I did it, it would be too forceful, because I'm an adult. Children's responses are regarded differently." Because young children link morality and adult authority so closely, the fragile "good child" identity may fare better in an environment where peers, not adults, bear messages that the child has misbehaved. And that "good child" identity may, in turn, lead a child to behave responsibly in the future.

Some research suggests that Japanese children maintain a positive identification with adults. Compared to their American counterparts, Japanese fifth-graders report more desire to please parents and teachers in their academic work.[12]

The Dark Side of Peer Control

As Japanese children quiet unruly classmates, evaluate classmates' behavior, and even intervene in fistfights, their problem-solving skills and their sense of responsibility for others are no doubt fostered. But peer control may also have a dark side. Research suggests that young children's moral judgments tend to be harsh and punitive and that adults may provide a welcome moderating influence.[13] Because of the strong emphasis on kindness, friendship, and inclusion in Japanese elementary classrooms, I generally feel very comfortable with the wide latitude given children to work out problems and to manage disruptive classmates. Students have responsibility for managing one another, but to exercise it in ways that are unkind or dictatorial would violate strong classroom norms. Yet I am troubled by practices such as allowing students to manage even fistfights. When a teacher stands by and watches a fistfight or even cheers on the weaker boy (see p. 127), doesn't she condone fighting as a means of problem solving? And when she fails to help the child being hit, doesn't she miss an important opportunity to model compassion? Similarly, standing by while children drop clay "bombs" on goldfish condones cruelty to animals, in the view of some American teachers who have discussed this incident with me.

My guess is that Japanese teachers shy away from intervention in fights both to foster children's own problem solving and because they believe, as an oft-quoted Japanese saying goes, that "both parties are to blame in a fight" (*ryōseikenbai*). If both sides are indeed at fault, then the impetus to intervene on behalf of the "victim" is reduced. In the several fistfights I saw in Japanese preschools, teachers processed the entire incident with the class: what led up to the fight, a blow-by-blow description of the fighting, how it was settled, and so forth. As much emphasis was given to the provocation (for example, name calling or exclusion from play) as to the physical aggression itself, with no implication that the person who started hitting was somehow worse than the person who engaged in name calling. Americans may wish to draw a clearer line between verbal and physical aggression.

Different from fistfights is aggression that occurs in the service of classroom management – for example, when a classmate hits the distracted monitor to remind him to do his job or punches a groupmate to stop her from clowning around during a cooperative activity. I saw several such incidents in which the classroom teacher looked on without comment. Again I felt uncomfortable – as if the teacher condoned, in the interest of group progress, behavior abusive to an individual. It's important to ask whether unchecked peer socialization might provide a foundation for later *ijime,* in which a group of students bully an individual child, often one who stands out from the group in some way.

Americans may find in Japanese elementary education many appealing techniques for involving students in classroom management: student-run class meetings, student involvement in disciplinary problem solving, leadership by students in quieting and managing the class. The low rates of problem behavior for Japanese youth (see chapter 8) suggest the power of these techniques. Yet certain Japanese practices – such as permitting children to hit one another in the service of classroom management – may violate widely held American values about the right of individuals to be free from physical assault. Joseph Tobin and colleagues note that some Japanese preschool teachers, too, are uncomfortable with the practice of allowing children to settle physical fights.

Pressure for Conformity

In Japanese classrooms, I often found myself amused or irritated by procedures suggesting that there is one correct way to do things: to arrange desk contents (pencils on the right!), to stow shoes (toes first!), to take notes from the blackboard (reproducing the elaborate system of underlining and boxes used by the teacher). The list goes on: The number of pencils, erasers, and handkerchiefs one brings to school is sometimes a matter of policy, not personal choice, and checks for "forgotten items" are conducted regularly in many classrooms. Schools provide rules governing students' use of time over vacations and weekends, asking, for example, that students rise early, exercise daily, and stay away from video parlors. Schools also regulate how students come to school (in neighborhood walking groups that arrive well before school actually begins), suggest an appropriate bedtime and wake-up time for students, and even suggest the appropriate timing of bowel movements (before school!).

Taken individually, the regulations and prescriptions governing student behavior seem harmless enough, particularly during the early elementary years. Yet they may, in subtle and not-so-subtle

142

ways, undermine students' willingness to think and act as individuals. A system that uniformly regulates the details of students' belongings and personal hygiene may accustom students to conform their behavior to that of peers, socializing them to feel anxious about any difference from peers. It may teach them to look to precedent when they approach a new task rather than rely on personal judgment.

Detailed regulation of children's behavior during the elementary years may accustom children to accept, during their later development, regulation Americans would consider arbitrary. Although this method may create tractable students and employees, it may not foster thoughtful, independent behavior. Accounts of Japanese junior high school education suggest that regulation of students' behavior during this period escalates, sometimes becoming harsh, authoritarian, and arbitrary.[14] Paradoxically, an education system that begins by having children generate rules ends up with a top-heavy structure of adult-imposed rules.

Rules about study materials, bedtime, and bowel movements may help elementary classrooms run efficiently. Students are prepared to initiate new activities quickly, with a minimum of wasted time. On the occasions when I forgot some element of my research apparatus, I envied the Japanese first-graders around me, whose training seemed to ensure they had the items *they* needed. Several adult Japanese friends have confessed that the tricks they developed in elementary school for remembering required belongings (for example, creating an acronym from the first letters of the items) they use even today to remember their datebook, wallet, handkerchief, and so forth. Yet whatever the efficiency, I found myself uncomfortable with the idea that there was a right way to arrange desk contents and that children should investigate whether classmates had brought the right belongings to school.

Beyond simple efficiency, rules may also provide a loyalty test. Commitment to the group is shown by willingness to stow one's backpack and point one's shoes in the right direction. Testing children's loyalty may become particularly important during the years of adolescent rebellion. A more benevolent interpretation of rules and regulations, suggested by Ineko Tsuchida, is that manners and orderliness are seen as essential to group life and therefore as a way of expressing respect and concern for others.

What often struck me as I sat in Japanese classrooms was the contrast between the *content* and the *process* of regulation. The content of regulations – for example, the fact that the apron for school lunch servers should be refolded in a particular way, according to a posted diagram – often seemed arbitrary or unimportant. Yet the methods for building compliance respected children's needs for meaning and autonomy. Children discussed, at length, why the apron needed to be folded in a standard way (to prevent wrinkles, make the unfolding predictable for the next child) and themselves took responsibility for helping and reminding one another. In contrast, accounts of American classrooms suggest that very reasonable rules – such as respecting the property of others and their right to learn – are sometimes imposed and enforced from above, with little opportunity for students to develop an understanding of or personal commitment to them.[15] As Americans look at Japanese education, we may find more of interest in the *process* by which children are helped to understand rules than in the content of the rules.

VARIATION AMONG JAPANESE TEACHERS

Japanese preschool and elementary teachers often tolerate a level of noise and chaos that is surprisingly high by American standards. The Japanese preschool studied by Joseph Tobin and colleagues was regarded as chaotic, uncontrolled, and too unstructured by American audiences who viewed it on videotape – a perspective not shared by Japanese audiences. "Organized chaos" is how another comparative study of U.S. and Japanese childcare centers described the Japanese setting.[16] In Japanese preschools, I dictated my observations into a tape recorder held right up to my mouth – a technique that had worked well when I tested it in American preschools. But in Japanese preschools, children's shouting and laughing obscured nearly half of my dictations – even though the children were rarely within even 2 feet of me.

144

Yet it's important to note, as has researcher Gary DeCoker, that Japanese preschool teachers vary in their expectations about discipline. One teacher at Trinity Preschool made more than a hundred statements in a single morning intended to shape children's behavior: "Let's sit up straight"; "Who's got a curvy back?" "Who's clapping out of rhythm?"; "Leaning against the stage is strange"; "Who's leaning against the stage?" All these statements came from the first 2 minutes of a rhythm exercise in one of the most structured Japanese preschools I observed, where children were being prepared to take entrance examinations to prestigious private elementary schools. In contrast, many teachers at other preschools made no direct requests for children to change their behavior during an entire morning.

All the preschools and elementary schools I observed had some periods during the day that were much freer than would typically be found in American schools, as children romped, unsupervised, throughout the school and grounds, beneficiaries of a national curriculum that extols "energetic children" and "vigorous outdoor play." But all schools had times when students were expected to listen attentively to classmates and teacher. The degree of self-control expected of children varied considerably across teachers and across schools. One elementary teacher, a 40-year classroom veteran who began teaching in 1945, swatted children's hands with a long fly swatter each time the "hands" committed mischief. (Her action was in violation of Japan's prohibition of corporal punishment in schools.) Much more common – and very surprising to Americans who watch them on videotape – were first-grade teachers who tolerated much noisy and disruptive behavior as long as most children were engaged in learning. Gentle, invisible guidance, based on the bond of trust between student and teacher, was the ideal to which most teachers aspired.

Yet I occasionally heard teachers yell at students. In the intensely close, familylike environment of a Japanese classroom, an occasional outburst of anger was forgiven by colleagues and administrators. Frequent yelling, in the one instance where I encountered it, was regarded as poor teaching, both by parents and by colleagues – much as it probably would be in the USA. Japanese principals told me they would offer personal help to a teacher who frequently yelled at students; if that failed, they would attempt to transfer the teacher to a nonhomeroom position, such as teaching music or calligraphy, or at least to an upper-grade position.

Discipline in Japanese Schools: Training or Culture?

I'm often asked how Japanese teachers learn their approach to discipline. How much is learned in teacher education courses? How much comes from their own childhood experiences? I don't know. The research of Nobuo Shimahara and Akira Sakai suggests that the training of new teachers emphasizes techniques for establishing warm, close relationships between teacher and students. Some postwar "democratic" educational philosophies actually continue traditional Japanese ideals regarding the relationship between student and teacher. Robert LeVine and Merry White cite Gunzo Kojima's 1959 description of *kyōikuai* ("love in education"):

> It is love in educational activities which generates the driving force . . . and which gives vitality to guidance. [The first kind of love is] . . . the natural human love which is common in other aspects of human life and which the teacher always has in his heart as he . . . watches the sound growth of the immature and inexperienced pupil . . . . The second is a conscious love with which the teacher finds within the pupil the potential for an ideal person, and endeavors for this fulfillment with sincere hope.[17]

Japanese teachers' magazines are filled with advice and activities designed to help teachers build bonds with withdrawn or difficult children, involve children in shaping class norms, and build a sense of "classhood." Accounts of Japanese childrearing, both historical and contemporary, underline the belief in children's innate goodness and the emphasis on harmony rather than obedience.[18] Spanning nearly 350 years, accounts of Japanese childrearing by three Western sojourners to Japan show remarkable continuity.[19]

> They raise their children attentively and gently. Even if a child fusses or cries all night, physical punishment would not be used. Using patience and gentleness, the child would be helped to un-

derstand; punishment or criticism would not be thought appropriate. They believe that children have not yet developed understanding, that understanding comes with age and experience, that children must be guided with patience and nurturance.

Françoys Caron, 1645

No matter how ill-behaved children are, you almost never see parents punish them. I've hardly even seen them scolded or glared at. Japanese children are probably the most troublesome children in the world, the most mischievous, and yet you couldn't find more pleasant or happy children anywhere.

J. C. Ridder H. van Kattendyke, 1860

In Japan immediate gratification of children's demands is a top priority. All those rules that we were so accustomed to in our own childhood – no eating in the living room; no jumping on the couch; no snacks before meals; in bed by a reasonable hour – must seem rather *kibishii* (strict) by Japanese standards, almost as if we were trying to make adults out of children before they were ready. Instead, the overriding principle in Japan always seems to be "Don't go against the child's wishes." . . . When our son has thrown tantrums in public, concerned strangers have, on the spot, produced balloons, candy, drinks, *takoyaki* [octopus meatballs], and even a can of corn soup. Though this is probably attributable in part to our son's foreign appearance, at one point we began to wonder whether the entire population didn't carry anti-tantrum supplies in their bags and briefcases.

David McConnell, 1990

Recent commentators also express concern, however, about the breakdown of traditional childrearing and the rejection of the traditional maternal role.[20]

SUMMARY

How do Japanese teachers handle misbehavior? The answers to this question echo the themes of previous chapters. Peers have an extensive role in managing behavior, whereas teachers' authority is muted. Understanding, not compliance, is the goal of discipline.

147

Teachers may appeal to "feelings" (of inanimate objects as well as people) to avoid a direct contest of wills with children. When teachers do intervene, it is often with strategies meant to bolster the "good child" identity and to foster children's connections to one another. In other words, the disciplinary arsenal aims at long-term "buy-in," not immediate compliance. By creating a lively, supportive yet self-critical environment, these disciplinary practices may have some important spin-offs for learning, as the next chapter explores.

7

LEARNING AND CARING

A Classroom Is a Place to Make Mistakes

A classroom is a place to make mistakes.

Let's raise our hands freely and make mistakes in our answers and ideas.

We shouldn't be afraid of making mistakes.

We shouldn't laugh at mistakes.

As we talk together, pooling our ideas, saying, "Isn't it this way?," "Isn't it that way?" in response to mistakes, we'll come to find something authentic.

And we'll all grow.

Let's feel easy about raising our hands.

Let's feel easy about making mistakes.

Let's create the kind of classroom where, if we make mistakes, someone will correct us, someone will teach us.

> Sign posted in a Japanese fourth-grade classroom

At a time when the traditional structures of caring have deteriorated, schools must become places where teachers and students live together, talk with each other, take delight in each other's company. My guess is that when schools focus on what really matters in life, the cognitive ends we now pursue so painfully and artificially will be achieved somewhat more naturally.

> Educational researcher Nel Noddings[1]

My INTEREST IN JAPANESE EDUCATION INITIALLY FOcused on discipline, group cooperation, and other aspects of children's social development. But as I spent time in Japanese classrooms, I came to see children's academic and social development as a single tightly woven fabric. To describe one without the other is to rip threads from that fabric, to destroy its pattern and integrity. Earlier chapters argued that at the heart of Japanese elementary education is an emphasis on experiences of belonging, contribution, and sense of shared purpose. In this chapter, I argue that these qualities may be important not just as they shape children's social development but also as they shape intellectual development.

Here I explore four qualities of learning in Japanese early elementary classrooms. First, children's own contributions drive instruction to a remarkable extent. Lessons are deliberately designed to involve children, emotionally as well as intellectually, and to elicit their ideas and feelings. Second, learning is social. It's a community endeavor in which students listen to one another and teach and support one another. Third, learning emphasizes process as well as product. Wholeheartedness, persistence, and thoughtfulness, as well as mastery of subject matter, are strongly valued. Finally, learning is reflective; the ubiquitous *hansei* permeates learning. Students ask themselves, "Did anything about this lesson change my thinking?"; "What would I do differently next time?"; "What did I learn today?"

STUDENT CONTRIBUTIONS TO LEARNING

Although rote memorization and drill may dominate classroom education at the junior high and high school level in Japan,[2] both ethnographic and large-sample studies suggest that Japanese elementary education emphasizes active student contributions to learning and *deemphasizes* rote memorization and drill, particularly in mathematics and science.[3] For example, Jack and Elizabeth Easley contrast Japanese and American mathematics instruction:

> Mathematics [in the Japanese schools studied] is treated more as a real-life, conceptual, theoretical subject to be thought about and explained to oneself than as a mechanical paper and pencil skill to be practiced. . . . By second grade, children are writing the equations and complete answers for problems in permanent notebooks, often having to explain in their own words why something was done in a particular way. . . . In America, primary school

math is generally regarded as a set of arbitrary skills – algorithms to be performed mechanically. . . . The idea of explaining reasons in notebooks does not fit into this conception, apparently.[4]

A study of first- and fifth-grade classrooms in Japan, China, and the USA concluded:

> If we were asked briefly to characterize classes in Japan and China, we would say that they consist of coherent lessons that are presented in a thoughtful, relaxed, and nonauthoritarian manner. Teachers frequently rely on students as sources of information. Lessons are oriented toward problem solving rather than rote mastery of facts and procedures. . . . The role assumed by the teacher is that of knowledgeable guide, rather than that of prime dispenser of information and arbiter of what is correct. . . . Lessons are not rote; they are not filled with drill. Teachers do not spend large amounts of time lecturing but attempt to lead the children in productive interactions and discussions. And the children are not the passive automata depicted in Western descriptions but active participants in the learning process.[5]

Learning Measurement in Mr. Yamamoto's Class

Mr. Yamamoto's first-grade mathematics lesson on measurement was typical of dozens of first-grade lessons I saw. One important idea shaped the lesson from beginning to end. The lesson quickly drew out children's own ideas, giving children many opportunities to evaluate their own ideas critically and to hear and respond to the ideas of other children. The classroom was noisy and active, as children worked both together and individually.

> Mr. Yamamoto began his lesson on measurement by asking children to clear their desks except for one pencil. He held up his own pencil. "How can we tell if yours or mine is longer?" he queried the class. No sooner were the words out of his mouth than a child volunteered, "Hold ours up next to yours," and children rushed to the front of the classroom to compare their pencils with Mr. Yamamoto's. "I won" or "I lost," Mr. Yamamoto exclaimed dramatically as he compared his pencil with each child's. Children were

noisily discussing whose pencils had won and lost when Mr. Yamamoto threw down the gauntlet: "Find the longest object you can and bring it up here. This time I will definitely win." With a gleeful smile, Mr. Yamamoto pulled his pointer from a hiding spot behind his desk, and children rushed to the front to compare their objects with the pointer.

Children lined up with a remarkable array of objects that they thought might "defeat" the pointer: their own height, towels, belts from clothing, seat cushions dangling from long pieces of elastic. But the pointer was longer. Seeing this, an enterprising group of students pulled all the cleaning rags out of the closet and tied them together in a long chain. The class cheered on this group of students and then exploded in groans when the rag chain turned out to be a bit shorter than the pointer.

Suddenly four boys who had been kneeling and conferring noisily in front of Mr. Yamamoto stood up, one boy balanced on the shoulders of another, "chicken-fight" style, while the other two boys held them steady. "You win, you win, you're taller," said Mr. Yamamoto, laughing, and the class laughed and cheered. As the students returned to their seats, Mr. Yamamoto passed out mimeographed sheets that had two lines drawn on them. He posed the following problem: "You can compare objects easily if you can put them next to each other, but what about if they're on paper and you can't move them? Then how do you compare them? Please investigate which line is longer. Circle it, and write on the back how you investigated."

Children spent several minutes investigating the lines. Some took out rulers or long or short objects (such as pencils or erasers) to measure the lines. Others used paper to mark the length of each line. Mr. Yamamoto asked children which line was longer; the whole class agreed on the answer. Then he asked them to explain how they investigated. Children discussed this for several minutes, with about one quarter of the class endorsing the idea that you can tell "just by looking."

"If you think you can tell what is longer just by looking, let's try this," said Mr. Yamamoto, handing out another mimeographed sheet. This sheet also contained two lines – but arranged at angles in an optical illusion that made the shorter line look longer. Children discovered this as they measured, and they shouted out comments like "What's going on here?," "I thought this was longer," "Weird, hah," and "Unbelievable." Mr. Yamamoto asked the children who previously thought they could tell length "just by looking" whether they still thought so; the children said no.

Then Mr. Yamamoto asked children to name all the different ways they investigated the length of the lines. The class discussed each one, and Mr. Yamamoto asked children to demonstrate on the board techniques that were not obvious to others, such as marking a piece of paper with the length of one line and then comparing it with the second line. "The students who are now fourth-graders discovered 10 different ways to compare the length of objects when they were in first grade. So let's think of some more. Talk within your groups about other ways to compare the lines."

Students conferred for several minutes and came up with some new ways, including using fingers to measure. Asking the whole class to measure the lines on the first printout using their fingers, Mr. Yamamoto posed the question, "Is the same line longer no matter what you measure it with?" Many children readily answered yes to this question, but the class discussed the issue for several minutes, as students attempted to explain why several classmates had obtained different results using different measurement methods. Class members offered explanations to the children who found contradictory results ("You used different fingers to measure"; "Maybe you didn't measure carefully"), and the class discussed these comments for several minutes.

Mr. Yamamoto then posed another challenge: "Measure whether your notebook or your desk is longer without

153

putting them next to each other. And remember – it's no good to tell just by looking, as we already found out." Students spent a few minutes measuring, using a variety of techniques; a child who used a small eraser said aloud to himself as he worked, "What a tedious way to measure a big desk." Then Mr. Yamamoto posed the final problem: "Let's measure the two ends of the classroom to see which is longer." No sooner were the words out of his mouth than the whole class sprang into action. Children pushed desks away from the back of the classroom. Many children spontaneously worked in pairs or small groups. Some children got down on the floor with tiny 10-centimeter rulers or pencils and carefully worked their way across the classroom. Others counted the tiles across the classroom floor. Several children lay down, hands outstretched, and measured the floor in human body lengths.

Measurements completed, students pushed the desks back into rows and began to report all the different methods they had used to measure the two ends of the classroom. Mr. Yamamoto listened quietly to their discussion, chiming in at the end to mention one method no one had used: pacing off the classroom. Mr. Yamamoto concluded the lesson: "Next time we're going to try using a ruler to measure. In preparation, I'm going to measure lots of things at home." He pulled a ruler from his drawer and brandished it, smiling. The monitors stood to announce that mathematics class was over.

ACTIVE LEARNING: DRIVEN BY IDEAS

What's the difference between learning about measurement in Mr. Yamamoto's class and learning it, say, by sitting at a desk filling in a workbook that provides measurement exercises? First, the lesson drew out children's own ideas in a way that a workbook could not: Children were forced to recognize and examine their own assumptions about measurement (for example, that you can tell relative length "just by looking"). The point of Mr. Yamamoto's lesson was not simply to build measurement skill (though students had many opportunities to practice measuring) but to build an understanding and appreciation of measurement: that you can't tell size "just by looking"; that different units (eraser lengths or finger lengths) can be used for measurement; that these different units might yield different numbers but should yield the same conclusions about relative length. In this lesson, the thinking of other children was a critical stimulus; learning was a social enterprise that entailed listening to fellow students and reconciling conflicting views, not simply recording one's own unchallenged ideas on a workbook page. Interestingly, Mr. Yamamoto raised, but never answered, a major conceptual issue: Is the relative length of two objects the same no matter how you measure them? Too, Mr. Yamamoto made measurement irresistibly interesting and important. It became a way to explore the classroom, work with friends, playfully challenge the teacher, and reveal deception.

Students' active learning took them not only to the floor of Mr. Yamamoto's classroom but to many other places inside and outside elementary schools. They went to surrounding neighborhoods to make maps and study safe routes to walk to school. They went to local parks to investigate playground equipment and rules. They went into the schoolyard to sketch the growth of the morning glories planted by the students. They went to all rooms in the school, including the utility rooms, to map them and meet all the people who "help the school." I quickly learned not to depend on electric outlets for my tape recorder, since lessons (particularly science and social studies) often took students outside the classroom.

All first-grade classes cared for animals and plants, and their natural changes catalyzed a number of lessons. For example, when three of six crabs in one first-grade class died over a one-week period, the teacher devoted a science class to investigation of the crabs' demise.

> Children observed the living and dead crabs and mentioned everything they noticed about them, including the fact that they all "stunk." Some children believed that the crabs smelled bad because their water was dirty; others in-

155

sisted that crabs "naturally" smell bad and cited experiences at the seashore as evidence. The teacher asked how they could find out which was true. After students raised many possible strategies – including a trip to visit the crabs' natural habitat! – they settled on the idea of cleaning the aquaria and seeing whether the crabs still smelled bad. The teacher asked the class to reason through the strategy: "If I change the water and the crab still smells, then which is it, water or crab, that smelled?"; "If I change the water, and then the crab doesn't smell, which is it, water or crab, that smelled?" The children raised their hands to predict which they thought would smell – water or crab – and the teacher tallied the predictions on the board. The class was about evenly split. The students then changed the water, cleaned the crab cages, and came up to smell the crabs again. Most thought that the crabs no longer stunk. The teacher asked several students to summarize what the class had done and found out and then offered his own opinion, focusing less on science than on responsibility training: "I think the water was so dirty the crabs died. Which do you think crabs like: clean or dirty water?" "Clean," answered most of the students. "All of you would rather be in a clean house, wouldn't you?" the teacher reasoned, and added, "There's a group to change the crabs' water, but if the rest of you remember, remind that group to change it."

Finally, the teacher asked the class what to do with the dead crab. "Bury it"; "Give it a funeral," volunteered the students, and one began humming a funeral dirge. The teacher agreed, and teacher and students took the dead crab out to the schoolyard, stopping at a utility closet on the way to get a shovel. Several boys argued over who would get to use the shovel and finally played "scissors-paper-stone" to select the grave diggers. The whole class now hummed the funeral dirge as they crowded around the grave. The period was over, and the teacher suggested that any students who wanted to make a grave marker and write an epitaph could do so during the upcoming 20-

minute recess. The students returned to the classroom. "Let's take good care of the crabs who are still living," was the teacher's final comment. Student monitors rose to announce, "Science class is over."

In another school, a mysterious white powder that appeared on some of the class's cucumber plants provoked a lesson very similar to the investigation of the crab death. Students were encouraged to observe the plants closely, hypothesize why some plants were covered with white powder, and devise ways to test their ideas.[6]

Not just children's predictions but also their active thinking of other sorts shaped the direction of many lessons. For example, problem creation (*mondaizukuri*) was a common technique in mathematics lessons. Children wrote their own word problems. Often children showed great eagerness to solve the problems they themselves had created: In one first-grade class devoted to creating word problems, children begged to extend mathematics class beyond the bell so that they could go on and solve the word problems they had written. (Maybe it helped that the students had suggested the kinds of candy, gum, and cookies they would "buy" in their word problems.)

A number of gamelike mathematics lessons featured the mathematics set each first-grader possessed: a box stocked with colorful tiles, gameboards, a clock, and other manipulative math materials. For example, in one first-grade class, pairs of students played the hand game "scissors-paper-stone" 20 times, with the victor coloring in one square in a 4×5 matrix after each round. The class then copied on the board different children's game boards and discussed whether different arrangements of squares could really represent identical scores. An American undergraduate science major who observed the lesson with me wrote the following narrative notes:

> Although the class period was designated for math, the actual time spent doing math problems was relatively small compared to the time spent playing and discussing the results of the game. I was particularly impressed with this because instead of spending class time on repetitive math problems, the teacher used the game to maintain the attention of the students as well as to induce them

to think about the relationship between the number and pattern of squares and the final outcome of the game. At each stage of the game the teacher asked her class to guide her in making the next step and as a consequence, I assume that she promoted much independent thought in the students. Throughout the process she used a warm tone of voice and kept a slightly puzzled facial expression in order to encourage the students to give answers to questions. I was very surprised by this because I expected Japanese math teachers to place more emphasis on practical problem-solving instead of on general conceptualization of mathematical and geometrical relationship.[7]

Drill and practice accounted for a small portion of the school day in the first-grade classes I observed. While students might spend 20 to 30 minutes writing ideographs or 5 to 10 minutes at the beginning or end of mathematics class responding to flashcards, the vast majority of lessons involved children as active thinkers – and often as active doers as well. Several teachers explained to me that drill and practice were best left to homework and that school lessons should take advantage of possibilities unique to the group setting, such as having children work together and benefit from each other's ideas. It's important to note, however, that students' ideas may have more opportunity to drive lessons in science and mathematics than in other subject areas, particularly as students advance through the grades.[8]

"WET" LEARNING: AN EMPHASIS ON WHOLEHEARTED INVOLVEMENT

I have a criterion for deciding whether to save or throw away the papers my son brings home from school. Is there anything "of him" in the work? Any idea, feeling, memory, aesthetic impulse of his? Or has he simply filled in the blanks with prescribed answers? By this test, I would save most of the work done by Japanese first-grade students, whose essays, diaries, artwork, and notebooks speak richly about themselves, their families, their experiences at school, their daily encounters with nature and science. Japanese use the English loan words *uetto* and *dorai* ("wet" and "dry") to describe

emotional styles. A "dry" approach is rational, logical, unemotional, and Western; a "wet" approach is personal, emotional, interpersonally complex, and Japanese. Most of the academic lessons I
saw in early elementary classrooms were "wet" learning. Lessons
were designed to spark children's personal interest and contribution, grip them emotionally, and involve them intimately with classmates. Even when the content was science or mathematics, learning
was often an emotional enterprise. Here's how the first-graders of
Ms. Hirabayashi's class studied sinking and floating.

> Students had prepared for this science lesson by bringing
> an odd assortment of plastic bottles from home. Ms.
> Hirabayashi explained that the class would make boats
> from the plastic bottles: "We'll decorate the bottles, put
> sand in them, and float them in water. Think about how
> things float as you plan your decorations, and make the
> most wonderful decorations you can imagine." After chil-
> dren met briefly in their small groups to share ideas about
> sinking and floating, they spent nearly 2 hours over the
> course of that day and the next transforming their bottles
> into boats, using colored paper and found objects. The re-
> sults were extraordinary: dragon boats, dinosaur boats,
> floating European castles, a pirate ship complete with flag
> and crew, a "candyland" boat, and a panoply of super-
> heroes and fairytale characters. (Before I knew it, I had
> used a whole roll of film on these fanciful creations.)
>   After 2 hours of work, the children lined up the bottles
> on a long counter to admire and study one another's work.
> The colorful procession of bottles, looking like floats in a
> holiday parade, decorated the classroom until the next
> morning's science class. The next day, Ms. Hirabayashi
> brought in several buckets of sand. With her instruction
> "Think about how your boat will float as you plan the
> sand," children began funneling sand into their bottles.
> When children then moved outside to float their boats in
> the school's fountain, the scene was dramatic. One or two
> boats floated with their decorations above water, but most
> toppled into the water, and a few sank. Children's atten-

tion was riveted on the boats; children shouted, "The water got me"; "Godzilla's soaked"; "Ultraman drowned." After a few minutes of watching, shouting and laughing, they retrieved their soaked creations and returned to the classroom.

Ms. Hirabayashi began the discussion by posing two questions: "Who was happy with the way your boat floated?" and "Who saw something about another person's boat you'd like to try on your own boat next time?" A 20-minute discussion by the whole class ensued. Children talked about which boats had sunk, floated, or tipped in various directions and volunteered their ideas about why, mentioning amount and placement of sand. Ms. Hirabayashi pointed out the similarity or contradiction among children's ideas and said, "What a magnificent reflection (*hansei*)!" to several children who had criticized their own designs. Finally, the students spent a few minutes in their small groups, discussing how they would decorate the boats and weight them with sand if they were going to do it again.

Why did Ms. Hirabayashi's students spend 2 hours decorating their boats? Many lessons began with discussions or activities that – at first blush – seemed irrelevant. In the lesson about water volume described in chapter 4, Mr. Yanagi spent the first 10 minutes having each child "introduce" the bottle he or she had brought from home. Along the way, the children volunteered information about the favorite drinks or liquids that had inhabited the bottles: "This is my favorite juice"; "I love vinegar, just like my dad." Mathematics lessons began with children naming their favorite sweets – and later making up word problems about buying those sweets. In Japanese class, students closed their eyes and imagined the sights and sounds of their recent field trip before writing about it. Art class – making pop-up cards for graduating sixth-graders – began with 10 minutes spent recalling the many ways the sixth-graders had helped the first-graders; students recalled, for example, how the "big brothers and sisters" of the sixth grade had cleaned the first-grade classroom and ministered to the first-graders who scraped knees on the playground. These beginnings were what some teachers called *sasoikake* – invitations. "If the *sasoikake* is good, the learning will be good," one teacher told me.

Another illustration of "invitations" to learn comes from research on Japanese and American preschool teachers. Look at Figure 1 and imagine that you and a preschooler sit facing each other. But instead of seeing each other, you each look at one side of the large easel that sits between you holding the four pictures shown in Figure 1. Your job is to describe the starred picture in such a way that the preschooler will select it from the four pictures. American teachers involved in this task significantly more often got right to the "point" and gave clues that immediately identified the target picture. Japanese teachers, in contrast, often invited children to the task by relating all the pictures to some shared experience of teacher and student or to the student's interests. A Japanese preschool teacher used the following description to help 5-year-old Yuki-chan choose the correct picture from Figure 1:

> Yuki-chan, a little while ago you were playing in the assembly hall, with Kazuo-chan. The principal and Teacher Hayashi were playing too. Remember? Everyone played with hoops. Remember how all the hoops were circles but there was just one hoop that was broken, at the top. Separated, by quite a bit. But I think the principal will fix it for us, because it is dangerous. At the top. Yuki-chan, which do you think it is? The one that's separated, by quite a bit.[9]

Only after the child selected the wrong picture did the teacher give further information: "Less than half is missing." For the Japanese preschool teachers, the goal of having the child select the correct answer often took a back seat to the teacher's efforts to interest children in the task and establish a feeling of mutuality.

The emphasis on personalized learning and on classroom goals of friendship, kindness, and helpfulness may have a cumulative impact on the way Japanese students approach learning. Researcher Keiko Moriya asked more than 1,000 English and Japanese children aged 7 to 17 to write everything they "felt and thought"

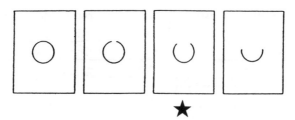

Figure 1. Communication game illustration. Child and adult sat on opposite sides of an easel. Each looked at a copy of the four drawings and gave clues that enabled the patner to pick the drawing marked with a star.

Source: Azuma, Kashiwagi, and Hess, 1981, p. 118, from Dickson, 1975.

after being read Shel Silverstein's book *The Giving Tree,* a simple picture book about a tree that only gives and a boy who only takes. Japanese children, compared with English children, more often reacted empathically to the story and more often conjectured about the feelings of the characters. English children, in contrast, more often reacted nonevaluatively, objectively describing what happened to each of the characters without reference to their emotions.[10]

A FOCUS ON PROCESS

How do we judge whether a classroom lesson is successful? For many lessons, our judgment depends on whether children acquire particular skills, information, or concepts. I think this is true for many lessons taught in Japanese as well as American schools. But I often felt a second strong force operating in Japanese classrooms: an emphasis on process. The point wasn't just to obtain a correct answer. The point was also to feel certain things while learning, to be engaged in a wholehearted way, and to reflect on one's work, whether or not these led to correct answers. Often teachers' comments underlined the connection between emotions and work: "If you're noisy, what's in your hearts won't be able to come up to your heads," a teacher cautioned students who were drawing their memories of a class trip to the zoo.

162

Third-grade science lesson, "Let's Make Magnets." Children work in small groups to find out what materials can be made into magnets.

Persistence and elaboration were often singled out for praise, quick-and-dirty work for criticism. "Clap if you think Jimbo-kun really worked hard," urged a first-grade teacher when a boy had finally managed to give a short speech in front of the class after several days of unsuccessful attempts. "Someone worked very hard on writing these sentences," another teacher said to the class, putting her arm around a child who had had great difficulty writing. The teacher's comment prompted applause. Pictures that filled the paper or were elaborate were held up by teachers as examples of children who "really had autumn in their hearts as they drew pictures of autumn." Pictures dashed off quickly were returned to their owners for elaboration: "Weren't there more classmates on your field trip? Why is just one child playing here?" or "Look how lonely

163

that chestnut looks on the paper. Can't you draw something to keep the chestnut company?" The same held true for compositions: "Some classmates were able to remember and write many things about our trip to dig sweet potatoes, others just a few. If you could write just a few, think and write at home, so we can all remember and write a lot on Monday." More elaborate work was valued, I think, as evidence of students' persistence and engagement.

The national curriculum, described in chapter 2, honors process in its emphasis on such goals as "Love of nature" and "Desire to contribute actively to family life." These goals can be measured *only* by emotional engagement, not by skills or knowledge. Sometimes process seemed to be the point of an entire lesson. One first-grade science lesson, called "juice play" (*shiruasobi*), had children bring in a variety of flowers and fruits from home, extract colors from them, and use the colors to make fold-dyed paper during a subsequent art class.

> Children spent the first 10 minutes of class introducing what they'd brought from home or picked in the class garden – grapes, a melon, an orange, a lemon, and many different kinds of leaves and flowers. The teacher asked students to introduce their flowers and leaves, telling the names and where they grew; she asked the children to predict what colors each would make. The children shouted out predictions, which the teacher wrote on the board. The teacher explained the three ways of extracting juice – grinding in a mortar and pestle (for leaves or hard fruits), massaging in a plastic bag with water (for flowers), and squeezing (for juicy fruits). She then instructed the students to work cooperatively with their four groupmates and to send one person from each group to obtain a container of water and a plastic bag for the group. Each student had an inexpensive, commercially produced "juice play kit" that contained a small mortar and pestle and an assortment of small dishes. Students set to work pulverizing, squeezing, and massaging. "I can't get any juice out of my leaves," shouted one child after about 5 minutes of

grinding. "I think it just takes a long time," counseled a nearby child.

The teacher announced that they would continue juice play for 25 minutes, "until the big hand is at the 10. So think about the time so you can do a good job within the allotted time." Children continued to grind, squeeze, and massage. Despite the difficulty of pulverizing the leaves in the mortar and pestle, a number of students seemed mesmerized by this task and kept grinding, making comments to neighbors like "Look, my leaves are totally smashed." Several students didn't move on to the other methods, despite a reminder from the teacher that "we'll end juice play when the big hand is at 10, so remember to try all the methods." Students traded fruits within their groups and shared the group's plastic bag. The classroom became wonderfully fragrant of melon, orange, and flowers. The teacher announced that the big hand had reached the 10; she was greeted by a loud chorus of protests. "We want more time" and "Not yet," shouted a number of children. "Well, OK, how much more time do you need?" They agreed on another 10 minutes, but students once again protested at the end of that time, and the teacher agreed to another 10 minutes. The children then saved the various juices in order to use them in their art lesson later that day: They would fold paper and dip it in the various colored juices, unfold it to see the patterns, and, finally, compare their predictions with the colors actually produced.

Many other researchers have commented on the Japanese focus on process, rather than product, particularly in learning the traditional Japanese arts.[11] Researchers Robert Hess and Hiroshi Azuma describe the American teaching approach as "quick and snappy," the Japanese approach as "sticky-probing."

In a study of science education, Azuma and Walberg (1985) compared Japanese and American teaching processes. Fifth grade teachers, four in each country, were asked to teach their pupils about the dissolution of substance in water. . . . All four American classes discussed what they planned or were going to do, the procedures that should be followed. . . . The teacher asked questions that could be answered in short sentences. Clear feedback or acknowledgment from the teacher immediately followed each child's response. The exchange moved at a brisk pace. Convergence of ideas was not a goal. . . .

All four Japanese classes, however, spent considerable time lingering over a substantive question, such as how to ascertain the density of a salt solution without testing it, whether or not some of the weight of the substance would get lost when it dissolved in water, whether salty taste is evidence of salty substance, and the like. The teacher probed and focused, but seldom gave clear feedback, and kept his own position vague. At the same time, he made sure that the discussion concentrated on the problem he posed at the beginning. After a lengthy discussion that divided the class into groups holding different opinions, an experiment was planned and executed as a means of resolving the conflict. These experiments were carefully designed to persuade students to adopt a conclusion that the teacher approved.

The American classes . . . were clear and snappy, encouraging divergent fluency. "Anything else? Anything different?" was the stimulus to which children kept responding. The discussion kept moving on, as if to linger on the same phrase or idea might threaten fluency. The Japanese classes were generally "sticky." The core of the sticky impression was taking time on the same topic, looking at it from varied perspectives and in a variety of conceptual frameworks.[12]

When teachers allowed students to spend an entire class period investigating measurement or sinking and floating, they were – like the teachers observed by researchers Hess and Azuma – emphasizing students' understanding rather than "quick and snappy" recall of information. They seemed to believe that a focus on understanding would eventually yield results, a view reminiscent of the long-term view of discipline explored in chapter 5.

A certain contrast between academic and nonacademic lessons puzzled me at first. Art, music, and physical education often seemed to be taken more seriously in Japanese classrooms than is often the case in the United States and to be less spontaneous and fun as a result. Yet academic subjects as taught in Japanese early elementary classrooms often seemed more personal and emotionally involving than they might be in America.

Why? I think the yardstick used by Japanese teachers – to measure both academic and "nonacademic" lessons – emphasized students' emotional and intellectual engagement, reflection, and persistence. "Even" art, music, and athletics should reflect these qualities. A few splashes of paint on a paper was not as good as a more elaborate work that reflected greater involvement and a thoughtful, self-critical approach. But the same emphasis on emotional engagement, applied to academic lessons, created a refreshing emphasis (from an American's point of view) on process. The point was to get the students to care about the lesson, to relate it to their own experience, to be active in pursuit of learning – even if it meant children on each other's shoulders or on the floor as they learned mathematics.

MISTAKES: A NATURAL PART OF LEARNING

The focus on process explains something that was at first very puzzling to me: Why did teachers often fail to correct children's mistakes? The first time I noticed this was during the very first days of my observations in a Japanese preschool.

A 3-year-old sat on the steps from the classroom to the playground. He had just put on his shoes in order to play outside, but he had put them on the wrong feet. A teacher noticed and said to the child, "Do you feel anything funny?" The child didn't recognize the problem. The teacher said, "Do your shoes feel funny?" The child still didn't understand the problem. The teacher said, "Look at Taro's shoes. Do they look the same as yours, or different?" The child compared the shoes but still didn't grasp the problem. The teacher continued this line of questioning for approximately 3 minutes, but the child still didn't understand. "Oh well, just go ahead and play," said the teacher, and the child went off to play with his shoes on the wrong feet.

167

Similarly, first-grade teachers often told students, "This is strange (*okashii*)" or "See if you can find anything strange about your paper" rather than explicitly identifying or correcting a mistake. The point was not so much to elicit the right answer as to foster thinking. Why correct a child's shoes when the "funny feeling" of having them on the wrong feet might wreak a conceptual breakthrough? A common technique in mathematics instruction was to have several students copy their solutions onto the board – often, among them, one or more incorrect approaches. Students would explain their thinking, including that which led to mistakes. The comparison of the various correct and incorrect problem-solving strategies would form the core of a lesson. Jack and Elizabeth Easley have noted the importance of mistakes in Japanese mathematics instruction:

> Children [in Japanese schools] are much less protected . . . from making serious mistakes in mathematics, a point which seems quite consistent with the Kitamaeno staff attitude toward social interactions. Be supportive, but don't direct or take over what someone else is doing for himself or herself. . . . As the children themselves often put it, they were expected to learn from their mistakes. . . . In American math classes, expression of erroneous thinking or other differences of opinion are usually not encouraged, and the form of discussion is expected to be fairly uniform. . . . Often, no one knows what Johnny did wrong and why. In Kitamaeno School, we saw a larger variety of mistakes, presumably because the children felt free to explore their ideas openly.[13]

A COMMUNITY OF LEARNERS

At first I felt uncomfortable when children's mistakes were bared for all to see. Don't children feel humiliated when they put an incorrect math solution on the blackboard? Or when their drawings are singled out as looking like stick figures? Quite soon I was reassured by the sense of community in the Japanese classrooms I studied. Friendliness, cooperation, and persistence dominated classroom values, and these were arenas of achievement available to *all* children. Lessons were challenging, and hence mistakes were an inevitable part of learning. Like the optical illusions presented by Mr. Yamamoto, answers were not always obvious or easy. Often teachers asked for a show of hands from students who had obtained correct and incorrect answers to a problem, and the show of hands for incorrect answers was often substantial. As we've seen, students who criticized their own thinking were warmly acknowledged, as were students who explained the thinking behind their mistakes, so that, as one teacher said, "Everyone in the class can learn from the students who tried to solve the problem this way." Mistakes became opportunities to help classmates rather than failures to be hidden.

Students' active role in managing academic activities was often as striking as their active role in managing discipline (see chapters 5 and 6). Students clapped for each other, gave each other permission to speak, evaluated each other's performance, and responded to each other's ideas. In some classrooms, students used hand signals to signify their agreement or disagreement with the student who was speaking or their desire to add a new idea; this allowed the student or teacher to lead a smooth, ordered discussion by knowing the category of contribution each student wanted to make. Often students ran discussions, with each student choosing the next student to speak or with the daily monitors serving as discussion leaders. Many classroom rituals emphasized *students'* role in each other's learning. For example, in many classrooms students routinely asked permission from their classmates before they read aloud and routinely asked, "Is this all right?" after they wrote on the blackboard. In many schools, students had pieces of blackboard which attached magnetically to the front blackboard, so that they could easily share their individual work with the class. A first-grade mathematics lesson illustrates a number of these themes.

Ms. Ogawa read a word problem to the class: "Seven children boarded a train, two got off, and three more boarded the train. How many were finally on the train?"

She asked children to write equations to represent the problem, and she asked several children, who had each written a different equation to represent the problem, to

169

put their equations on the board. Hiro's equations were very puzzling to the class: $3 - 2 = 1$ and $7 + 1 = 8$. Hiro himself could not explain his reasoning, although he tried for several minutes. Ms. Ogawa asked whether anyone in the class could explain his reasoning, but no one volunteered. When she asked, "Do Hiro's equations represent the problem correctly?," most students answered no. Ms. Ogawa again encouraged Hiro to explain his equations: "Tell us what you were thinking as you wrote these." After another unsuccessful attempt to reconstruct his own thinking, Hiro looked distressed, and Ms. Ogawa said, "Touch my hand in a baton touch and empower me to speak for you. And I will try to speak your thoughts." Hiro reached out his fingertips to touch Ms. Ogawa's, and she explained that the first equation might represent the net difference between people who boarded and left the train. She went on to help the class reason through why Hiro's equations represented the problem correctly. At the end of class, Ms. Ogawa asked Hiro to tell the class "how you felt when everyone in the class said your solution was wrong." "I didn't feel good," Hiro said. "I think he was very courageous to try and give an explanation when everyone thought he was wrong," said Ms. Ogawa, and the class looked to Hiro and burst into applause.

REFLECTION

Self-evaluation or reflection – *hansei* – finds its way into each chapter of this book. *Hansei* undergirds discipline, group formation, efforts to foster the "whole child's" development, and academic learning as well. Whatever the subject matter, reflection seemed to be a part of learning. During a first-grade music class, each han (fixed small group) first performed a song for the class and then gave its own *hansei* on "what was good and what needs to be improved." After sharing these reflections with the class, the members of the small group invited the class to add to the group's own *hansei*. A first-grade art lesson began by having students strike

170

athletic poses as if they were throwing, kicking, or running. Students admired each other's poses and selected "Masa-kun, who really looks like he's throwing," to stand on the teacher's desk and model for the students to draw. When students finished drawing, they taped up their renditions of Masa on the blackboard, and the teacher led a discussion: "Which drawings best capture Masa's pose?"; "Which look like real people rather than stick figures?"; "Which best fill the paper?" The discussion concluded by having each child identify ways to improve his or her drawing the next time. In the same way, students evaluated their science projects, compositions, and math solutions. "Who compared yours with other people's and thought it was good?" "Who compared yours with other people's and found something you'd like to improve?" "If you were doing this again, what would you do differently?" "What did you learn from doing this?" Teachers seemed to feel that such evaluation and synthesis was more powerful when it came from the students themselves.

What if the students didn't raise the points the teacher wished to bring out? Sometimes, to be sure, teachers simply added their own thoughts to those raised by the students. But I was surprised that some lessons ended with a question mark. First-graders spent a period creating math word problems and identifying similar "types" of problems; the teacher did not reveal what she meant by "types," so children tried classifying them in various ways. "Aren't there additional types of problems?" the teacher asked a half dozen times over the course of the lesson, as children wrote more problems, trying to think of new "types." The array of problems mushroomed: simple addition and subtraction, comparison of two numbers, addition of two numbers and subtraction of a third number from their sum, comparison of two sums, and so forth. Still the teacher called for "more different types of problems" and ended the class by asking children to "continue to make up problems with your friends, and see if you can think of any types that we didn't think of today."

A mathematics lesson in another first-grade class left children to think on their own about whether two different ways of solving a mathematics word problem were actually both correct. In another

171

school, a fifth-grade teacher told his class they would devote the day's mathematics lesson to "discovering the beauty of using letters to represent unknowns." Students spent the entire class period suggesting the advantages of letters to represent unknowns, compared with question marks or the geometric shapes (rectangles, triangles) often used to represent unknown quantities in primary grade textbooks. The students came up with several advantages. For example, the alphabet, unlike a question mark, can distinguish multiple unknowns – one to represent the price of pencils, another to represent the price of erasers, and so forth. Letters, unlike geometric shapes, are standard symbols that can be written easily in horizontal formulas. The students continued to suggest, discuss, and list on the board or discard potential advantages of letters as unknowns, but the teacher continued to ask, "Aren't there more advantages?" The lesson ended with the teacher's comment "Did we think of all the reasons letter unknowns are useful? See if you can think of more." After each of these lessons, I found myself puzzling: What *are* the various types of word problems? What are the advantages of letters used to represent unknowns? The fact that I continue to puzzle over these issues years later is, I think, precisely the point.

TOLERANCE OF DIVERSITY

Recent educational reforms in Japan have focused on the need for increased "individuality" and "internationalization" in Japanese schooling.[14] It's easy to see why these areas have been identified for improvement. The 627 hours devoted to social studies (and its primary grades precursor, Daily Living) during the elementary years focus almost exclusively on the students' school, community, region, and country, until sixth grade, when some attention is given to international cultural, sports, and peacekeeping organizations.

Although U.S. elementary curricula, too, tend to start with a local focus, by sixth grade most American students have studied some foreign countries; many have had the opportunity to study some other cultures in depth and to study cross-cultural issues such as the immigrant experience and cultural conflict. In many American elementary schools, a wide range of artistic, literary, and research activities are designed to build students' empathy for and interest in diverse cultures. American elementary teachers sometimes criticize America's multicultural education for failing to go beyond "the three F's: food, festivals, and famous people." Yet our exposure to diverse cultures is considerably more than many Japanese students receive. The call for "internationalization" of Japan's curriculum is relatively recent, and it remains to be seen how elementary schools will respond.

As noted above, visitors to Japanese classrooms are often struck by the single "right" way to do things: to stow desk belongings, to fold the chef's apron after serving lunch, to choose the belongings to bring to school. Sometimes, too, there are "right" answers to questions of culture. I observed one first-grade social studies lesson that asked students to brainstorm items – holidays, flowers, foods, and so forth – associated with each season of the year. When one student volunteered "Christmas" for the list of winter items, the teacher declined to put it on the list, asking, "Can't you think of a more Japanese winter holiday?" The teacher passed over several responses until finally a student mentioned Japanese New Year. Similarly, the teacher ignored students' protests that they could swim and play baseball year-round, and she put these items only in their "proper" seasonal categories. In another first-grade class, studying "how our mothers spend their time," the teacher ignored children's reports that their mothers worked outside the home. By recording in the class bar graphs only the time mothers spent on traditionally female tasks, such as cooking, cleaning, and childcare, the teacher sent a strong message about the proper work of mothers.

With respect to emotions, too, one sometimes senses a careful socialization of the "correct" emotions. On one level, it's refreshing to enter a Japanese classroom and see that the month's goal is "Let's be cheerful" or "Let's be energetic" – goals that recognize that children's needs go beyond academics. Yet these goals too suggest a "correct" way to feel. Why should children make an effort to be cheerful if it doesn't come naturally? One comparison of Japanese and American preschools found that Japanese educators tended to

173

emphasize socialization of appropriate emotions, whereas American educators tended to emphasize self-expression.[15]

Japanese textbooks may present a narrow "party line" regarding Japanese history and values. In one well-known textbook approval case, the Ministry of Education requested that a poem in a sixth-grade textbook be changed so that the poet's description of a river would conform to the officially recognized onomatopoeia for a river's sound. "We can only conclude from this that the Ministry's inspectors feared that children might get the idea that it was all right to play with the national language in ways which would encourage them to think of it as something belonging *to them* rather than as something whose use is controlled by the State *for them*," write Teruhisa Horio and Stephen Platzer.[16]

Paradoxically, though, Japanese teachers may – in some areas such as mathematics and science instruction – nurture diversity of student thinking to a much greater extent than do American teachers. For example, in mathematics and science, Japanese teachers are more likely than American teachers to encourage the expression of disagreement and to highlight the many different approaches to problems. However, Japanese teachers encourage disagreement more frequently in science than in social studies, according to Ineko Tsuchida's study of 40 fourth-grade science and social studies lessons by 10 Japanese teachers.[17]

The Japanese curriculum, with its substantial devotion to art, music, physical education, and hands-on learning, may be much more responsive to diverse learning styles than are many American curricula. Yet in other ways – what constitutes mothers' work, a winter holiday, an emotion appropriate to group life – Americans may find in Japanese practice an intolerance of diversity, an encroachment on what we think is properly a matter of individual opinion.

Is this intolerance of diversity an inevitable cost associated with Japanese academic achievement? The areas of particularly high achievement for Japanese schools – science and math – are precisely the ones for which Japanese elementary teachers successfully foster diverse thinking as part of instruction. In contrast, areas such as social studies, where an "official" view of Japanese society may predominate, are often viewed as weaknesses of Japanese educa-tion.[18] Japanese educators may find it much safer to foster diverse student thinking in mathematics and science – where students are unlikely to overturn the theory of gravity – than in social studies, where students might easily discover uncomfortable contradictions between the official view of Japan as a harmonious, cooperative society and the events of Japanese history.

Social studies textbooks have provoked some of the most bitter conflicts over Ministry of Education review. For example, the minis-try's request that history textbooks call Japan's World War II mili-tary activities in Asia an "advance" rather than an "invasion" pro-voked an international diplomatic incident. Education critics Teruhisa Horio and Stephen Platzer provide an interesting perspec-tive on another textbook screening incident:

> The Education Ministry's inspector declared that it was not per-missible to use the word *kenka* (fight, brawl, squabble) in a Japa-nese language textbook. The author of this text was told that to be acceptable, the story he was relating had to be reworked so that the phrase "they went to the next village to rumble with the boys there" could be replaced with "they went to the next village to have a sumo match with the boys there." Are the Ministry of Education's textbook inspectors really so foolish as to think that simply by proscribing the word *kenka* they can safeguard the harmoniousness which they want to represent as the essence of Japaneseness?[19]

The values emphasized in Japanese classrooms are, I believe, somewhat different from the values that many Americans would choose to emphasize. I think many Americans would find Japanese classrooms too weak in their emphasis on individual rights and tolerance of diversity and too strong in their emphasis on harmony and conformity. Yet there's little reason to suggest that weak em-phasis on diverse thinking is an inevitable "cost" associated with Japanese practices. In fact, I would make the opposite argument: that Japanese education would be strengthened by expanding the welcome for diverse thinking – now pretty much confined to math-ematics and science – to other curricular areas as well.

SUMMARY

There's an extraordinary gap between the American media's portrayal of drill and memorization in Japanese elementary schools and the active, idea-driven learning that researchers have observed. Media portrayals may reflect an assumption that Japanese elementary schools are, like Japanese secondary schools and cram schools, focused on drill and memorization. Too, media coverage may reflect Americans' own assumption that academic achievement is produced by a focus on drill and performance, not a focus on understanding. Although more research is needed, particularly outside the areas of mathematics and science, I think existing research supports the following tentative conclusions about Japanese early elementary education:

- That skills tend to be learned as part of some larger, meaningful pursuit – not as an end in themselves.
- That lessons elicit children's own ideas and feelings and help children reflect on them.
- That teachers work hard to create a community of learners who respond supportively to one another's thoughts and feelings.
- That teachers emphasize the process, as well as the outcome, of learning.
- That wholehearted involvement, persistence, and thoughtful problem solving are regarded as important goals for children's learning.
- That reflection (*hansei*) is a pillar of academic learning.

Early elementary lessons generally rested on a view of children as active learners rather than simply passive recipients of information. This view recognizes that children have their own powerful ideas about how the world works – scientifically, socially, morally – and that learning must engage and shape those ideas, not simply superimpose information or procedures that children memorize and then forget. Again and again I found Japanese lessons striking for the welcome they gave children's own powerful ideas and the help they gave children to examine these ideas in a thoughtful, critical, sustained way.

Do you have the same amount of water if you pour it into a taller, narrower glass? Do 10 colored boxes scattered across a sheet represent as big a score as a block of 10 boxes next to one another? What are the reasons for rules in a park? Children's powerful ideas were welcome in part because of the structure and content of the lessons: a sustained, relaxed focus on a single major issue over one or more entire class periods; plenty of "invitations" to connect the lesson with personal experiences; activities that engaged children (often physically and emotionally as well as intellectually) with what was being studied.

I was impressed by the faith teachers seemed to place in children's own capacity for self-evaluation and by teachers' reluctance to short-circuit children's own reflection by providing answers and judgments. Yet the welcome for children's ideas may hinge as much on sense of community within the classroom as it does on lesson content and presentation. Children listened and responded to one another's ideas – clapping for one another, correcting, congratulating, devising explanations for students who were having difficulty. Would any of this have been possible without the community-building and group-building efforts described in chapters 3 and 4?

Both American and Japanese educators recognize the importance of opportunities for children to learn from their mistakes. But the crucial infrastructure for exploring mistakes – or for any kind of challenging learning – may be a classroom where all students know and care about one another as people, know how to talk and listen to one another respectfully, and have the safety provided by strong, shared class norms of kindness, helpfulness, and "putting our strength together."

8

WHAT IS A SUCCESSFUL SCHOOL?

The more the school cares about students, the more students care about matters of schooling.
Thomas Sergiovanni, *Moral Leadership*

Japanese children learn a lifelong lesson that is the cor-
nerstone of the efficiency and success of modern Japan:
Each person has a role to fulfill as best he or she can.
Deborah Fallows

DELIBERATELY OR NOT, SCHOOLS PROFOUNDLY SHAPE
children's social and ethical development. Schools can motivate children by rewards and punishments or by an appeal to what
is right. Schools can allocate opportunities for leadership to all children equally or to the best-behaved and highest-achieving children
disproportionately. Schools can emphasize competition among
children or shared goals accessible to all: persistence, doing one's
best, friendliness, helpfulness. Since schooling profoundly shapes
children's social and ethical development, it's odd that we so often
define successful schools purely in terms of academic achievement.

JAPANESE SCHOOLS: DO THEY FOSTER SOCIAL AND ETHICAL DEVELOPMENT?

Japanese schools are often lauded for their academic achievements.
But do they also foster children's ethical and social development?
We find sharp differences of opinion on this question. Childhood
and youth indicators of failed social and ethical development – such

178

as delinquency, school dropout, and self-destructive behavior – generally appear to be substantially lower in Japan than in other industrialized countries, including the United States. As the U.S. Study of Education in Japan notes, "by comparison with various other industrialized nations, including the United States, delinquency in Japan is mild and infrequent."[1]

School-Related Problems

In contrast to this relatively optimistic American assessment, Japanese educators and the Japanese public are profoundly concerned about problems of elementary and secondary students, including *ijime* (bullying), *ochikobore* (students who fall behind academically), *tōkōkyohi* (school refusal), and school violence. Many of these problems begin in elementary school, and common sense suggests a connection between these problems and the downward pressure exerted by the examination system.

Figure 2 provides data on *tōkōkyohi* (school refusal), the term applied to students absent from school more than 50 days during the year because of "dislike of school." The rate of school refusal in Japan has increased more than threefold among junior high students since 1966 and now amounts to 7.5 students per 1,000. During the same period, the rate has nearly doubled among elementary students but is still relatively low, affecting fewer than 1 student per 1,000. Comparable statistics are not available for the United States, but principals of American elementary schools tell me that it's not unusual in an elementary school of 400–800 students to have 1 or more students who persistently stay home from school. Such a very rough reckoning suggests that the American experience may not be greatly out of line with the nearly 1 in 1,000 Japanese elementary students who miss more than 50 days a year of school because they dislike school. Comparisons are complicated, however, by the fact that 40% of parents of Japanese school refusers do not push unwilling children to go to school;[2] in many U.S. states, truancy laws would not permit leniency. On the other hand, the Japanese rate may underestimate the problem, because many school refusers attend special counseling centers where they may continue their

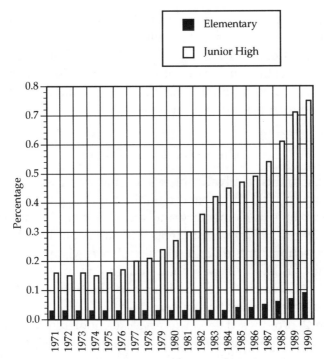

Figure 2. Percentage of Japanese students refusing to attend school 50 days or more per year, 1971–1990.

Source: Monbushō Shōtō Chūtō Kyōikukyoku, 1992.

schooling and thus escape the school-refusal statistics. Research suggests that a variety of events precipitate school refusal in Japan, including problems with classmates, teachers, and schoolwork (37%); personal circumstances such as illness (26%); and problems in family life such as family discord or a sudden change in family circumstances (26%).[3]

Violence in Schools

In his book *Shogun's Ghost*, Kenneth Schoolland describes several horrifying incidents of bullying that have occurred in Japan's middle schools and high schools. Figure 3 provides data on bullying, a

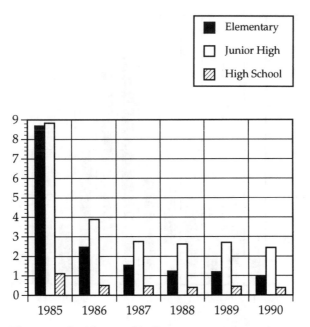

Figure 3. Incidents of bullying per 1,000 students.

Source: Sōmucho, Seishōnen Taisaku Honbu, 1991, based on data from Ministry of Education, Science, and Culture

problem that was the focus of intense national concern and intervention in the mid-1980s. For 1991, the figures shown amount to a little less than 1 incident of bullying for every two Japanese elementary schools and 1.2 incidents per middle school. As shown, reported bullying has declined sharply since the mid-1980s, when national statistics were first collected. The decline is sometimes attributed to increased awareness and intervention on the part of educators.[4] Unfortunately, we do not know how much bullying goes unreported. As shown in Figure 4, bullying peaks at junior high and occurs at a much higher rate in larger schools (Figure 5). Table 8 breaks down by type all reported incidents of bullying in Japanese elementary schools during 1990.

Unfortunately, the seriousness of the reported incidents is difficult to judge. What proportion are the kinds of teasing, threats,

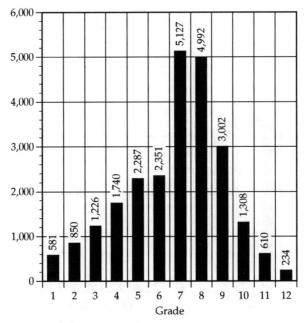

Figure 4. Incidents of bullying by school grade.

Source: Sōmucho, 1991, p. 257, based on data from Ministry of Education.

and exclusion that are also familiar, if unpleasant, features of life in many American schools? What proportion represent the kind of intense, ongoing cruelty that has led several Japanese students to take their lives? Only about 16% of the reported bullying incidents in elementary schools involve use of force. Insults, exclusion, and humiliation account for the majority of incidents.[5] Principals – who report the information that ultimately becomes the statistics – have told me that they report only repeated, systematic attempts to humiliate or coerce a classmate, not one-time incidents. A low rate of police involvement suggests that relatively few of the incidents are serious. In 1989, police provided "guidance" *(hodō)* to a total of 314 students as a result of bullying incidents: 278 middle school students, 35 high school students, and 1 elementary student.[6]

Shogun's Ghost also describes use of corporal punishment in Japanese middle schools. Although prohibited by law, corporal punish-

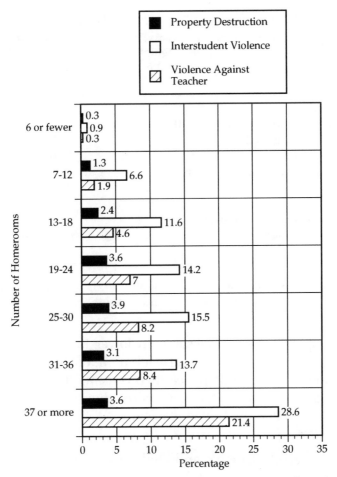

Figure 5. Percentage of Japanese Junior Highs reporting selected types of violence, by school size.

Source: Sōmucho, 1991, based on data from Ministry of Education.

ment is practiced by some Japanese middle school teachers, according to many sources.[7] In 1991, 331 teachers were disciplined for using corporal punishment.[8] Ministry of Education statistics for 1991 report 713 incidents of violence against teachers, 1,859 incidents of violence among students, and 518 incidents of property destruction in Japan's 11,290 middle schools. The number of inci-

Table 8. *Bullying Incidents in 1990, by Type*

	Elementary (11,999 incidents) (%)	Junior High (17,651 incidents) (%)
Verbal insults	15.9	19.8
Being teased, made fun of	24.0	22.4
Having belongings hidden	8.6	6.8
Being ostracized	23.0	12.8
Being ignored by group	6.3	6.0
Physical force	16.9	22.7
Blackmail	1.9	6.2
Forced, intrusive friendliness (*osekkai shinsetsu*)	1.5	1.3
Other	1.9	2.1

Source: Sōmucho, Seishōnen Taisaku Honbu, 1991, p. 258, based on data from Ministry of Education, Science, and Culture.

dents in high schools was substantially lower. In the same year, 780 incidents of school violence, nearly all in middle schools, were serious enough to result in police involvement; 466 of these were violence against teachers.[9] Japan has roughly half the number of schoolchildren that the United States has.

Self-destructive and Delinquent Behavior

Figure 6 provides statistics on the arrest of American and Japanese minors. Once again, statistics suggest a relatively low incidence of serious offenses by Japanese youth. Other data suggest, however, that Japanese youth manage to engage in some self-destructive behavior even without easy access to illegal drugs. Police detained more than 22,000 minors for "guidance" (*hodō*) for thinner sniffing in 1990.[10] Once again, it's difficult to know what to make of the statistics without knowing more about how they are collected. Do they underestimate problems to create an impression of a harmonious society, as some critics suggest, or overestimate problems to obtain increased funding, as others have conjectured? The fact that

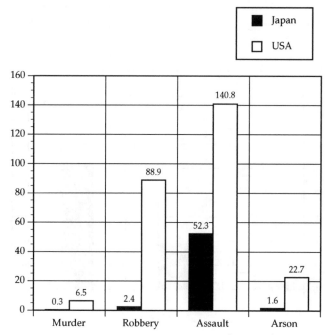

Figure 6. Arrests of persons under 18 per 100,000 for 10- to 18-year-olds.

Source: Hōmushō Hōmusōgōkenkyūjo, 1990, pp. 408–409, 452–53 (1988 data).

police even bother to collect and publish statistics on minors' pedestrian crosswalk violations may say a great deal about the frequency of serious crime – or about the tolerance for deviations from proper conduct.

Youth suicide – one of the few problems for which reasonably objective comparable data are available – is often thought by Americans to be very common in Japan, an impression that probably stems from the Japanese media's intense coverage of examination-related suicides. As Figure 7 shows, however, the most recent international comparisons indicate that the suicide rate for American 15- to 19-year-olds is nearly three times that of their Japanese counterparts. A survey of 3,000 high school students found that Japanese students reported *fewer* feelings of stress, academic anxiety, depression, and aggression than their Chinese and American peers.[11]

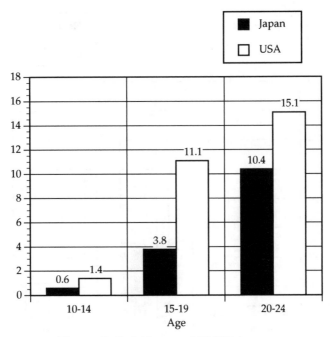

Figure 7. Suicides per 100,000, by age.

Source: Sōmucho, 1991, and U.S. National Department of Health and Human Services, National Center for Health Statistics, Hyattsville, MD, 1992.

Japanese teen pregnancy and abortion rates are among the lowest in the world, despite the fact that most Japanese teens (60%) approve of sexual relations among their peers with appropriate contraception.[12]

Liking for School

Of course, the relatively low rate of various problems among Japanese youth may not be attributable to schooling; it may be attributable to family influences or other qualities of the society. Yet observers who have actually spent time in Japanese preschools and elementary schools, including schools serving less advantaged populations, uniformly comment on children's eagerness, involvement, and active role in school life.[13]

186

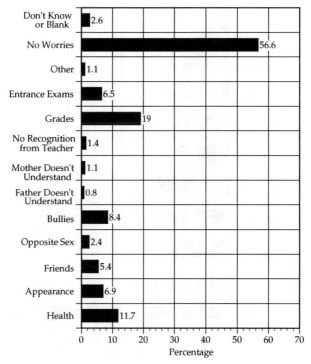

Figure 8. Worries of Japanese fourth- to sixth-graders.

Source: Sōmucho, 1991, p. 54 (data from NHK Broadcasting Research Institute, "The Activities and Attitudes of Elementary Students," 1989).

More than 80% of Japanese fifth- and sixth-graders report that they are completely satisfied or mostly satisfied with their school life. (The comparable figure for Japanese middle school students is only 60%.) Similarly, over 85% of Japanese fourth- to sixth-graders describe themselves as happy.[14] As Figure 8 shows, over half of the fourth- to sixth-graders polled by the NHK Broadcasting Research Institute said that they had no worries or problems; about one quarter worried about grades or entrance examinations, and only 8% worried about bullying. As Figure 9 shows, the picture is strikingly different for Japanese junior high students, only 8% of whom say they have no problems or worries; 75% of junior high students report worrying about school and examinations. In their study of

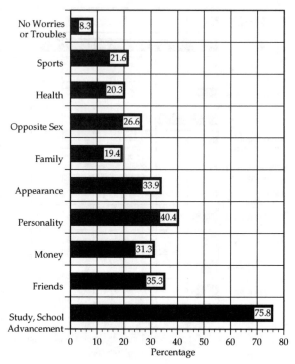

Figure 9. Worries of Japanese Junior High students.

Source: Sōmucho, 1991, p. 55 (data from Nihon Seishōnen Kenkyūjo, Primary Panel Study of Junior High Students, 1988)

Chinese, Japanese, and American students, researchers Harold Stevenson and James Stigler found that Asian elementary students liked school more than their American counterparts did.[15] Ineko Tsuchida's study of Japanese and American fourth-graders also found greater liking for school among the Japanese students.[16]

Summary

A few conclusions seem justified from the various data. First, Japanese education, even at the elementary level, is not free of problems. The bullying, school refusal, and school violence that have so disturbed the Japanese public and press do extend beyond the incidents reported in newspaper headlines. Second, most problems increase dramatically at junior high (the final stage of compulsory education in Japan and the peak of cram-school attendance), echoing the recommendation of Japanese educators that education for this age group needs reform. Finally, for serious problems (such as suicide and major crimes), for which cross-national data are most likely to be comparable, Japanese rates do appear to be substantially lower than those in the United States. Japanese rates of youth suicide, drug use, and violent crime have generally remained steady or fallen over recent decades.[17] Without minimizing the seriousness of problems such as school refusal, bullying, and school violence, the numbers suggest that Japanese schools do "succeed" socially with a very high percentage of students, losing relatively few students to school dropout (see chapter 1), delinquency, and self-destructive behavior.

Because of the many ways Japan and the USA. differ, it will never be possible to prove that elementary schools in one country or the other more effectively promote children's commitment to schooling. In any case, differences between the two countries mean that strategies that are effective in Japan might not work, or might not be regarded as appropriate, in the United States. Yet the strategies used by Japanese preschools and elementary schools are remarkably similar to approaches that have been successful in promoting children's academic and social development in U.S. schools. In fact, American educators interested in promoting children's fullest social and ethical development *independently* came up with many of the practices routinely used in Japanese schools. A subsequent section of this chapter describes the Child Development Project and other homegrown American approaches that rest on principles similar to those widely found in Japanese elementary schools.

MEETING CHILDREN'S NEEDS: A KEY TO EDUCATIONAL SUCCESS

American research and theory suggest that when schools meet children's needs, children come to care about school. Three basic psy-

189

chological needs – belonging, autonomy, and competence – may be particularly important to children's attachment to school.[18] Let's look briefly at each of these basic psychological needs.

"Belonging" refers to the child's need for close, supportive relationships. That such relationships are fundamental to children's healthy emotional and social development is basic to Western, as well as Japanese, theories of human development.[19] As we have seen, Japanese elementary schools foster such relationships in many ways. They make friendliness and cooperation central, clear goals of classroom life. They emphasize *everyone's* belonging to the class and the school community and scrupulously avoid ability grouping, individual awards, and other practices that imply that some members are more valued than others. Teachers expend much effort nurturing familylike small groups where children feel comfortable and able to speak up.

"Autonomy" describes the child's need to feel some control over the environment and to be free of undue or arbitrary restraint. As we've seen, Japanese schools provide for young children's autonomy in many ways. All children assume leadership in rotation. Children help shape the goals and rules by which they live. Discipline emphasizes self-evaluation rather than evaluation by the teacher, and self-management rather than adult control.

"Competence" is the child's need to pursue activities regarded as worthwhile. Children naturally explore the world and try to make sense of it – even without rewards or encouragement from others. Much research shows that children are young scientists, constantly trying to explain the physical and human world around them. Children are likely to find school gripping and important if it helps them in their quest to make sense of the world. As noted in chapter 7, lessons in Japanese schools are often driven by children's own thinking and by their involvement in tasks that are likely to be inherently interesting – crafting boats that float, designing the ideal playground, exploring each room of the school, using measurement to understand the world around them. Such meaningful child-driven activities are much more likely to meet children's need for competence than would a focus on isolated "basic" skills. The breadth of the Japanese curriculum and the emphasis on effort and participation rather than on competition further increase the likelihood that *all* children – not just an academically able few – will find areas of competence and feel themselves to be valued members of the school community.

In summary, Japanese preschool and early elementary classrooms have many qualities that help them effectively meet children's basic needs for autonomy, belonging, and competence. In response, children are likely to come to care about school and about the values emphasized there. I have pointed out, in prior chapters, aspects of Japanese educational practice that I think many Americans would find troubling, such as allowing children to fight or to handle dangerous tools. Yet none of these is central to Japanese education. What *is* central is a set of values deeply consonant with widely held American values. The next section briefly spotlights successful American approaches that are based on some of the same fundamental principles as Japanese elementary schooling.

AMERICAN APPROACHES: THE CHILD DEVELOPMENT PROJECT

At a California elementary school, kindergarteners are planning a class aquarium. They brainstorm all the plants and animals they would like and then discuss which ones are feasible: Which need salt water, rather than fresh? Which fish might eat each other? They list their top choices and talk about how many they can buy within the $20 budget. At the end of the class meeting, they reflect on how the meeting went: Did they show respect for one another?

To the Japanese teachers who have watched this California class on videotape, the setting is exotic: a carpeted classroom where children can gather cross-legged on the floor around their teacher. But the lesson is familiar: a class project that invites children's ideas, joins children in planning a shared project, and melds social and intellectual development as children both think about marine biology and reflect on whether they showed respect for one another's ideas.

191

This California classroom was videotaped as part of the Child Development Project (CDP), a school change effort developed by American researchers and teachers. CDP's aim is to help students become good learners *and* good people, with an emphasis on qualities such as concern for others, responsibility, thoughtfulness, and motivation to learn.

The Child Development Project targets many facets of schooling: what is taught, how it is taught, how students relate to one another and to teachers, how norms for student and adult behavior are developed and enforced.[20] Interestingly, this project – based in American basic research and theory – *independently* arrived at many of the same practices that are at the heart of Japanese elementary education. Central to the Child Development Project is the effort to make the school a "caring community of learners" in which:

- All children are valued, contributing members.

- Students are motivated by a personal commitment to responsible, caring behavior rather than by rewards and punishments.

- The curriculum is meaningful and engaging to children.

How do elementary schools pursue these goals? Table 9 lists major components of the Child Development Project and examples of each component. The similarities between the Child Development Project and the Japanese practices outlined in chapters 2–7 are striking. Both emphasize a school-wide sense of community and discipline that promotes personal commitment to values. Both emphasize explicit discussion of values, such as kindness and responsibility, and methods of instruction that capitalize on children's intrinsic motivation.

I chose the Child Development Project for Table 9 because of my own familiarity with it and because of the careful longitudinal research demonstrating its positive effects on American children in their academic as well as social and ethical development. But I think many other homegrown approaches, successful in American settings, fit some of the same basic principles outlined for the Child Development Project. For example, James Comer's School Devel-

Table 9. *Major Goals and Practices of the Child Development Project*

Caring, supportive relationships	Students and teachers get to know one another as people through daily opportunities to share ideas and experiences as part of class meetings, class "unity building" activities, shared planning, literature discussions, etc.
	Much collaborative learning; deemphasis of competition
	Shift away from techniques that stigmatize or reward individual children (e.g., names on board, reprimands) toward discussion of "what kind of class we want to be" and reflection on progress
Intrinsic motivation	Emphasis on values, not rewards and punishments, as the reason to behave responsibly
	Subject matter that is intrinsically interesting: literature instead of textbooks, hands-on activities, choice
	Shift away from praise and criticism by teacher and shift toward questions and comments that focus students' attention on the learning
	Teachers draw out children's questions and thinking; learning is meaning-centered
Attention to ethical and social dimensions of learning	Students explore what it means to be a principled, caring person as they study history, literature, and other subjects
	Children help shape class and school norms based on their desire to be treated with kindness, fairness, etc.
	Children frequently reflect on whether they are showing kindness, responsibility, fairness, etc., in their daily work and lives together

193

opment Project and New York's innovative Central Park East schools emphasize caring, supportive relations among students and between students and adults and opportunities for all students to contribute to the life of the school.[21] These projects draw on American traditions and research – including Dewey's vision of progressive education; "attachment" theory, which recognizes emotional bonds as fundamental to development; and intrinsic motivation. Albert Shanker, president of the American Federation of Teachers, recently wrote:

> The problem is that [American] schools are not organized in a way that gives teachers and students a chance to develop close and caring relationships. . . . Elementary school children spend one year with a teacher – just long enough to *start* feeling comfortable – and then they move on to a new teacher. Why shouldn't elementary and junior high school students stay with the same group of kids for three or four years? Why shouldn't . . . the class be broken down into small groups so each group can . . . get to know one another?
>
> These ideas are sound in educational as well as emotional and moral terms. Students who are connected with another adult, and with one another, are less likely to drop out. And they are more likely to work and shape one another up – and thus to enjoy a measure of success in school work.
>
> Mentoring [outside of school] can fill an important need for the many youngsters who have no close or caring relationship with an adult. But we are kidding ourselves if we think we can make a dent in this enormous problem with ad-hoc arrangements. We should stop working around the edges of the main institution concerned with children – the schools – and concentrate on making our schools moral communities.[22]

Despite the growing awareness that close relationships are crucial to children's development, educators who would make this happen must swim against other very strong currents in U.S. education: an obsession with achievement test results, an assumption that academic excellence requires competition, and the notion that learning occurs most efficiently when children are grouped by ability.

194

THINKING ACROSS CONTEXTS: LIMITATIONS OF JAPANESE IDEAS IN AMERICAN SETTINGS

I can think of two major reasons to reject Japanese practices as a source of ideas for our own educational practice. First, they may run counter to widely held American values. Second, they may be impractical here. Prior chapters have explored some aspects of Japanese preschool and early elementary education that may run counter to American values. This section explores conditions that may make it difficult to use ideas drawn from the Japanese context.

Children's Status

Japanese children live in what one American researcher has called a "privileged world." By all the usual indices – infant mortality, malnutrition, child abuse, family stability, parental drug abuse, poverty – Japanese children are extraordinarily fortunate, even compared with children in other advanced industrialized nations.[23] Few Japanese teachers, but many American teachers, must somehow educate children whose families – poor, alienated, or stressed – do not always meet children's basic need for food, shelter, and adult attention.

The disciplinary practices used in Japanese schools aim to develop stable, trusting relationships between adults and children and among children. Would Japanese teachers be able to use these techniques if many students came to school – by virtue of their early experience – mistrustful of adults? As noted in chapter 6, much research suggests that young Japanese children are given wide latitude for misbehavior and that the focus of maternal efforts during the preschool years is on building a warm, close relationship to the child, not on obedience.

In contrast, it's likely that conflict with adults and punishment are much more common experiences in the lives of young American children. This raises the possibility that Japanese disciplinary approaches, if used with American children, might not work as readily. Yet disciplinary practices focused on building stable, caring relationships may be especially critical for children who have had disrupted or difficult relationships outside of school. James Comer, a distinguished psychiatrist who has worked to restructure schools serving poor minority children in the United States, writes:

> All the money and effort expended for educational reform will have only limited benefits – particularly for poor minority children – as long as the underlying developmental and social issues remain unaddressed. Yet most teachers and administrators are not trained to organize and manage schools in ways that support the overall development of students.[24]

The importance of stable, caring relationships in children's development is a central principle in much American theory and research on child development and is the crux of some of the best-regarded American programs for educating poor minority children. Even in Japan – where children lead a "privileged" early life that includes strong parental support, universal health care, and a high proportion of stable, two-parent families – schools devote considerable time and attention to building trusting, sustained relationships between children and adults. Doesn't it follow that this effort deserves even more attention in American settings?

Curriculum

As noted in chapter 2, Japan has a national curriculum, with tight control of textbooks. The national control of curriculum and textbooks means that the same content – often the same lesson – is taught to schoolchildren throughout Japan. So, for example, I saw quite similar "Mothers' Work" lessons taught in first-grade classrooms in three different Japanese schools. In all three schools, the students had investigated, as homework, the mother's activities over a 24-hour period. Although the three teachers introduced the lesson using different personal examples and had the children engage in different activities (e.g., drawing and writing), the basic point of the lesson was more or less the same across classrooms: to develop an appreciation of the mother's work and a specific commitment to help her.

The complete sets of lessons in all subject areas that Japanese teachers have at their disposal are, I think, an extraordinary resource. Typically, each lesson is dominated by a single important goal for children's learning – for example, to discover that heat rises or that measurement is useful – and a single problem to explore in depth. Information provided in the teacher's manual often illuminates the thinking children are likely to bring to the problem, supporting teachers' treatment of children as active, thoughtful participants whose ideas should help drive the lessons. Supported by such frugal, carefully crafted lessons and examples, Japanese teachers are free to focus on how they will interest and motivate students – not on culling important concepts and information from textbooks and teachers' manuals jam-packed with lists of new concepts, information, vocabulary, and application problems. A critique of American science textbooks has noted that the average American science lesson contains more new vocabulary than a foreign-language lesson and that textbooks feature attention-grabbing sidebars worthy of *Ripley's Believe It or Not* but irrelevant to the science concepts under study.[25]

The focused, coherent lessons experienced by Japanese students may help them develop habits of mind that are important to learning. One study suggests that Japanese fourth-graders have a coherent, organized mental "script" of a mathematics lesson that enables them to attend selectively to important information, whereas American children attend equally to important and unimportant information – presumably because they have not developed clear expectations about what mathematics lessons include.[26] The pressure on American teachers to create original curriculum materials, rather than to provide skilled interpretations of standard curricula, may be broadly detrimental to American education:

> In America, teachers are judged to be successful when they are innovative, inventive, and original. Skilled presentation of a standard lesson is not sufficient and may even be disparaged as indicating a lack of innovative talent. It is as if American teachers were expected to write their own play or create their own concerto day after day and then perform it with expertise and finesse.

These two models, the skilled performer and the innovator, have very different value in the East and West. It is hard for us in the West to appreciate that innovation does not require that the presentation be totally new, but can come from thoughtful additions, new interpretations, and skillful modifications.[27]

One lamentable gap in our knowledge of Japanese education is how Japanese *teachers* feel about the curriculum they teach. Do they wish for more latitude in choosing the content and goals of their lessons and in selecting topics of interest to the particular children they teach? Japanese elementary teachers do have some room for innovation, both within regular subjects and within the nationally designated periods for class-chosen activities. For example, elementary classes I observed studied local pollution-related diseases, took oral histories of local weavers, and read novels outside the standard curriculum. In all cases, however, these activities received relatively little time, and teachers had to submit lesson plans in advance to the principal, noting the titles of nonapproved texts. Japanese teachers interested in a "whole language" approach to reading told me they envied American teachers' freedom to choose books and focus on interesting issues raised by books rather than on recall of information.

I have mixed reactions to the calls for a national curriculum in the USA. Japan's national curriculum ensures that all children study subject matter of agreed-upon importance but still allows teachers, principals, and local boards of education some room to pursue particular local and personal interests. A strength of the Japanese curriculum is its focus on subject matter from children's daily lives: potatoes and cabbage worms from the class garden as examples of growth and development; mapping the school as the introduction to geography. A paradox of the standardized Japanese curriculum – at least in the areas of mathematics and science – may be that it supports and frees teachers to be *more* responsive to the individual thinking of the children they teach, because lesson plans highlight students' thinking. Too, Japanese teachers are largely free of the onerous task of locating and reviewing good curricula. Yet in reading and social studies, the Japanese curriculum is less impressive, particularly in the upper grades. As children get older, language instruction tends to focus on factual recall and detailed analysis of texts rather than on the important ideas raised by a work of literature. Social studies – in the early years an opportunity to map the neighborhood and study the local sewer system – becomes increasingly focused on memorization of names and dates in the upper elementary years.

My guess is that a national curriculum would prove too confining for many American educators, whose freedom to study particular issues of interest – local conflicts, problems of concern to students, topics in the news, the literature and culture of newly arrived class members – can help create a curriculum meaningful to students and responsive to their needs. Japan's national curriculum creates friction even in that relatively homogeneous country. For example, teachers from Kyushu have complained to me that the science curriculum is not appropriate to the seasonal changes and local biology of their very southern climate.

Yet Japanese practices underline a striking gap in American elementary education: a sound *process* for defining what is important to teach children and bringing this to bear on the taught curriculum. Although professional groups in the United States regularly debate what is central to education in various subject areas, their deliberations have limited influence on the de facto curriculum, which is defined in great part by standardized tests and commercial textbooks. So in a sense there is already a national curriculum in the United States – but not one that lays out, thoughtfully and frugally, the knowledge, thinking, and attitudes central to children's development.

Status

As discussed in chapter 2, Japanese teachers enjoy a great deal of prestige, as measured by compensation and by other indices. They also report more influence on school policy and more help from their fellow teachers than do American teachers.[28] Japanese families tend to place great importance on education and imbue teachers with an almost sacred status.[29] How different the situation is for many American teachers, who daily find evidence that they are not regarded as professionals: poor compensation, endless paperwork, "teacher-proof" curricula, incentives and accountability systems that equate learning with factory production, major school redesign efforts that largely exclude the teacher's voice. Such offenses may be more than unpleasant; they may destroy the very conditions needed, within a school, to create and sustain excellent teaching.

American research suggests that school improvement hinges on a sense of community and collaboration among teachers – conditions easily undermined by top-down control and a focus on "accountability."[30] For teachers as well as students, learning requires the emotional safety needed to take risks and to recognize and learn from mistakes. When high status and professional treatment are lacking, so too may be the safety to learn. In the current climate of education bashing in the United States, who can blame the American math educator who said, "I'm sick and tired of hearing about the Japanese"?[31] Yet who can see such attitudes as fertile ground for educational improvement?

Comparative studies of Japanese and American families suggest that Japanese parents are more indulgent of young children but that they also emphasize respect for authority more strongly.[32] Hence Japanese teachers, bolstered by a strong cultural emphasis on respect for authority, may have an easier job than their American counterparts. Perhaps it's easier to focus on warm, friendly relations with children, "educational love," and "playing with children" when the status and authority of teachers is firmly established, as it appears to be in Japan.

Assessment

Few systematic data are available about testing practices in Japanese elementary schools. Many teachers I studied gave short tests at the end of units in mathematics, social studies, and other areas to check on whether students had mastered important concepts – "to test my teaching," as one Japanese first-grade teacher phrased it. Many Japanese teachers use unit tests produced by publishers, but there is also a national organization of Japanese teachers opposed to commercially produced tests.[33] What can be said with certainty is that standardized tests play nowhere near the role in Japanese elementary schooling that they do in the United States, where school funding, real-estate prices, and legal sanctions may all hinge on standardized test scores.

Having read many horror stories about the downward pressure exerted by Japanese college entrance examinations, I was surprised to find that Japanese teachers individually, or with grade-level colleagues, chose whether and how they would evaluate students' progress. Although education during the upper elementary grades may become more focused on the entrance examinations to junior high taken by the small percentage of students (5%) who attend private or national schools, what is striking in the early and middle years of elementary school is teachers' freedom to focus on children's social and ethical growth and on children's understanding of subject matter, not on their performance on externally imposed measures.

That standardized testing can be the enemy of good teaching is hardly a new point, but it is one that needs to be emphasized in comparing Japanese and American schools. Although some researchers have argued that entrance examinations positively influence Japanese educational achievement, exactly the opposite case can also be made: that elementary achievement is high because Japanese teachers are free from the pressure to teach to standardized tests. Japanese teachers are simultaneously supported by clear national objectives that emphasize social, ethical, and intellectual development and free to teach for understanding rather than drill students for test performance.

SUMMARY

In this chapter, we've explored differences between Japanese and American early elementary education that may make Japan's "lessons" difficult to apply in the United States. As we've seen, Japanese children are well cared for. Teachers enjoy high status, support from a coherent and generally thoughtful curriculum, and relative freedom from the tyranny of standardized tests, at least during the early years of elementary school. They are supported by a national curriculum that emphasizes social and ethical, as well as intellectual, development. Given these differences, what lessons can we reasonably learn from Japan?

Most striking, I think, is the attention Japanese schools devote to children's social and ethical development. In a society often described as homogeneous, teachers spend a great deal of time helping children build friendships and a sense of shared purpose within the classroom and school. In a society where most children are well cared-for economically and socially, children's social and personal development is nevertheless central to the elementary curriculum. If children's social and personal development demand so much attention in a society like Japan, shouldn't they demand even more in the United States?

Second, Japanese schools do not "just" nurture children's social and personal development. They also pursue an ambitious academic agenda. But this agenda is pursued without emphasizing competition among students. Lessons and all other school activities are carefully designed with an eye to students' social, personal, *and* intellectual development. And so Japanese schools are able to escape the pendulum swing between social development and academic rigor that has blemished American educational history.[34]

Like some American schools, Japanese schools find the key to success in meeting children's own needs – for belonging, friendship, contribution, exploration of the world around them. The quest to meet children's needs is integral to some of America's most successful educational programs and yet strongly antithetical to other powerful forces in American education. What, then, should we be looking for as we look at education for our children?

9

SUMMARY: QUESTIONS TO ASK OURSELVES

> A learning space needs to be hospitable not to make learning painless but to make the painful things possible, things without which no learning can occur – things like exposing ignorance, testing tentative hypotheses, challenging false or partial information, and mutual criticism of thought. Each of these is essential to obedience to truth. But none of them can happen in an atmosphere where people feel threatened and judged.
>
> Parker J. Palmer[1]

> The Japanese quest for character improvement is close to being a national religion.
>
> Thomas Rohlen[2]

THE FIRST PART OF THIS CHAPTER REVIEWS SEVEN QUALI-ties of Japanese preschool and early elementary education that I see as central to its success. The second part lays out questions about elementary education designed to help us define what we want in schools serving young children.

SEVEN CENTRAL QUALITIES OF JAPANESE EDUCATION FOR YOUNG CHILDREN

1. Focus on the Whole Child

As I sat in Japanese elementary classrooms, I often felt as if I was at summer camp or at a scout meeting – settings broadly focused on the whole child's development. The rhythms of the Japanese school day, week, and year recognize that children have many needs: to

203

play, to create things of beauty, to form lasting relationships with fellow students and with adults. Japanese preschoolers spend most of their time in free play, and elementary school students devote more than one third of their instructional hours to nonacademic subjects such as art, music, and physical education. Approximately 30 days of Japan's famed longer school year are set aside for shared, pleasurable activities such as Sports Day, Arts Day, camping, festivals, and school trips, activities that often rally the whole student body and faculty in weeks of shared planning and preparation. The national Course of Study – which forbids instruction in letters and numbers before elementary school – is striking in its emphasis on social and ethical, as well as intellectual, development.

2. Emphasis on Prosocial Values

To enter a Japanese elementary classroom is to confront clear, explicit values. Students study under banners that proclaim class goals: "Let's become friends," "Let's get along well and put our strength together," and "Let's be kind children who easily say 'I'm sorry' and 'Thank you.'"

But values do not just inhabit banners. They find their way into the content and process of academic lessons, class meetings, chores, and many other aspects of school life. Daily, Japanese students discuss their aspirations and reflect on their progress toward such goals as kindness, cooperation, responsibility, and persistence – goals that enable all children, whatever their academic skills, to achieve in ways that are recognized and valued.

3. Building a Supportive Community in the Classroom

How do you transform a collection of 35 students into a classroom community – a group in which all students feel valued, heard, and responsible? To build a sense of community in the classroom, Japanese teachers provide many chances for students to get to know one another as people, to have fun together, and to collaborate in shaping classroom values and practices. Close, trusting relationships – among students and between students and teachers – are seen as central to education. Early elementary students and their teachers

204

stay together for all or nearly all activities of the school day, including lunch. Typically the entire teacher-class unit stays together for 2 years. Japanese teachers who visit our schools often ask how American teachers manage to build a sense of classhood in the face of ability grouping, "pull-out" programs, separation from the class at lunch, and multiple outside teachers for subjects like music and physical education.

As chapter 4 explored, one building block of classroom community in Japan is the small fixed groups found in all elementary classrooms and nearly all preschool classrooms. These groups are the units for many activities: Children eat, work, play, plan, and have discussions within these fixed groups several times a day, dozens of times a week. These groups differ sharply from the single-purpose, ability-based groups found in many American elementary schools. In Japanese schools, groups are familylike. They embrace members of different abilities and personal qualities, share a great range of activities each day, and stay together for an extended period (as long as 2 years at the preschool level, an average of 3 months in first grade). The groups are expected to provide an emotional home base where even the shyest child comes to feel comfortable, connected, and able to speak up.

4. Methods of Discipline That Promote a Personal Commitment to Values

Japanese teachers invest a great deal in the long-term goal of building children's commitment to responsible behavior. Yet in the short run they often tolerate remarkably noisy and disruptive behavior. "If American kids acted like that, they'd all get sent to the principal's office every day" is how my 9-year-old described student behavior in the Japanese school he attended for 4 months. Japanese teachers often keep a low profile as authority figures. Instead of using rewards, punishment, or adult authority to motivate children, teachers try to build students' capacity to self-manage. *Children* quiet classmates before lessons, lead class meetings, make class rules, and solve problems that arise. Like the teacher I saw who waited patiently for 17 minutes while the daily student monitors struggled to quiet the class, teachers see discipline as something that must come from within children. Undergirding their approaches is a firm belief that children will *want to* behave responsibly if their bonds of friendship to classmates and teacher are sufficiently strong.

5. Children's Thinking, Problem Solving, and Discussion Help Drive Classroom Life

In Japan's early elementary classrooms, children's own thinking helps drive classroom life – in academic lessons and in "nonacademic" activities. As chapter 2 explores, cooperation – and the struggles and successes it engenders – is, effectively, *the* curriculum of Japanese preschool education. During both the preschool and early elementary years, teachers treasure shirked chores, breakdowns in cooperation, and even fistfights as catalysts to discuss "what kind of class we want to be" and "what promises we need in our class."

Academic lessons, too, are often driven by children's own problem solving and thinking – a point that has been well documented in cross-national studies of elementary mathematics instruction.[3] Japan's national elementary curriculum is designed so that children's own observations and thinking *can* drive instruction. For example, science focuses on plants and animals that children observe first-hand in the classroom and class garden, rather than the more exotic species (penguins and salmon) featured in American texts.[4] Japanese children discuss the reasons for rules they find in public parks, reflect on why the boats they built from plastic bottles sank or floated, and map the neighborhood. As students delve into these pursuits, teachers question and challenge children but rarely need to lecture, for students' own observations and hypotheses can drive lessons.

Nor do Japanese teachers need to show their caring for children by uncritical acceptance of children's ideas. All children belong, and all are important class members (see items 1 to 3). Critical, lively discussions are thus possible.

6. "Wet" Learning

Japanese use the English words *wet* and *dry* – *uetto* and *dorai*, as they are pronounced in Japanese – to describe emotional styles. A "dry" approach is rational, logical, unemotional; a "wet" approach is personal, emotional, interpersonally complex. Many of the academic lessons I saw were "wet" learning. They were designed to spark children's personal interest, grip them emotionally, and involve them intimately with classmates. By comparison with their Japanese counterparts, American students have been described as lonely and isolated, toiling individually at worksheets.[5] In Japanese classrooms, even science or mathematics learning is often an emotional enterprise. Children might spend 2 hours decorating the plastic bottle "boats" they would use to study sinking and floating in science class, or start science class by having each child tell a brief personal story about the fruits, flowers, or containers brought from home to use in the day's experiment.

Learning is active. It takes children to the floor (where children try out as many ways as they can to measure it – including human body lengths), to every room in the school (where they investigate who is in the room and what kind of work they do to help the school), to the schoolyard (where they sketch the flowers and vegetables in the class garden), and to the neighborhood (where they study the sewer system and the play equipment in local parks). Learning is also interpersonally complex, as students work in four-person groups on remarkably demanding projects. Even preschoolers make *kamishibai* (paper dramas), in which the children of a small group jointly devise a story and each individual child draws one frame of the shared story. Finally, many lessons emphasize process. The point isn't simply to obtain a correct answer. It is to be engaged in a wholehearted way and to reflect on one's work, whether or not these lead to correct answers.

7. Reflection (*Hansei*)

Hansei pervaded daily activities in the Japanese schools I studied. Children reflected, in their small groups, on whether they had worked together well. Children reflected individually on their personal goals for self-improvement ("To stop punching other children on the playground"; "Not to talk when the teacher is talking"). As a class, children reflected on the activities of the past hour, day, week, and school term, discussing or privately thinking about a variety of questions: Did I do anything kind for others? Anything naughty? What did I like best today at school? Least? Did I volunteer my ideas? Did I do anything to help others? Did I do my very best? Such ubiquitous reflection focuses children's attention – gently yet persistently – on what it means to be a good member of the school community and on one's own shortcomings in that endeavor.

A Model of Education's Underpinnings

Why do I think these seven qualities are important to the success of Japanese education? Schools that meet children's needs – for belonging, autonomy, meaningful contribution – are likely to be rewarded with children who care about school. In their preschool and early elementary classrooms, Japanese children are likely to find friendship, a diverse curriculum, and daily reminders that they are responsible and important members of a school they have helped to shape.

QUESTIONS FOR REFLECTION

A theme that runs through this book is the importance of *hansei* (reflection) in Japanese schooling for young children. Personal and collective reflection, by students and by teachers, is a central practice in Japanese elementary schools. More often than not, the lesson, the school day, the week, the semester, the school year end with reflection. What did we learn? What did we do well and poorly? What should we do differently next time? My guess is that the heartfelt self-evaluation that often results is infinitely more powerful than the externally imposed tests, evaluations, and incentives through which outsiders may attempt to produce educational excellence.

What questions should we be asking ourselves about education for young children? The following questions grow from the work and thinking of Japanese and American educators. They are the questions that I ask myself, as a parent, when I visit a school.

Does the School Welcome the Whole Child?

Children have many needs: to make sense of the world, to make friends, to contribute to others' well-being, to create things of beauty. Does a school recognize these many needs? Does it emphasize art, music, class meetings, and service to others as well as reading and mathematics? Or must children leave their needs for friendship, contribution, and artistic expression outside the schoolhouse door?

Do School Practices Foster Children's Social and Ethical As Well As Intellectual Development?

It is shocking to note how many school improvement efforts in the United States evaluate *only* whether a given program improves students' academic achievement – as though schools could somehow perform a surgical strike on children's intellects without profoundly shaping their social and ethical development. Critical to children's social and ethical development are close, trusting relationships with adults and children and opportunities to contribute to the well-being of others. Schools that value supportive relationships make them central to schooling, emphasizing student collaboration and contribution rather than competition and ability grouping. Studies conducted in American preschools suggest that didactic, skills-focused preschooling may increase students' aggressiveness during elementary school, compromise their ability to take into account the needs of others, and even increase their antisocial behavior at adolescence.[6] My guess is that heavily didactic, skills-focused early programs fail to meet children's needs for friendship, belonging, and meaningful learning and thereby undermine children's bonds to one another and to schooling.

Intentionally or not, school shapes children ethically, socially, and intellectually. Are *all three* considered in designing every feature of school life?

209

Do Values of Kindness, Fairness, and Responsibility Permeate All Activities?

Schools promote and undermine values in many ways. Reading instruction can provide a host of opportunities to explore, through literature, what it means to be a principled, caring human being – or no grist for reflection. Class and school meetings can offer many opportunities for children to discuss values such as kindness and fairness as they come up in daily school life – or little opportunity for students to hear the needs and perspectives of others. Rich and heartfelt discussions of the values that govern humane life can arise in the course of just about any subject matter or school activity if such discussions are valued and if the level of trust supports them.

Do *All* Members of the School Community Contribute to It in Ways That They Themselves, and Others, Value?

Too often a small number of students dominate the contributions to a school: students who are particularly talented or responsible or, conversely, who have been afforded particular opportunities because they are thought to be "at risk." Yet the structure of schooling can allow *all* children to contribute in meaningful ways. Students can have daily responsibility for leading class meetings, solving problems that arise in the daily life of the school, and maintaining the school environment. They can voice their aspirations for the school, shape classroom and school life, and strive toward goals they have helped create. Academic activities and special events can celebrate the participation and contributions of all students rather than the accomplishments of a few.

Do Disciplinary Practices Build Children's Personal Commitment to Responsible Behavior, Rather Than Their Reliance on Adult-Imposed Rewards and Punishments?

Rewards and punishments are seductively effective in the short run. As all parents know, a threat or a promise produces action much more quickly than a discussion. But for democracy to function, children must develop a personal commitment to such values as responsibility, fairness, and honesty. Adult-imposed rewards and punishments are not likely to foster such a commitment. In fact, they are likely to undermine it by distracting children's attention from the more important and enduring reasons to behave responsibly. To understand the values that help human beings live together humanely, students need many opportunities to discuss and apply these values to their own lives at school and to hear the needs and perspectives of others, adults as well as children. As an American educator put it: "When children first start dressing themselves, we don't immediately expect them to coordinate beautiful outfits. Why, then, should we expect children to behave responsibly without lots of practice and mistakes?"[7] Children need many opportunities to discuss moral issues as they arise in daily life.

Do Children's Ideas Help Drive Instruction?

Eleanor Duckworth writes that it is "exhilarating to find that your own ideas can lead you somewhere. Few feelings are likely to be as effective in getting you to keep on thinking about things on your own."[8] Children have powerful ideas about the social, ethical, and physical world around them: about what is fair, why objects sink or float, what a family is. By engaging these powerful ideas – and helping children to reflect critically on them – schools can foster children's intellectual growth. And as they do, children will come to see school as a place that supports their efforts to make sense of the world rather than a place that provides arbitrary, meaningless hurdles.

Does the Curriculum Cover Subject Matter of Agreed-Upon Importance?

On both a state and national level, American educators have done much careful thinking about the content that is important in various subject areas. In the words of Jere Brophy and Janet Alleman, the curriculum "should be driven by major long-term goals, not just short-term coverage concerns," and should center on important ideas taught for understanding, not just memorization.[9] Yet in the

211

United States, standardized tests and commercial textbooks often define an actual curriculum that departs sharply from these ideals. The Japanese example – as well as many American schools – demonstrates that it *is* possible to cover subject matter of agreed-upon importance while still having children's ideas help drive instruction.

Do Students and Teachers Actively Reflect on Their Own Behavior and Learning and Continuously Try to Improve It?

The late educational researcher Ralph Tyler said, "We don't learn from our mistakes; we learn from thinking about our mistakes." As many researchers have pointed out, good educational practice cannot be mandated or forced; ultimately it depends on educators' active reflection and striving for self-improvement. But reflection and striving for self-improvement are fragile. They can easily be undermined by outside evaluation, which too often shifts attention from self-improvement to self-protection. They can easily be undermined by isolation, which robs educators of diverse perspectives on their own practice. Developing a climate of active self-evaluation within a school is challenging because of the many people a school brings together – teachers, administrators, staff, parents, students. To create a climate of shared, self-critical reflection is probably more difficult in the USA than in Japan because American schools bring together diverse cultures and give parents, as well as educators, a voice. Yet, as we've seen, some promising models in U.S. schools do build the kind of community among students, and among adults in a school, that can support critical self-reflection and growth.[10]

SUMMARY

A key to Japanese business success, in the view of many commentators, is its focus on long-term goals rather than on short-term profitability. A similar point might be made about Japanese education – that it focuses on children's long-term internalization of values rather than on their immediate compliance, and on the creation of committed, responsible learners rather than on next year's test scores. Many American educators, too, are calling for a renewed emphasis on education's long-term goals and on the conditions – such as meaningful curriculum and caring, collaborative relationships among students – needed to achieve those long-term goals. Yet, unlike their Japanese counterparts, American teachers often find themselves in a hostile environment, where concern with "accountability" and with mastery of a skill-and-drill curriculum can undermine the very classroom conditions needed to foster children's long-term growth.

In the history of American education, the pendulum has swung back and forth between "opposing" emphases on intellectual rigor and on students' social development.[11] Japanese preschools and elementary schools – and many American schools as well – demonstrate that the pendulum need not swing. Friendship, belonging, and kindness can go hand-in-hand with intellectual rigor. But schools must build children's self-critical reflection and their shared sense of purpose, rather than "motivate" them through competition. *All* students can experience the exhilaration of seeing their ideas "lead them somewhere" and of contributing to the well-being of others – pleasures likely to be far more enduring than stickers or praise.

But to make this happen widely, we need a broad, and shared, vision for young children's education. This vision must recognize that schooling inevitably shapes children's ethical and social as well as intellectual development, and must deliberately organize every aspect of schooling to foster children's development in all three areas. In other words, a "good" science curriculum must come to be seen as one that promotes collaboration among students, genuine interest in science, and personal commitment to scientific honesty, as well as mastery of scientific concepts. This vision of education must recognize that, for students within a school, close, supportive human relationships are not just an amenity. They are essential to children's ethical and social development. They are also essential to the "painful" task of rigorous learning. Japanese schooling for young children – because of both its strengths and shortcomings – provides a powerful mirror for our own reflection.

213

APPENDIX
Characteristics of the Preschools Studied

The facilities I studied in 1979 were all *yōchien* (preschools) and included public and private facilities in Tokyo and several other parts of Japan. Their characteristics are described briefly in the table that follows. As shown, six preschools were private, seven local public, and two national public. Roughly 58% of Japan's preschools are private, 41% public, and fewer than 1% national (Ministry of Education, 1992).

Pseudonym	Description
National University Preschool	Affiliated with prestigious public university in Tokyo; 171 students
Western Tokyo Preschool	Public preschool, middle-class Tokyo neighborhood; 159 students
Trinity Preschool	Christian preschool, offering after-school special instruction in art, English, gym; 200 students
Our Shepherd Preschool	Catholic-affiliated preschool in mixed middle-class Tokyo neighborhood; 81 students
Private University Preschool	"Escalator" preschool for prestigious private women's university in Tokyo; 250 students
Central Japan City Preschool	City-operated preschool in midsize Japanese city, central Honshu; 176 students
Western Japan Public Preschool	City-operated western Japan preschool; western Honshu; 103 students
National University Preschool, Western Japan	National university-operated preschool, western Honshu; 160 students

Provincial Private Preschool	Private school about 2 hours from Tokyo. Emphasis on counseling and educational placement; 320 students
Tokyo Ward Public Preschool	Public preschool of 69 students, middle-class residential Tokyo neighborhood
Tokyo Central Ward Preschool Number One	Ward-run public preschool, mixed residential and commercial area; 270 students
Tokyo Residential Ward Public Preschool	Ward-run public preschool; 240 students
Yamamiya Private Preschool	Private family-run preschool, 1 hour from Tokyo, Progressive Christian origins, emphasis on "international citizenship" and "Christian nurturance"; 120 students
Tokyo Local Preschool	Neighborhood private preschool, affluent Tokyo neighborhood; 140 students
Buddhist Preschool	Private Tokyo preschool affiliated with Buddhist temple. Emphasizes training for entrance examinations to elite elementary schools; 254 students

NOTES

INTRODUCTION

1. The findings cited in the introduction are documented in more detail in subsequent chapters. Japanese academic achievement is reviewed in Lynn, 1988, and Stevenson and Stigler, 1992. The comparative data on preschool activities are from Stevenson and Stigler, 1992, and the presentation by Harold Stevenson at the Conference on Social Control in Early Childhood Education, Green Gulch, CA, October 26–29, 1987. Both William Cummings (1980) and Merry White (1987a) have noted the emphasis in Japanese elementary education on social and personal development and its likely connection to academic achievement. However, popular accounts of Japanese achievement generally ignore these qualities.
2. For readers interested in late elementary schooling, I recommend Nancy Sato's (1991) thoughtful ethnographic study of fifth- and sixth-grade classrooms in Tokyo public schools serving two quite different populations.
3. Lewis, 1984, reports my original study. Peak, 1991, documents child-centered discipline, and Stevenson and Stigler, 1992, document emphasis on free play.
4. Fukuzawa, 1992; Shimizu, 1992; White, 1993.
5. Stevenson & Stigler, 1992.
6. LeVine and White, 1986; Rohlen, 1976; and White, 1987a, explore the connections between learning and character development in historical and contemporary Japanese thought. Hiroko Hara and Hiroshi Wagatsuma (1974) and Hideo Kojima (1986) describe the history of Japanese childrearing beliefs and practices, including beliefs about young children's inherent godliness.

1. A BRIEF BACKGROUND ON JAPAN'S EDUCATIONAL SYSTEM

1. Merry White, 1987a, provides a lively, engaging overview of Japanese education, with emphasis on familial and cultural determinants of

educational outcomes. The U.S. Study of Education in Japan (1987) provides a breadth of data on Japanese educational practices and policy in a brief, readable volume. Harold Stevenson and James Stigler (1992) report comparative data, from a large multiyear study of U.S., Chinese, and Japanese classrooms, on classroom teaching, student behavior, and family attitudes and practices. William Cummings's 1980 study integrates observational, survey, and policy data on Japanese education and raises many issues that sparked my initial investigations of Japanese education.

2. Monbushō [Ministry of Education, Science, and Culture], 1992.
3. Tobin, Wu, and Davidson, 1989, make this argument, which is also supported by the evidence presented in Boocock, 1989; DeCoker, 1989; and Peak, 1991.
4. Kathy Uno, 1984, traces the historical roots of these two types of institutions, and Roberta Wollons, 1993, explores the foreign and native influences on Japanese preschool education. Gary DeCoker, 1989, and Lois Peak, 1991, both find more similarities than differences between *hoikuen* and *yōchien*, and DeCoker makes the case that other types of distinctions (e.g., formality, intensity, academic focus) are more meaningful than that between part-day and full-day care. Tobin et al., 1989, note the historical differences between *yōchien* and *hoikuen* and suggest these are breaking down. Boocock, 1989, and Peak, 1991, discuss the curricular and program differences between the two settings.
5. These are 1989 estimates of tuition, fees, and school lunch for public and private preschools, respectively. They are provided by Ministry of Education, Science, and Culture, 1992.
6. U.S. Study of Education, 1987; Monbushō, 1992.
7. Tobin et al., 1989.
8. Monbushō, 1992.
9. Monbushō, 1974, p. 107 (translation by Japan Private Kindergarten Federation).
10. Boocock, 1989.
11. Monbushō, 1992.
12. Cummings, 1992.
13. Quoted in LeVine and White, 1986, p. 92.
14. Ministry of Education, 1992.
15. National instructional guidelines, nationally approved textbooks, national subsidies, and teacher rotation are some of the practices that

reduce variability. These are described in Cummings, 1980; Rohlen, 1983; and U.S. Study of Education, 1987.

16. Monbushō, 1991.
17. Masami Kajita, Japanese teachers' career histories, paper presented at the Conference on Teaching and Learning in Japan, Green Gulch, CA, April 9–12, 1992.
18. Monbushō, 1992.
19. Summaries of achievement data are provided by Burstein and Hawkins, 1992; Lynn, 1988; and Stevenson and Stigler, 1992.
20. Burstein and Hawkins, 1992; Stevenson and Lee, 1990.
21. In the sample studied by Stevenson and Stigler, 1992, 10% of fifth-graders took mathematics in an after-school school.
22. Kashiwagi et al., 1984, document the correlates of academic achievement in Japanese and American children. Lewis, 1992, reviews evidence on creativity.
23. Cummings, 1980; Schiller and Walberg, 1982; Stevenson and Stigler, 1992; Torrance, 1980.
24. National Council on Educational Reform, 1986; White, 1988.
25. Ministry of Education, 1992.
26. U.S. Study of Education, 1987, p. 19.
27. Ibid., p. 17.
28. Monbushō, 1989b.
29. Horio and Platzer, 1988.
30. Monbushō, 1992, gives recent statistics; history of plans is described in Monbushō, 1991, p. 192.
31. U.S. Study of Education, 1987, p. 5.
32. Duke, 1973, provides a history of the Teachers' Union. Cummings, 1980; Horio and Platzer, 1988; Rohlen, 1984; and Schoppa, 1991, provide accounts of particular policy disputes as well as theoretical perspectives on ministry-union conflict.
33. Horio and Platzer, 1988.
34. Rohlen, 1985–86, p. 128.
35. Rohlen, 1983; Shimahara, 1992.
36. Sōmucho, Seishōnen Taisaku Honbu [Prime Minister's Office, Policy Headquarters for Children and Youth], 1991 (1988 data).
37. Simons, 1987, describes a "cram school" for preschoolers. Peak, 1992, describes the many varieties of preschool training for Japanese children, including examination-focused training.

219

2. THE PRESCHOOL EXPERIENCE

1. Monbushō, 1989a, p. 1. Unless otherwise noted, translations are mine.
2. Kotloff, 1988; Peak, 1992a; Stevenson and Stigler, 1992; Tobin et al., 1989.
3. All names are pseudonyms.
4. Kotloff, 1988, p. 4.
5. Ibid., p. 5.
6. Hendry, 1986; Peak, 1992a.
7. Hendry, 1986, p. 142.
8. Monbushō, 1986; these and subsequent survey data are from the latter half of the school year.
9. Monbushō, 1989a, p. 3.
10. Ibid., pp. 8–9.
11. Simons, 1987.
12. Monbushō, 1986, p. 32.
13. Tobin et al., 1989; U.S. Study of Education, 1987.
14. Stevenson and Stigler, 1992, p. 79.
15. Tobin et al., 1989.
16. Stevenson and Stigler, 1992.
17. Peak, 1992a.
18. Ibid., p. 59.
19. DeCoker, 1989.
20. For example, Stevenson and Stigler, 1992, report that 90% of American mothers but only 36% of Japanese mothers taught the alphabet to their preschoolers at home. The same authors report an achievement advantage for Japanese students as early as the first grade of elementary school.
21. See, e.g., DeVries, Reese-Learned, and Morgan, 1991; Schweinhart, Weikart, and Larner, 1986; and Stipek, Feiler, Daniels, and Milburn, in press.

3. THE WHOLE CHILD GOES TO ELEMENTARY SCHOOL

1. Cummings, 1980, p. 13, italics omitted.
2. Monbushō, 1992.
3. Of the school goals from 150 Japanese elementary schools documented by Kashiwagi (1985), about half are focused on persistence and academic effort, the other half on social and personal develop-

ment. The greater emphasis I found on social and personal development probably relates to the grade level (first grade) and to a different method (I recorded not just school goals but all goals meant to be read by children, including group and class goals).

4. Befu, 1986; Duke, 1986; Holloway, 1988; Singleton, 1989.
5. Holloway, 1988; Stevenson and Stigler, 1992.
6. Peak, 1991.
7. The variation between control and chaos is best illustrated by reading across a number of accounts such as Bedford, 1979; DeCoker, 1989; Hendry, 1986; Ohanian, 1987; Peak, 1991; Sano, 1989; Sato, 1991; White, 1987a.
8. Connell and Wellborn, 1991; Deci and Ryan, 1985; Lewis, Battistich, and Schaps, 1990; Solomon, Watson, Battistich, Schaps, and Delucchi, 1992.
9. Shimahara and Sakai, 1992, pp. 156–157.
10. Ibid, p. 156; see also Rohlen, 1989.
11. Dickson, 1975. For a full description of the task, see Dickson, Hess, Miyake, and Azuma, 1979.
12. Azuma and Kashiwagi, 1987.
13. Kobayashi, 1990; LeVine and White, 1986; Rohlen, 1976; Singleton, 1989.
14. Peak, 1986.
15. Kajita et al., 1988.
16. Abiko, 1986.
17. Sato and McLaughlin, 1992, p. 365.
18. Goya, 1993, p. 126.
19. Easley and Easley, 1983, pp. 47–48.
20. Battistich, Solomon, Watson, and Schaps, 1994, p. 3.
21. U.S. Study of Education, 1987. See also Barrett, 1990, for additional international comparisons and a case for school year lengthening.
22. Ito, 1994.
23. Fujita, 1989; Sato, 1991.
24. Peak, 1991, pp. 59–60.
25. Fujita, 1989; Peak, 1991.
26. Murakami, 1991; Schoolland, 1990.
27. Hara and Wagatsuma, 1974.
28. Horio and Platzer, 1988.
29. Sato, 1991, and see chapter 2.
30. Connell and Wellborn, 1991; Deci and Ryan, 1985; Solomon, Watson et al., 1992.

4. THE SMALL GROUP: A HOME BASE FOR CHILDREN

1. Holloway, 1988.
2. Goldberg and Maccoby, 1965.
3. Kajita, Shiota, Ishida, and Sugie, 1980.
4. Peak, 1991; Tobin et al., 1989.
5. Ineko Tsuchida and Catherine Lewis, Responsibility and learning, paper presented at the Conference on Teaching and Learning in Japan, Green Gulch, CA, April 9–12, 1992.
6. Kajita et al., 1980. My guess is that these diverse strategies reflect both the multiple goals teachers hold for groups – to build belonging, ease classroom management, and positively shape students' academic and social development – and teachers' keen appreciation of the natural history of groups. First, groups must provide children with a sense of belonging, an emotional home base. Then groups could be used to stretch children's capacities socially and academically.
7. Quoted in Sugie, 1988, p. 425.
8. Sugie, 1988, provides an interesting history of cooperative learning in Japan, noting that several works published by Japanese school practitioners in the 1910s and 1920s integrated Dewey's work with an emphasis on techniques for supporting cooperative small-group learning. He reports that these early works were concerned with many of the same themes that characterize contemporary Japanese educational practice, including the importance of student interaction to learning and the negative effects of competitive motivation for learning.
9. Kajita et al., 1980; Sugie, 1988; Tsuchida, 1992.
10. I could not locate systematic studies of the frequency of ability grouping in U.S. schools. However, several portraits of American elementary school life, such as Goodlad, 1984, and Hallinan, 1987, suggest that ability grouping is "as common as daily recess" and that tasks children engage in often require little cooperation (e.g., round-robin reading, filling out workbook pages, writing or drawing individually). However, these portraits predate the recent interest in cooperative learning in the United States. Baseline data from a 1992 study of 24 elementary schools in six districts across the United States found that 60% of the 472 teachers grouped their children for reading, and 72% of these used same-ability grouping at least some of the time (Dissemination Baseline Study, Developmental Studies Center, Oakland, CA).

11. Some of the most widely known and most carefully studied forms of cooperative learning in the United States employ rewards for group performance. See, for example, Slavin, 1989.

12. Solomon, Watson, et al., 1992, have studied a model of cooperative learning that emphasizes collaborative social processes and intrinsic motivation for learning; Brandt, 1989–90, includes articles by several researchers (Shlomo Sharan and David and Roger Johnson) that provide evidence on the success of cooperative learning models that emphasize students' collaborative process rather than external incentives. See also note 11.

13. As Bronfenbrenner, 1973, notes, group cohesiveness increases conformity of judgments in experimental research employing the Asch Paradigm.

14. Schoolland, 1990.

15. Ibid. Also Murakami, 1991.

16. Battistich, Solomon, & Delucchi, 1993.

17. Solomon, Watson, Battistich, Schaps, and Solomon, 1990. But see also note 13.

18. Marshall, 1988.

5. THE ROOTS OF DISCIPLINE: COMMUNITY AND COMMITMENT

1. Quoted in Kobayashi, 1964.

2. McLaughlin, Talbert, Kahne, and Powell, 1990, p. 220.

3. Doi, 1973; Hara and Wagatsuma, 1974; Vogel, 1963.

4. Stevenson et al., 1987.

5. deCharms, 1968.

6. Kajita et al., 1988.

7. Monbushō, 1978, pp. 54–55.

8. Easley and Easley, 1983, pp. 40–41.

9. Conroy, Hess, Azuma, and Kashiwagi, 1980. Given documented socioeconomic status differences in disciplinary techniques, it is important to note that the samples were socioeconomically matched, with the Japanese and American samples each including lower- and middle-class mothers.

10. Lewis, 1981.

11. For a review, see Lepper, 1983.

12. Aronson and Carlsmith, 1963; Lepper, 1973.

13. Ibid.
14. Lepper and Greene, 1975.
15. Ibid.
16. Hamilton, Blumenfeld, Akoh, and Miura, 1989.
17. Stevenson and Stigler, 1992.
18. Kashiwagi, 1986; Fukuya, 1990.
19. Guilford, 1968; Stevenson and Lee, 1990; Uchihashi, 1983.
20. Kurita, 1990; Nagano, 1983.

6. DISCIPLINE: HOW PEERS AND TEACHERS MANAGE MISBEHAVIOR

1. Easley and Easley, 1983, p. 41.
2. Bronfenbrenner, 1973; Johnson, 1962.
3. Peak, 1991.
4. Hara and Wagatsuma, 1974; H. Kojima, 1986.
5. Dienstbier, Hillman, Lehnhoff, Hillman, and Valkenaar, 1975.
6. Damon, 1977.
7. Conroy et al., 1980.
8. See DeVos, 1973; Doi, 1973; Hendry, 1986; Lanham, 1956; and Vogel, 1963, for discussions of exclusion as a disciplinary technique.
9. Between 1975 and 1990, 750,000 teachers received training in Assertive Discipline, a single U.S. classroom behavior management system. Hill, 1990, notes that during that period, Lee Canter & Associates, the company offering Assertive Discipline, grew from a small business into a multimillion-dollar enterprise with 75 full- and part-time employees. In 1990 alone, it was estimated that 50,000 teachers would take the 1-day seminar in Assertive Discipline and 35,000 teachers would take the 5-day graduate-level course. A 1992 survey of 489 elementary teachers in 24 schools across the United States found that 38% of teachers gave points or awards for good behavior "always" or "usually," and another 36% did this "sometimes" (Dissemination baseline data, Developmental Studies Center, Oakland, CA).
10. Thomas Rohlen, comments at the Conference on Teaching and Learning in Japan, Green Gulch, CA, April 9–12, 1992.
11. Tobin et al., 1989, p. 30.
12. Hamilton et al., 1989. Merry White, 1993, also notes a stronger identification of Japanese youth with adults.
13. Bronfenbrenner, 1973; Johnson, 1962. Schoolland, 1990, explores the dark side of peer control in Japanese education.

14. White, 1993; Fukuzawa, 1989.
15. Sarason, 1983.
16. Fujita and Sano, 1988.
17. G. Kojima, 1959, cited in LeVine and White, 1986, pp. 107–108.
18. See notes 4 and 8.
19. Caron, 1645/1967, p. 166; Kattendyke, 1860/1964, pp. 202–203; McConnell, 1990, p. 20. I am indebted to Hiroshi Watanabe for locating the first two quotations.
20. Hara, in press.

7. LEARNING AND CARING

1. Noddings, 1988, p. 36.
2. Fukuzawa, 1989; Rohlen, 1983.
3. Easley and Easley, 1983; Stigler and Stevenson, 1991; Tsuchida, 1993.
4. Easley and Easley, 1983, pp. 42–43.
5. Stigler and Stevenson, 1991, p. 14.
6. The water volume lesson, crab death investigation, and other science lessons involving students in prediction, debate, and experimentation may well be examples of the Japanese teaching method "hypothesis-experiment-instruction" described by Gyo Hatano and Kayoko Inagaki, 1991.
7. Nathaniel Chuang, field notes, February 16, 1990.
8. Tsuchida's 1993 comparison of fourth-grade science and social studies lessons in Japanese and American classrooms suggests this.
9. Azuma, Kashiwagi, and Hess, 1981, provides the example I translate. Dickson et al., 1979, provides a description of the task and results.
10. Moriya, 1989. Like many studies of interpersonal awareness, this research found girls to be more empathic and interpersonally concerned than boys. Interestingly, Japanese boys were closer to English girls than to English boys in their level of interpersonal concern.
11. Hess and Azuma, 1991; Umesao, 1990.
12. Hess and Azuma, 1991, pp. 6–7.
13. Easley and Easley, 1981, p. 12.
14. Provisional Council on Educational Reform, 1985.
15. Tobin et al., 1989. For additional examples, see Hendry, 1986, and Peak, 1992a.
16. Horio and Platzer, 1988, p. 174.
17. Stevenson and Stigler, 1992; Stigler, Fernandez, Yoshida, and Hatano, 1992; Tsuchida, 1993.

18. Rohlen, 1983, 1985–86.
19. Horio and Platzer, 1988, pp. 174–75.

8. WHAT IS A SUCCESSFUL SCHOOL?

1. U.S. Study of Education, 1987.
2. Homusho Jinkenyōgokyoku, 1989, p. 38.
3. Monbushō Shōtō Chūtō Kyōiku Kyoku, 1992, p. 9.
4. Sōmucho, Seishōnen Taisaku Honbu, 1991.
5. Ibid., p. 258.
6. Ibid. (These statistics exclude incidents that occurred outside school within youth gangs.)
7. Fukuzawa, 1989; White, 1993.
8. Reported in White, 1993, p. 86, based on Asahi News Service report of December 26, 1991.
9. Monbushō, 1992.
10. Sōmucho, 1990, p. 271. Police provided *hodō* to 21,552 minors for thinner sniffing and to 986 for stimulant use *(kakuseizai)* in 1989.
11. Stevenson, Chen, & Lee, 1993.
12. White, 1993, p. 191.
13. See, for example, Easley and Easley, 1983; Sato, 1991; Tobin et al., 1989; White, 1987a.
14. Somucho, 1991, pp. 52–55, 60–61, 88–89.
15. Stevenson and Stigler, 1992.
16. Tsuchida, 1993.
17. Somucho, 1991, p. 240.
18. I am indebted to Marilyn Watson for pointing out the connection between meeting children's needs and internalization of values. Watson, Solomon, Battistich, Schaps, and Solomon, 1989, and Connell and Wellborn, 1991, provide data on educational application of the attachment theory developed by Deci and Ryan, 1985.
19. Bowlby, 1969; Doi, 1973.
20. Solomon, Watson, Battistich, Schaps, and Delucchi, 1992.
21. See, for example, Comer, 1988, on the School Development Project and Bensman, 1987, on the Central Park East schools.
22. A. Shanker, "Where we stand: Mentoring reconsidered," *New York Times,* March 20, 1994, p. E7.
23. Boocock, 1987. See also Shwalb, 1993, for a discussion of the connection between Japanese childrearing and preschool life.

24. Comer, 1988, p. 48.
25. Linn, Songer, and Eylon, in press.
26. Yoshida, 1993.
27. Stevenson and Stigler, 1992, pp. 167–68.
28. Sato and McLaughlin, 1992.
29. White, 1987a.
30. McLaughlin et al., 1990.
31. Stigler and Perry, 1987, p. 1.
32. Kobayashi-Winata and Power, 1989; Power and Kobayashi-Winata, 1992.
33. Nihon Kyoshokuin Kumiai, 1974.
34. Kliebard, 1987.

9. SUMMARY: QUESTIONS TO ASK OURSELVES

1. Palmer, 1983.
2. Rohlen, 1976, p. 128.
3. Stigler et al., 1992; Yoshida et al., 1993.
4. Okamoto, Calfee, Varghese, and Chambliss, 1992.
5. Stevenson and Stigler, 1992.
6. DeVries et al., 1991; Haskins, 1985; Schweinhart et al., 1986.
7. Penny Rix, personal communication, December 1992.
8. Duckworth, 1991, p. 2.
9. Brophy and Alleman, 1991, p. 13.
10. Bensman, 1987; Comer, 1988; Solomon, Schaps et al., 1992.
11. Kliebard, 1987.

REFERENCES

Abiko, T. (1986). Seclusionism of culture and education in contemporary Japan. In T. Taura (Ed.), *Kikokushijo no Kyōiku mondai ni kansuru sōgōteki jisshōteki kenkyū* [Interdisciplinary research on the education of returnee students] (pp. 60–72). Nagoya: Nagoya University Faculty of Education.

Abiko, T., & George, P. S. (1986, December). Education for early adolescents in Japan, U.S.: Cross-cultural observations. *National Association of Secondary School Principals Bulletin*, pp. 74–81.

Aronson, E., & Carlsmith, J. (1963). Effect of severity of threat on the valuation of forbidden behavior. *Journal of Abnormal and Social Psychology, 66*, 584–588.

Azuma, H., & Kashiwagi, K. (1987). Descriptors for an intelligent person: A Japanese study. *Japanese Psychological Research, 29*, 17–26.

Azuma, H., Kashiwagi, K., & Hess, R. D. (1981). *Hahaoya no kōdō taido to kodomo no chiteki hattatsu* [Maternal attitudes and behavior and children's intellectual development]. Tokyo: University of Tokyo Press.

Azuma, H., & Walberg, H. (1985). *Kagakuteki gainen no shutoku, teichaku, ten-i ni oyobosu kyōjuhōhō no eikyō* [The influence of teaching method on acquisition, retention, and transfer of scientific concepts]. In T. Inagaki (Ed.), *Department of Curriculum and Instruction research report* (pp. 208–277). Tokyo: Faculty of Education, University of Tokyo.

Battistich, V., Solomon, D., & Delucchi, K. (1993). Interaction processes and student outcomes in cooperative learning groups. *Elementary School Journal, 94*, 19–32.

Bedford, L. (1979). Rakuto kindergarten: Observations on Japanese pre-schooling. *Harvard Graduate School of Education Association Bulletin, 23* (2), 18–20.

Befu, H. (1984). Civilization and culture: Japan in search of identity. *Senri Ethnological Studies, 16*, 59–75.

Befu, H. (1986). The social and cultural background of child development in Japan and the United States. In H. Stevenson, H. Azuma, & K. Hakuta (Eds.), *Child development and education in Japan* (pp. 13–27). New York: Freeman.

Bensman, D. (1987). *Quality education: The story of the Central Park East schools.* New York: Kramer Communications.

Boocock, S. S. (1987, March). *The privileged world of little children: Preschool education in Japan.* Paper presented at the annual meeting of the Comparative and International Education Society, Washington, DC.

Boocock, S. S. (1989). Controlled diversity: An overview of the Japanese preschool system. *Journal of Japanese Studies, 15,* 41–66.

Bowlby, J. (1969). *Attachment.* New York: Basic.

Brandt, R. (1989–90). Cooperative learning [Special issue]. *Educational Leadership, 47*(4).

Bronfenbrenner, U. (1973). *Two worlds of childhood: U.S. and U.S.S.R.* New York: Pocket Books.

Brophy, J., & Alleman, J. (1991). Activities as instructional tools: A framework for analysis and evaluation. *Educational Researcher, 20*(4), 9–23.

Burstein, L., & Hawkins, J. (1992). An analysis of cognitive, noncognitive and behavioral characteristics of students in Japan. In R. Leestma & H. J. Walberg (Eds.), *Japanese educational productivity* (Michigan Papers in Japanese Studies, No. 22, pp. 173–224). Ann Arbor: University of Michigan Center for Japanese Studies.

Caron, F. (1967). *Beschrijvinghe van het machtigh Coninckrijck Iapan* (1645). [Nippon okoku shi/The ideology of imperial Japan]. Tokyo: Heibonsha.

Comer, J. (1988). Educating poor minority children. *Scientific American, 259*(5), 42–48.

Connell, J. P., & Wellborn, J. G. (1991). Competence, autonomy, and relatedness: A motivational analysis of self-system processes. In M. R. Gunnar & L. A. Sroufe (Eds.), *The Minnesota Symposia on Child Development, 23* (pp. 43–77). Hillsdale, NJ: Erlbaum.

Conroy, M., Hess, R., Azuma, H., & Kashiwagi, K. (1980). Maternal strategies for regulating children's behavior: Japanese and American families. *Journal of Cross-Cultural Psychology, 11,* 153–172.

Cummings, W. (1980). *Education and equality in Japan.* Princeton: Princeton University Press.

Cummings, W. (1992). Examining the educational production function: British, American, and Japanese models. *Advances in Educational Productivity, 2,* 21–39.

Damon, W. (1977). *The social world of the child.* San Francisco: Jossey-Bass.

deCharms, R. (1968). *Personal causation: The internal affective determinants of behavior.* New York: Academic Press.

Deci, E. L., & Ryan, R. R. (1985). *Intrinsic motivation and self-determination in human behavior.* New York: Plenum.

DeCoker, G. (1989). Japanese preschools: Academic or nonacademic? In J. J. Shields (Ed.), *Japanese schooling: Patterns of socialization, equality, and political control* (pp. 45–58). University Park: Pennsylvania State University Press.

DeVos, G. (1973). *Socialization for achievement.* Berkeley and Los Angeles: University of California Press.

DeVries, R., Reese-Learned, H., & Morgan, P. (1991). Sociomoral development in children from direct-instruction, constructivist, and eclectic kindergarten programs. *Early Childhood Research Quarterly, 6,* 449–471.

Dickson, W. P. (1975). [Picture book communication game manual; list of every explicitly personalized message.] Unpublished.

Dickson, W. P., Hess, R. D., Miyake, N., & Azuma, H. (1979). Referential communication accuracy between mother and child as a predictor of cognitive development in the United States and Japan. *Child Development, 50,* 53–59.

Dienstbier, R. A., Hillman, D., Lehnhoff, J., Hillman, J., & Valkenaar, M.C. (1975). An emotion attribution approach to moral behavior: Interfacing cognitive and avoidance theories of moral development. *Psychological Review, 82,* 229–315.

Doi, T. (1973). *The anatomy of dependence.* Tokyo: Kodansha International.

Duckworth, E. (1991). Twenty-four, forty-two, and I love you: Keeping it complex. *Harvard Educational Review, 61*(1), 1–24.

Duke, B. (1973). *Japan's militant teachers: A history of the left-wing teachers' movement.* Honolulu: University of Hawaii Press.

Duke, B. (1986). *The Japanese school: Lessons for industrial America.* New York: Praeger.

Easley, J., & Easley, E. (1981, May). *Kitamaeno School as an environment in which children study mathematics themselves.* Talk given to the Faculty of Education, University of Tokyo, and unpublished report, Bureau of Educational Research, University of Illinois.

Easley, J., & Easley, E. (1983). Kitamaeno School as an environment in which children study mathematics themselves. *Journal of Science Education in Japan, 7,* 39–48.

Fallows, D. (1990, September 9). The lifetime lessons of Japan's schools. *Washington Post,* Outlook section.

Fujita, M. (1989). "It's all mother's fault": Childcare and the socialization of working mothers in Japan. *Journal of Japanese Studies, 15,* 67–92.

Fujita, M., & Sano, T. (1988). Children in American and Japanese day care centers: Ethnography and reflective cross-cultural interviewing. In H. T. Trueba & C. Delgado-Gaitan (Eds.), *School and society: Learning content through culture*. Westport, CT: Greenwood.

Fukuya, M. (1990). *Dai 21 kai kokusai hikaku chōsa hōkokusho: Toshi kankyō no naka no kodomotachi* [Report of the 21st international comparative survey: Children in urban environments]. Tokyo: Fukutake Shoten.

Fukuzawa, R. E. (1989). *Stratification, social control, and student culture: An ethnography of three Japanese junior high schools*. Unpublished doctoral dissertation, Northwestern University.

Goldberg, M., & Maccoby, E. (1965). Children's acquisition of skill in performing a group task under two conditions of group formation. *Journal of Personality and Social Psychology, 2*, 898–902.

Goodlad, J. (1984). *A place called school*. New York: McGraw-Hill.

Goya, S. (1993, October). The secret of Japanese education. *Phi Delta Kappan*, 126–129.

Guilford, J. (1968). *Intelligence, creativity, and their educational implications*. San Diego: Knapp.

Hallinan, M. T. (1987). Ability grouping and student learning. In M. T. Hallinan (Ed.), *The social organization of schools* (pp. 41–70). New York: Plenum.

Hamilton, V. L., Blumenfeld, P. C., Akoh, H., & Miura, K. (1989a). Japanese and American children's reasons for the things they do in school. *American Educational Research Journal, 26*, 545–571.

Hamilton, V. L., Blumenfeld, P. C., Akoh, H., & Miura, K. (1989b). Citizenship and scholarship in Japanese and American fifth grades. *American Educational Research Journal, 26*, 44–72.

Hara, H. (in press). Shitsuke revisited. In D. Shwalb & B. Shwalb (Eds.), *Classic studies of Japanese human development: Retrospects and prospects*. New York: Guilford.

Hara, H., & Wagatsuma, H. (1974). *Shitsuke* [Childrearing]. Tokyo: Kobundo.

Haskins, R. (1985). Public school aggression among children with varying day-care experience. *Child Development, 56*, 689–703.

Hatano, G., & Inagaki, K. (1991, April). *Motivation for collective comprehension activity in Japanese classrooms*. Paper presented at the annual meetings of the American Educational Research Association, Chicago.

Hendry, J. (1986). *Becoming Japanese: The world of the Japanese preschool child*. Honolulu: University of Hawaii Press.

Hess, R. D., & Azuma, H. (1991). Cultural support for schooling: Contrasts between Japan and the United States. *Educational Researcher, 20,* 2–8, 12.

Hill, D. (1990, April). Order in the classroom. *Teacher Magazine,* 70–77.

Holloway, S. (1988). Concepts of ability and effort in Japan and the United States. *Review of Educational Research, 58,* 327–345.

Hōmushō Hōmusōgōkenkyūjo, (1990). *Hanzai hakusho* [White paper on crime]. Tokyo: Ōkurasho Insatsukyoku.

Hōmushō Jinkenyōgokyoku [Ministry of Justice, Bureau of Human Rights Protection]. (1989). *Futōkoji no jittai nitsuite* [The situation of school refusers]. Tokyo: Ōkurasho Printing Bureau.

Horio, T., & Platzer, S. (1988). *Educational thought and ideology in modern Japan.* Tokyo: University of Tokyo Press.

Ito, Y. (1994). Kyōshi bunka gakkō bunka no nichibei hikaku [Teacher culture, school culture: A Japan-U.S. comparison]. In T. Inagaki, & Y. Kudomi (Eds.), *Nihon no kyōshi bunka* [The culture of teachers in Japan] (pp. 140–156). Tokyo: University of Tokyo Press.

Johnson, R. (1962). A study of children's moral judgments. *Child Development, 23,* 327–354.

Kajita, M., Ishida, S., Ito, A., Mizuno, R., Sugimura, S., Nakano, Y., & Ishida, H. (1988). Gakushū shidō yōshiki no kokusai hikaku [An international comparison of instructional methods]. *Bulletin of the Faculty of Education, Nagoya University, 35,* 137–162.

Kajita, M., Shiota, S., Ishida, H., & Sugie, S. (1980). Shō-chūgakkō ni okeru shidō no chōsateki kenkyū [Survey of teaching methods in elementary and junior high schools]. *Bulletin of the Faculty of Education, Nagoya University. 27,* 147–182.

Kashiwagi, K. (1985). Educational goals at Japanese elementary schools. Unpublished report. Shirayuri College Department of Child Development and Juvenile Culture, Tokyo.

Kashiwagi, K. (1986). Personality development of adolescents. In H. Stevenson, H. Azuma, & K. Hakuta (Eds.), *Child development and education in Japan* (pp. 167–185). New York: Freeman.

Kashiwagi, K., Azuma, H., Miyake, K., Nagano, S., Hess, R., & Holloway, S. (1984). Japan-US comparative study on early maternal influences upon cognitive development: A follow-up study. *Japanese Psychological Research, 26,* 82–92.

Kattendyke, J. C. R. V. (1964). *Uittrekesel uit het dagboek van W. J. C. Ridder H. v. Kattendyke gedurende zijn verbliht in Japan in 1857, 1858 en 1859* [Nagasaki kaigun gunshujo no hibi/Days with the Nagasaki navy] (1860). Tokyo: Heibonsha.

Kliebard, H. (1987). *The struggle for the American curriculum.* New York: Routledge & Kegan Paul.

Kobayashi, V. (1964). *John Dewey in Japanese educational thought.* Ann Arbor: University of Michigan School of Education.

Kobayashi, V. (1990). Ecological perspectives on kyoyo and aesthetic quality: Japan and America. *Senri Ethnological Studies, 28,* 83–90.

Kobayashi-Winata, H., & Power, T. G. (1989). Childrearing and compliance: Japanese and American families in Houston. *Journal of Cross-Cultural Psychology, 20,* 333–356.

Kojima, G. (1959, September). *The philosophical foundations for democratic education in Japan.* International Christian University. Excerpted in LeVine & White, 1986, pp. 107–108.

Kojima, H. (1986). Childrearing concepts as a belief-value system of the society and the individual. In H. Stevenson (Ed.), *Child development and education in Japan* (pp. 39–54). New York: Freeman.

Kotloff, L. (1988). *Dai-ichi Preschool: Fostering individuality and cooperative group-life in a progressive Japanese preschool.* Unpublished doctoral dissertation, Cornell University.

Kurita, Y. (1990). The culture of the meeting: The tradition of "yoriai" or village meeting. *Senri Ethnological Studies, 28,* 127–140.

Lanham, B. (1956). Aspects of childcare in Japan: Preliminary report. In D. Haring (Ed.), *Personal character and cultural milieu* (pp. 565–583). Syracuse: Syracuse University Press.

Lepper, M. (1973). Dissonance, self-perception, and honesty in children. *Journal of Personality and Social Psychology, 25,* 65–74.

Lepper, M. (1983). Social control processes, attributions of motivation, and the internalization of social values. In E. T. Higgins, D. Ruble, & W. Hartup (Eds.), *Social cognition and social behavior: Developmental perspectives* (pp. 294–330). San Francisco: Jossey-Bass.

Lepper, M., & Greene, D. (1975). Turning play into work: Effects of adult surveillance and extrinsic rewards on children's intrinsic motivation. *Journal of Personality and Social Psychology, 31,* 479–486.

LeVine, R. A., & White, M. I. (1986). *Human conditions: The cultural basis of educational development.* New York: Routledge & Kegan Paul.

Lewis, C. C. (1981). The effects of parental firm control: A reinterpretation of findings. *Psychological Bulletin, 90,* 547–563.

Lewis, C. C. (1984). Cooperation and control in Japanese nursery schools. *Comparative Education Review, 32,* 69–84.

Lewis, C. C. (1989). From indulgence to internalization: Social control in the early school years. *Journal of Japanese Studies, 15,* 139–157.

Lewis, C. C. (1992). Creativity in Japanese education. In R. Leestma & H. J. Walberg (Eds.), *Japanese educational productivity* (Michigan Papers in Japanese Studies, No. 22, pp. 225–266). Ann Arbor: University of Michigan Center for Japanese Studies.

Lewis, C. C., Battistich, V., & Schaps, E. (1990). School-based primary prevention: What is an effective program? *New Directions for Child Development, 90,* 35–59.

Linn, M. C., Songer, N. B., & Eylon, B. (in press). Science. In D. Berliner & R. Calfee (Eds.), *The handbook of educational psychology.* New York: Macmillan.

Lynn, R. (1988). *Educational achievement in Japan.* Armonk, NY: Sharp.

Marshall, H. (1988). Work or learning: Implications of classroom metaphors. *Educational Researcher, 17,* 9–16.

McConnell, D. L. (1990, March). Childrearing in the preschool years as a window on Japanese culture. *Kyoto International Cultural Association Newsletter, 16,* 19–23.

McLaughlin, M. W., & Talbert, J., with Kahne, J., & Powell, J. (1990, November). Constructing a personalized school environment. *Phi Delta Kappan,* 220–235.

Ministry of Education. (1974). *Kindergarten accreditation standards (summary)* (Japan Private Kindergarten Federation [Nihon Shiritsu Yōchien Rengokai], Trans.). Ministry of Education Ordinance No. 32.

Ministry of Education, Science, and Culture. (1992). *Statistical abstract of education, science, and culture.* Tokyo: Ministry of Education, Science, and Culture Research and Statistics Planning Division.

Monbushō [Ministry of Education, Science, and Culture]. (1978). *Shōgakkō shidōsho: Dōtokuhen* [Elementary instruction: Moral education]. Tokyo: Ōkurasho Insatsukyoku.

Monbushō. (1986). *Yōchien kyōiku no arikata nitsuite* [The nature of preschool education]. Tokyo: Monbushō.

Monbushō. (1989a). *Yōchien kyōiku yōryō* [Guidelines for preschool education]. Tokyo: Gyosei.

Monbushō. (1989b). *Shōgakkō gakushū shidō yōryō* [Course of study for elementary schools]. Tokyo: Monbushō.

Monbushō. (1991). *Wagakuni no bunkyō shisaku* [Japan's education policy]. Tokyo: Monbushō.

Monbushō. (1992). *Monbu tōkei yōran* [Summary of educational statistics]. Tokyo: Monbushō.

Monbushō Shōtō Chūtō Kyōikukyoku [Ministry of Education, Bureau on Elementary and Middle Grades Education]. (1992). *Tōkō kyohi (futōkō)*

mondai nitsuite [On the problem of school phobia (school refusal)].
Tokyo.

Moriya, K. (1989). A developmental and cross-cultural study of the interpersonal cognition of English and Japanese children. *Japanese Psychological Research, 31*, 108–115.

Murakami, Y. (1991). Bullies in the classroom. In B. Finkelstein, A. Imamura, & J. Tobin (Eds.), *Transcending stereotypes: Discovering Japanese culture and education* (pp. 190–196). Yarmouth, ME: Intercultural Press.

Nagano, S. (1983, April). *Docility and lack of assertiveness: Possible causes of academic achievement in Japanese children.* Paper presented at the Conference on Japanese Education and Child Development, Center for Advanced Study in the Behavioral Sciences, Stanford, CA.

National Council on Educational Reform. (1986). *Summary of Second Report on Educational Reform.* Tokyo: Government of Japan.

Nihon Kyoshokuin Kumiai [Japan Teachers' Union]. (1974). *Hyōka to testo* [Evaluation and tests]. Tokyo: Okumura Insatsu Kabushiki Kaisha.

Noddings, N. (1988, December 7). Schools face "crisis in caring." *Education Week,* p. 36.

Ohanian, S. (1987, January). Notes on Japan from an American schoolteacher. *Phi Delta Kappan,* 360–367.

Okamoto, Y., Calfee, R., Varghese, S., & Chambliss, M. (1992, April). *A cross-cultural comparison of textbook designs.* Paper presented at the annual meeting of the American Educational Research Association, Washington, DC.

Palmer, P. (1983). *To know as we are known: A spirituality of education.* San Francisco: Harper Collins.

Peak, L. (1986). Training learning skills and attitudes in Japanese early educational settings. In W. Fowler (Ed.), *Early experience and the development of competence* (New Directions for Child Development No. 32, pp. 111–123). San Francisco: Jossey-Bass.

Peak, L. (1991). *Learning to go to school in Japan.* Berkeley and Los Angeles: University of California Press.

Peak, L. (1992). Formal pre-elementary education in Japan. In R. Leestma & H. J. Walberg (Eds.), *Japanese educational productivity* (Michigan Papers in Japanese Studies, No. 22, pp. 35–68). Ann Arbor: University of Michigan Center for Japanese Studies.

Power, T. G., & Kobayashi-Winata, H. (1992). Childrearing patterns in Japan and the United States: A cluster analytic study. *International Journal of Behavioral Development, 15*, 185–205.

Provisional Council on Educational Reform. (1985, June 26). *First report on educational reform.* Tokyo: Government of Japan.

Rawl, R., & O'Tuel, F. (1982). A comparison of three prereading approaches for kindergarten students. *Reading Improvement, 19,* 205–211.

Rogoff, B. (1990). *Apprenticeship in thinking: Cognitive development in social context.* New York: Oxford University Press.

Rohlen, T. (1976, Spring). The promise of adulthood in Japanese spiritualism. *Daedalus,* 125–143.

Rohlen, T. (1983). *Japan's high schools.* Berkeley and Los Angeles: University of California Press.

Rohlen, T. (1984). Conflict in institutional environments: Politics in education. In E. S. Krauss, T. P. Rohlen, & P. G. Steinhoff (Eds.), *Conflict in Japan* (pp. 136–173). Honolulu: University of Hawaii Press.

Rohlen, T. (1985–86, Winter). Japanese education: If they can do it, should we? *American Scholar,* 29–43.

Rohlen, T. (1989). Order in Japanese society: Attachment, authority, and routine. *Journal of Japanese Studies, 15,* 5–40.

Sano, T. (1989). Methods of social control and socialization in Japanese day-care centers. *Journal of Japanese Studies, 15,* 125–138.

Sarason, S. B. (1983). *Schooling in America.* New York: Free Press.

Sato, N. (1991). *Ethnography of Japanese elementary schools: Quest for equality.* Unpublished doctoral dissertation, Stanford University School of Education.

Sato, N., & McLaughlin, M. W. (1992, January). Context matters: Teaching in Japan and in the United States. *Phi Delta Kappan,* 359–366.

Schiller, D., & Walberg, H. J. (1982). Japan: The learning society. *Educational Leadership, 39,* 411–412.

Schoolland, K. (1990). *Shogun's ghost: The dark side of Japanese education.* New York: Bergin & Garvey.

Schoppa, L. (1991). *Education reform in Japan: A case of immobilist politics.* New York: Routledge & Kegan Paul.

Schweinhart, L. J., Weikart, D. P., & Larner, M. B. (1986). Consequences of three curriculum models through age 15. *Early Childhood Research Quarterly, 1,* 15–54.

Sergiovanni, T. (1992). *Moral leadership: Getting to the heart of school improvement.* San Francisco: Jossey-Bass.

Shimahara, N. (1992). Overview of Japanese education: Policy, structure and current issues. In R. Leestma & H. J. Walberg (Eds.), *Japanese educational productivity* (Michigan Papers in Japanese Studies, No. 22, pp. 7–33). Ann Arbor: University of Michigan Center for Japanese Studies.

Shimahara, N., & Sakai, A. (1992). Teacher internship and the culture of teaching in Japan. *British Journal of Sociology of Education, 13*, 147–162.

Shimizu, K. (1992). *Shido:* Education and selection in a Japanese middle school. *Comparative Education, 28*, 109–129.

Shwalb, D. (1993). The source of Japanese school readiness: Preschool or family? On Peak's *Learning to go to school in Japan. Cross-Cultural Psychology Bulletin, 27*, 25–28.

Simons, C. (1987). They get by with a lot of help from their kyoiku mamas. *Smithsonian, 17*, 44–53.

Singleton, J. (1989). Gambaru: A Japanese cultural theory of learning. In J. J. Shields (Ed.), *Japanese schooling: Patterns of socialization, equality, and political control* (pp. 8–15). University Park: Pennsylvania State University Press.

Slavin, R. E. (1989). *Cooperative learning: Theory, research, and practice.* Englewood Cliffs, NJ: Prentice-Hall.

Solomon, D., Schaps, E., Watson, M., & Battistich, V. (1992). Creating caring school and classroom communities for all students. In R. Villa, J. Thousand, W. Stainback, & S. Stainback (Eds.), *Restructuring for caring and effective education: An administrative guide to creating heterogeneous schools* (pp. 41–60). Baltimore: Paul H. Brookes.

Solomon, D., Watson, M., Battistich, V., Schaps, E., & Delucchi, K. (1992). Creating a caring community: Educational practices that promote children's prosocial development. In F. K. Oser, A. Dick, & J. L. Patry (Eds.), *Effective and responsible teaching: The new synthesis* (pp. 383–396). San Francisco: Jossey-Bass.

Solomon, D., Watson, M., Schaps, E., Battistich, V., & Solomon, J. (1990). Cooperative learning as part of a comprehensive program designed to promote prosocial development. In S. Sharan (Ed.), *Cooperative learning: Theory and research* (pp. 231–260). New York: Praeger.

Sōmucho, Seishōnen Taisaku Honbu [Prime Minister's Office, Policy Headquarters for Childcare and Youth]. (1990). *Seishōnen hakusho* [White paper on children and youth]. Tokyo: Ōkurasho Insatsukyoku.

Sōmucho, Seishōnen Taisaku Honbu. (1991). *Seishōnen hakusho* [White paper on Children and Youth]. Tokyo: Ōkurasho Insatsukyoku.

Sōmucho, Seishōnen Taisaku Honbu. (1992). *Seishōnen hakusho* [White paper on children and youth]. Tokyo: Ōkurasho Insatsukyoku.

Stevenson, H. W., Chen, C., & Lee, S. Y. (1993). Mathematics achievement of Chinese, Japanese, and American children: Ten years later. *Science, 259*, 53–58.

Stevenson, H. W., & Lee, S. Y. (1990). Contexts of achievement. *Monographs of the Society for Research in Child Development, 55*(1–2).

Stevenson, H. W., & Stigler, J. (1992). *The learning gap: Why our schools are failing and what we can learn from Japanese and Chinese education.* New York: Summit.

Stevenson, H. W., Stigler, J. W., Lucker, G. W., Lee, S., Hsu, C., & Kitamura, K. (1987). Classroom behavior and achievement of Japanese, Chinese, and American children. In R. Glaser (Ed.), *Advances in instructional psychology* (Vol. 3, pp. 153–204). Hillsdale, NJ: Erlbaum.

Stigler, J. W., Fernandez, C., Yoshida, M., & Hatano, G. (1992, May). *Children's thinking during mathematics instruction in Japanese and American elementary school classrooms.* Paper submitted for publication.

Stigler, J. W., & Perry, M. (1987). *Cross-cultural studies of mathematics teaching and learning: Recent findings and new directions* (Working Paper 87–06–06). University of Chicago, Benton Center for Curriculum and Instruction.

Stigler, J. W., & Stevenson, H. W. (1991, Spring). How Asian teachers polish each lesson to perfection. *American Educator,* pp. 12–46.

Stipek, D., Feiler, R., Daniels, D., & Milburn, S. (in press). Effects of different instructional approaches on young children's achievement and motivation. *Child Development.*

Sugie, S. (1988). Cooperative learning in Japan. *Chukyo University Bulletin of the Faculty of the Liberal Arts, 29,* 395–428.

Tobin, J., Wu, D. Y., & Davidson, D. H. (1989). *Preschool in three cultures.* New Haven: Yale University Press.

Torrance, E. P. (1980). Lessons on giftedness and creativity from a nation of 115 million overachievers. *Gifted Child Quarterly, 24,* 10–14.

Tsuchida, I. (1993). *Teachers' motivational and instructional strategies: A study of fourth grade U.S. and Japanese classrooms.* Unpublished doctoral dissertation, University of California, Berkeley, School of Education.

Uchihashi, K. (1983). Making the most of masterly expertise. In T. Ishii et al. (Eds.), *A look at Japanese technological development* (pp. 13–20). Tokyo: Foreign Press Center.

Umesao, T. (1990). Tradition of culturedness in modern Japan. *Senri Ethnological Studies, 28,* 1–12.

Uno, K. S. (1984). Day-care and family life in late-Meiji/Taisho Japan. *Transactions of the Asiatic Society of Japan, 19,* 17–31.

U.S. Study of Education in Japan. (1987). *Japanese education today.* U.S. Department of Education. Washington, DC: Government Printing Office.

Vogel, E. (1963). *Japan's new middle class.* Berkeley and Los Angeles: Universitiy of California Press.

Watson, M., Solomon, D., Battistich, V., Schaps, E., & Solomon, J. (1989). The Child Development Project: Combining traditional and developmental approaches to values education. In L. Nucci (Ed.), *Moral development and character education: A dialogue* (pp. 51–92). Berkeley, CA: McCutchan.

White, M. (1987a). *The Japanese educational challenge.* New York: Free Press.

White, M. (1987b). The virtue of Japanese mothers: Cultural definitions of women's lives. *Daedalus, 116,* 149–163.

White, M. (1988). *The Japanese overseas: Can they go home again?* New York: Free Press.

White, M. (1993). *Material child: Coming of age in Japan and America.* New York: Free Press.

Wollens, R. (1993). The black forest in a bamboo garden: Missionary kindergartens in Japan, 1868–1912. *History of Education Quarterly, 33,* 1–35.

Yoshida, M., Fernandez, C., & Stigler, J. W. (1993). Japanese and American students' differential recognition memory for teachers' statements during a mathematics lesson. *Journal of Educational Psychology, 85,* 610–617.

INDEX

Imp. characteristics of school
that reflect Japanese culture?

Aspects of Japanese schools
work in America?